MW00803204

Poets and the Fools Who Love Them

Also by Richard Katrovas

The Woman with a Cat on Her Shoulder

The Great Czech Navy

Swastika into Lotus

Raising Girls in Bohemia: Meditations of an American Father

Scorpio Rising: Selected Poems

The Years of Smashing Bricks: An American Memoir

Prague Winter

The Republic of Burma Shave

Mystic Pig: A Novel of New Orleans

Dithyrambs

Prague, USA

The Book of Complaints

The Public Mirror

Snug Harbor

Green Dragons

Poets and the Fools Who Love Them

2/7/2022

For Melissa,
with affection
and vast
respect.

A Memoir in Essays

Richard Katrovas

Louisiana State University Press   Baton Rouge

Published by Louisiana State University Press
lsupress.org

Copyright © 2022 by Richard Katrovas
All rights reserved. Except in the case of brief quotations used in articles or reviews, no part of this publication may be reproduced or transmitted in any format or by any means without written permission of Louisiana State University Press.

LSU Press Paperback Original

Designer: Barbara Neely Bourgoyne
Typeface: Adobe Text Pro

Library of Congress Cataloging-in-Publication Data are available at the Library of Congress.

ISBN 978-0-8071-7663-4 (paperback) — ISBN 978-0-8071-7744-0 (pdf) — ISBN 978-0-8071-7745-7 (epub)

I dedicate this book to the memory
of the beautiful American poets
Robert L. Jones and Bruce H. Boston

ARS POETICA

I. The wild green man chased himself around a tree, crying,

> "The green man chased a wild crying tree!
> The tree chased a wild man and cried, 'Green!'"

II. The green of one wild tree
   turned the man into a crying man.

III. Truly I heard in the wild green the crying
    both of men and trees.

—KARENMARIA SUBACH

there will be trees
each death
there will be trees

—BRUCE H. BOSTON

CONTENTS

xi   Acknowledgments

1   Introduction

4   My Father's Job Was Crime

14   Name-Dropping

23   My Penchant for Violence: Poets and Physical Courage

35   Their Fathers' Queer Sons: The Apotheosis of Larry Levis

50   My Gorgons

59   Local Poets

68   Shakespeare, on Acid

78   My Wicked Thirties

88   Fresno, California: "Armpit of America" and Breeding Ground of American Poets

98   Poetry Is a Dead Art

102   What Poets Know: Dry and Wet Knowing

109   The Magic Book: Why I Thought Publishing a Book Would Change Everything

121   Take My Wife, Please: Poetry Readings and Stand-Up

Contents

133   AWP and Me: A Meditation

143   A Privateer in the Arts: Arnold Johnston's *Where We're Going, Where We've Been*

154   Soul Retrieval

165   Straight and Normal: Poets and Drugs in the New Age

177   "The Raggedy-Ass Masses": Poets and Democracy

192   The Dick and the Donald: White Privilege and Flimflam

205   A Dead Dog and a Boy

223   Index

ACKNOWLEDGMENTS

Portions of this book first appeared in the following publications: *Blackbird, James Dickey Review, Los Angeles Review, Meluzina, Offbeat, St. Petersburg Review, storySouth, What Falls Away Is Always: Writers over 60 Talk about Writing and Death, Xavier Review.*

"Poetry Is a Dead Art" and "The Magic Book" first appeared in *Raising Girls in Bohemia: Meditations of an American Father* (Three Rooms Press, 2014). Parts of "A Dead Dog and a Boy" appeared, in very different form, in *The Republic of Burma Shave* (Carnegie Mellon University Press, 2001).

Portions of Stanley Kunitz's poem "The Layers," from *The Collected Poems* (W. W. Norton & Company, 2000) copyright © 2000 by Stanley Kunitz, appear here with permission of W. W. Norton & Company.

I thank the teachers of my youth: Glover Davis, Carolyn Forché, Philip Levine, Robert Mezey, Gregory Orr, Stanley Plumly, Gerald Stern, Mark Strand, James Whitehead, Miller Williams. I thank my friends, enemies, former colleagues, and ex-wives (and the combinations thereof) who have been my teachers: Krista Angelique, Andrei Codrescu, Gerald Costanzo, Moira Crone, Barbara Cully, Stuart Dybek, Robert Eversz, Arnold and Deborah Johnston, Rodger Kamenetz, Sydney Lea, Betty Lewis, Trevor Top, Dominika Winterová, David Wojahn, Gail Wronsky, Hana Zahradniková.

I thank Jaimy Gordon and Karenmaria Subach for reading and commenting on this book, and I thank Elizabeth Gratch for deftly copyediting the manuscript; any remaining infelicities are entirely my fault.

And I thank Ema Katrovas, Anna Katrovas, and Ella Katrovas, who surpass me in every important way and to my unsurpassable delight.

Poets

and the

Fools
Who
Love
Them

Introduction

In this book, I'm concerned with the social role and relevance of poets more than with poetry; indeed, there is little verse seasoning these essays. I want to understand how and why I glommed on to the role of poet while awaiting my father's release from federal prison and while living in housing projects with my dying mother and four siblings on welfare.

From when I was eleven, I fancied myself a poet. By the time I entered college, only sex was as important to me as poetry, though really they were aspects of the same excitement, the same Life-Is-Worth-Living recurring revelation. I bumbled into the community of poets at the same time as non-onanistic sex became gloriously available to my late-teens self, and in this I know I'm not unique among poets or, for that matter, members of most other social groups, though *community of poets* has as odd a ring as *gang of priests* or *herd of bears;* that is, in all three cases the object of the preposition doesn't jibe with the nature of the collective: some priests may be pedophiles, but the priestly ideal runs counter to such miscreant behavior as is associated with gangs, and of course bears are solitary creatures, avoid others of their kind except in mating or nurturing young. Many poets, more like bears than priests, seem simply to be solitary by nature, though like priests, they hold something of an exalted status, and for poets that status is paradoxical: there is no more paradoxical social role, more exalted yet scoffed at, than poet. The fact that raw and nasty desire links the nescient young poet's new enterprise to the heady, abstract effusions she or he likely hides in her dresser drawer, in the folds of unmentionables, is the strongest indication that such a person is on a path fraught with fools: it is common wisdom that the lyrical and sexual impulses idle singularly in the loins where Romantic Love and Terror of Extinction grasp hands, Thelma and Louise–like, and again and again, after soulful kisses, raise plumes of dust as they accelerate toward lingering suspension.

I want to understand better this profession I stumbled into, one that affirms, sanctions, that role I chose as an early-1960s prepubescent. In the 1950s and 1960s, poets seeking equal institutional status with scholars often seemed out of their proper position, like lab rats donning white coats and goggles. I recall a Brit Lit professor commenting deadpan, in the early 1970s, when I was an undergraduate, that only the work of dead authors should be taught, and he didn't have to add that the longer they'd been dead the better. His attitude was typical, such that death indeed was the divide in English departments, the psychic border between scholars and creative writers at that phase in institutional history when literature was still canonical, therefore of the divine, whereas creative writing was at best practical, pedestrian, pedagogical.

Once even born poets lived, barely lived, so the story went, in garrets. By now every English department supports at least a couple, or more accurately, the popular creative writing program keeps many a creaky old English department afloat. That by now the American Dream of upward mobility is as potent a feature of American citizenship for poets as for food truck operators, hairstylists, and lounge singers is a legitimate point of national pride, even for those of us who abhor the very idea of national pride. Other cultures may celebrate their poets more gaudily than that of the United States, but none except America has cobbled together a system that not only rewards poets with gainful employment but may even lure individuals of modest talent—not quite born poets—to take up the sacred vocation of Erato as a path to a lifelong gig with tenure and a retirement account.

I was always going to be a poet, even before I discovered the vast network of American poetry, the innumerable opportunities to commune with like-minded folks and to share my efforts, and by declaring this, I mean not to self-aggrandize, to set myself above or apart. The fact that I, as a kid, felt destined to be a poet, to live the life of a poet to the extent that I held any image in my hormone-fogged noggin as to what that life might look and feel like, never fostered delusions of grandeur. I give that boy some small credit for leavening his ambition with humility and for conceiving of his future in anything but grandiose terms.

Yet soon after entering my first poetry workshop in 1973, I learned that most other students were taking the course because they assumed it would proffer an easy A or simply because they'd not been accepted into the College of Business and had to major in *something,* so wandered into English, a major that offered courses they assumed, often correctly, would be loosey-goosey and fun. I was too naive, too stupid even, to resent such as they, but I despaired, at least a little, to learn that not everyone else in that classroom felt destined to be a poet. In time I came to see that a curriculum of "requirements" and "electives" is a metaphysical smorgasbord at which some items the customer is force-fed and others she or he may choose among, but I hardly noticed that creative writing was migrating, even as I was matriculating, from a General Education elective to a respectable major with a host of requirements. I was having fun, living a haphazard, concupiscent life in paradisal San Diego as other young men my age and a little older were disengaging from a war, the various muddled phases of which had spanned our lifetimes. My childhood had been fraught, by first-world standards, with disruption and loss, insecurity and deprivation, but poetry had saved my life in adolescence, and the community of poets became my gang, my posse, my tribe, my true family, as I gamboled into adulthood.

Careening through the seventies, I had no idea how close I was coming, again and again, to spinning out, ruining my life, smashing my soul into the hardpan of inscrutable and sumptuous Southern California. I had no idea how I would "unite / My avocation and my vocation / As my two eyes make one in sight," as Robert Frost framed such ambition. I didn't fret much about the future, didn't plan and prepare from year to year, semester to semester, or even day to day. I didn't know it then, but I was rolling through life on the fumes of a faith I'd acquired as a boy, a faith that I was blessed, that somehow everything was going to work out.

Such is the glory of fools, and such has been the glory of my good life in this too often wretched world among earthly angels, among poets.

My Father's Job Was Crime

Work is much more fun than fun.
—NOEL COWARD

We are the work we do, and if we're lucky, it is indistinguishable from play. If we're not lucky, play is what we feel we have to do to compensate for work, for what we are and how that makes us feel. If we are not lucky, then work and play are a diabolical dichotomy.

My father was a criminal. Being one was his work, and because his crimes, his job, entailed trickery and subterfuge, a kind of acting, of charming, his criminal acts were also a form of play. I, his eldest spawn, became a poet. Robert Frost said that poetry is "play for mortal stakes," but many endeavors may be seen as that, and being a con man, even a low-rent con like my daddy, Dick, was to assume a livelihood, a job, a form of work that was also play for mortal stakes.

I last laid peepers on Dick in the early 1990s. He'd been out of prison for a while, was married to an RN he'd buttered up through the mail from the joint and lived with her in a single-wide on an impressive expanse of verdant property a few miles outside of Tallahassee, Florida. The Worm of Glory had wiggled and eaten into his heart, and as a consequence, Dick had been forgiven by Heaven though not pardoned within the federal penal system. For more than twenty years, I'd assumed he was dead, but then, through casual googling, found documents regarding his last legal mess and, on a whim, phoned the listed home number.

For roughly a year, we chatted every couple of weeks, though I hated talking to him, hated his Jesus talk, his unceasing proselytizing. In early

July 2016, his nurse wife phoned me in Prague to say that Dick had died. For purely selfish reasons of genetic entanglement, I was relieved that he'd made it into his eighties but even more deeply relieved that he was kaput.

Recently, I spent a day working around the house, dusting nooks that rarely get cleaned, throwing stuff away—Ellie's sixth grade folders of multiplication tables and fill-in-the-blank Michigan history assignments—that should have been jettisoned annually rather than stored. I was enjoying myself, feeling that satisfaction of accomplishing mundane tasks at which I'd peered soulfully for months, such as clearing the foyer of winter coats that would not be required for at least half a year, hauling them in plastic tubs down to the basement. I felt a little guilty because it was June, a month designated for single-minded concentration on my "real" work, on writing projects and university stuff, that is, of sitting quietly and tapping on my laptop, reading books and students' writing and taking notes. Performing household tasks was, in the moment, a guilty pleasure, and I wasn't blind to the irony: my "work" entailed sitting quietly and thinking, moving my hands a little, but even as my daily workout is for health reasons only, puttering around the house, hauling plastic tubs, scrubbing, dusting, ejecting the jetsam of conspicuous consumption, was actually a kind of recreation, a respite from my sedentary labor.

In the midst of such activity, I inevitably reflect upon Robert Frost's "Two Tramps in Mud Time," though, alas, I never encounter hobos shambling through my home shaming me into paying them to perform my housework. On this occasion, I thought about work, about my dead ex-con daddy Dick's work ethic, how he indeed had one. I thought about how lucky I am to call what I am paid to do "work." I thought about the many shitty jobs I performed through my teens and twenties, how deeply nostalgic I sometimes feel recalling repetitive tasks, especially the ones that made my body ache at night and compelled me to swear in the dark that I would not spend the rest of my life digging holes in and hauling dirt from San Diego's hardpan or schlepping "herbal French cosmetics" door-to-door in East LA and Watts.

When I was a young man, daily physical work was a condition to be escaped. Having said this, I'm tempted to launch into a meditation on Philip Levine's poetry, how he was indeed the American poet of labor, of daily physical labor's effects on a young person's body, mind, and soul—no, this is not the time. I'm reminded of John Adams's famous progression in his May 12, 1780, letter to his wife, Abigail:

> I must study Politicks and War that my sons may have liberty to study Mathematicks and Philosophy. My sons ought to study Mathematicks and Philosophy, Geography, natural History, Naval Architecture, navigation, Commerce, and Agriculture, in order to give their Children a right to study Painting, Poetry, Musick, Architecture, Statuary, Tapestry, and Porcelaine.

Well, quite the autodidact, Dick developed techniques for persuading bank tellers and merchants to exchange cash for worthless paper and for trading in illegally acquired automobiles. He performed these tasks as a means of supporting a growing family on the highways of America.

During the years of the *Godfather* movies, I, like most folks, delighted in the ways that the "organized" aspect of organized crime played out as a daily grind like most other enterprises, noting how, the murder and mayhem notwithstanding, it was like any other lifestyle choice, any other profession, any other job. There was nothing organized about Dick's shenanigans, though there was a daily rhythm and practical purpose grounded in necessity: when he scored, we ate.

It is easy now to liken my childhood to that of someone born into a prehistoric hunter-gatherer family unit. Dick would drop us off in the most degenerate motels on the edges of towns and cities and venture forth alone. He would return, after many hours, bearing prepared food in white bags; he might as well have been hauling a gutted carcass over a blood-smeared shoulder.

And I suppose distinguishing between work as a modern activity and what it was when "primitive" folks did it is essential to conceiving of art's shifting role in a world both improved and devastated by technological advancement. Philip Levine's Everyman factory worker is fast becoming an anachronism, in America anyway, if not in China and Indonesia, but more to the point, all forms of remunerative work, whether within a corporate or private contractor paradigm and whether in the public or the private sector, are morphing in ways that stock market speculators seek to predict and social scientists exist to understand but which poets must sniff like approaching rain in summer. My father's job was crime, and by some twisted, zany reckoning, crime may be considered as a no-less-essential element in both the Body Politic and the great Capitalist Clusterfuck—that gargantuan, seething mating ball of snakes—than poetry, than noncommercial art generally.

By kiting checks in the time of pre-computerized banking, Dick probed, tested that system, possibly, in some tiny, grotesque way, compelled it to get better. What I'm suggesting is similar to the hacker argument: by hacking into data-rich systems, the hacker forces institutions out of complacency. By then getting caught, judged, and incarcerated, Dick was fodder for both the public and private aspects of the incarceration industry. Of course, taken to something like a logical conclusion, this line of thinking celebrates the terrorist's contribution to the economic order and potentially accepts war as an economic necessity, arms manufacturing as an economic engine. The same convoluted rationale by which the vast underbelly of the global economic order is not so much justified as accepted applies no less to stealthy property crimes than to the production and dissemination of poetry, among other noncommercial artifacts. Both represent work that inspires the formation of burgeoning cottage industries.

Crimes of stealth and subterfuge, of trickery, now best exemplified by all scams perpetrated online, give rise to internet security companies and all other cyber-protection enterprises, private and public; poetry production and consumption, the issue of the radical egalitarianism of 1960s antiwar counterculture, transformed humanities higher education, gave rise to the cottage industry of Creative Writing. My father's job was crime, the kind of nonlethal transgressions that poke and fiddle, mess with the gears of commerce. No more accomplished than Dick, I, too, poke and fiddle, mess with the gears of commerce, though more obliquely. My poems, all poems, are checks written on a metaphysical account. Good poems clear; bad ones bounce. Either way, though, a metaphysical doughnut and cup of coffee won't likely get you through to lunch. It is indeed "difficult to get the news from poetry," but stomachs growl, and pituitary glands secrete, miserably every day for lack of calories and caffeine. Work and play, that diabolical dichotomy, slouch toward Bethlehem on the shifting sands of Intrinsic-Extrinsic value. Ezra Pound walked his "old bitch gone in the mouth" through Hieronymus Bosch's *Garden of Earthly Delights* (the center panel) right into any *Where's Waldo* composition; of course, he didn't scoop and bag the poop, and lest I get arrested by the pun police, let me state simply that poems are a shadow currency, even as paintings and other art objects are, potentially, commodities.

I mean that poems, shadow currency, possess only intrinsic value (the cost of the paper notwithstanding), whereas paintings and other plastic arts objects, possessing the potential for marketability, are full-fledged artifacts of the economic order. One cannot sell, or put up for auction, an exquisite sonnet, but one may purchase with it, so to speak, prestige within a coterie. A painting or sculpture potentially possesses the same exchange value as a '67 Mercury station wagon or twenty or thirty Maserati GranCarios. Noncommercial art—"high" or "low"—occupies the same niche as most humanities scholarship, one that is determined exclusively by intrinsic valuation and is subsidized within a patronage system more complex, more convoluted even, than that class-based system of centuries past in which aristocrats and potentates funded both the arts and scholarship and thereby determined, more often than not, both content and dissemination. Poets and painters, who did not have patrons and who did not possess independent means, produced art at their peril and were the Starving Artists by turns idealized and abandoned to their own devices in the putrid alleys of bourgeois nostalgia. Universities are the new arts patrons, sustaining activities deemed to possess value incompatible with the machinery of market imperatives . . . maple syrup poured into a gas tank. The Elizabethan literary scholar's peer-reviewed monograph lays claim to knowledge; the academic poet's thin volume exists, in part, as a reenactment of sixteenth-century indulgences, though in reverse, as though the church paid the sinner for his sin. What nineteen-year-old wouldn't prefer to compose free verse romps rather than arid, lockstep analyses of antique texts?

Shadow currency has nothing to do with what are variously called underground economies and black markets. There is a symbiotic relation between official and unofficial economies, though eventually the latter drains away the efficacy of the former. All forms of shadow currency—poems, stories that track daily life, essays such as *this* odd-duck ditty—circulate through the collective life of the mind like prayers through a Texan megachurch; even as the collection plates glean wads of greenback tithing, Betsy May flicks a prayer for Bobby Jo's great-aunt Millie Lou's cancer, Danny

Junior mumbles one for Dolly Lynn's daddy's drinking problem, and everybody, all 4,296, are praying in unison, through the inspired megaphonic heart of the pastor, for all the murdered babies in Planned Parenthood clinics across this great, if humanism-afflicted, nation.

From 1953, when I was born, until 1960, when Dick was caught the first time, and between 1963 and 1964, when he was nabbed the second time, I cohabited in the back seats of innumerable automobiles with two, three, finally four siblings. I spent uncountable hours with my chin, temple, or forehead on the seat between my parents, listening. My father often schemed the future, and the word *legitimate* repeated cricket-like, especially at night when the green glow of the speedometer dusted his forearms, and he spoke hushed and dreamily to my mother. He would find the perfect town or city in which we could settle down. He would start a legitimate business, and we would lead legitimate lives among the legitimate American purveyors of commercial legitimacy. My head lolled between and just behind them, and I was comforted in my long-distance stupor by the fairy tale of legitimacy.

I have not seen my sister, third born and four years younger than I, since I was thirteen and Dick hustled our brother, a year my junior, and me away from Norfolk, Virginia, away from our crumbling mother and three younger siblings. He stole a truck and hocked our band instruments, shiny school-issued trumpets, and drove us to San Diego, where we were swiftly adopted by his younger sister and her navy officer husband. Then he disappeared but was eventually caught and incarcerated. I have not seen my sister in more than fifty years, though over the past few months, we've conducted a spirited email correspondence. One day, googling dreamily, I stumbled across the virtual version of our mother's gravesite in Elizabeth City, North Carolina. There was a single bouquet of words below a photograph of her tombstone, a cryptic elegy I traced back to my sister.

She is spirited, articulate, very bright. She is a semiretired crime scene investigator. In our first exchange, she needed me to prove I am her brother. She has helped put a lot of criminals in prison by "dumpster diving for body parts," as she describes the fieldwork of her thirty-year career, and then testifying as an expert witness. As a consequence of her work, she must be very careful regarding all online activities. I answered questions only I can answer, and thousands of words then flowed between us.

She is a staunch Republican who is willing to look past my liberal biases, and though we have already had several knock-down, drag-out political arguments, we've so far been able to retreat to a shared position of civility by shifting to the concrete particulars of quotidian existence.

She is an amateur astronomer and owns a fancy telescope. She sometimes hosts a "witches' coven," a bevy of tough, smart, retired professionals who practice, as far as I can gather, a semiserious form of matriarchal, pre-Christian nature worship. She loves animals, owns numerous rescue K9s, and lives on several acres of lush woods on the lip of a national park (she has sent me photos). Her husband of forty years is a retired army NCO. Though I wish she were not a right-wing adherent, I am very proud of her; I like and respect her. I have infuriated her at least three times when I have expressed political views she found condescending, or, rather, when I have expressed my progressive views in what she perceived to be a condescending manner. I am learning not to be condescending, even as my loathing of aspects of her worldview swells in proportion to my epistolary equanimity. She is glad that I found her, that we found each other, though we have made no plans yet to meet in the flesh.

She hates our father. It seems that after he dropped our brother and me off in San Diego, he returned to Norfolk and beat our dying mother just short of a coma (this is what I imagine, not exactly what my sister said). The last time I saw our mother, she could not stand for long without falling and wept unceasingly. She was doomed, and I cannot fathom why Dick would have assaulted her, though I believe my sister is a truth teller, a woman who as a girl witnessed her sick mother being brutalized by her criminal father.

There are forty-six months between my birth and hers. In photos I've not seen in decades but recall vividly and inexplicably, I recognize the nine-year-old girl I last saw her to be. She was a third child of five, so smack-dab in the middle of two sets of brothers; the older two ignored her, and the two younger were, alas, in her charge as our mother's muscles atrophied and bones grew brittle.

My sister has a very uncluttered conception of justice and in one of our scores of email exchanges expressed consternation that Dick lived a serene final two decades in the sweet embrace of his Lord. My sister isn't religious, though she is comfortably in league, politically, with fundamentalist Christians. She is certain that religious faith was Dick's final scam, though I, having suffered through so many of his muddleheaded diatribes, am persuaded that he himself, indeed, may have been the final victim, and beneficiary, of his final scam. His fear of death, I could feel over the phone, was exquisite, his moldering guilt filmed over with righteous celestial pardon. He scammed his own guilt, and my sister, who witnessed a particular brutality I did not, is galled that our father did not expire writhing in the throes of self-loathing.

My sister does not yet know that on several occasions he beat me, with a belt and his open hands, leaving welts and bruises that lasted for weeks. Once, he punched me in the face, knocking me out. But on those relatively rare occasions, I felt as though I deserved the pain he inflicted upon me. The rage that is the reverse side of that psychic coin stamped the face on my darker moments until the recent past.

I loved him, longed for him to get out of prison, drive us away from the projects, from welfare, from wary, distant relatives. I longed for legitimacy, though, alas, I became a poet and, by so doing, forsook all claims to legitimacy except in the rarified realm in which shadow currency won't pay for your breakfast at IHOP but may, if you're more or less "successful," render your name a household word in dozens of homes across America.

My sister judges our father an evil monster, but I think she is wrong. He was at least a little evil because it is true that evil is banal, and he was that. But he wasn't a monster. A monster's unmediated purpose, his job, is to hurt and destroy. Our father wanted to take care of us, take care of our mother. I don't know why he lied rapid-fire in every conversation or how he maintained such towering self-regard despite everyone around him, surely in prison, reminding him minute by minute of his indisputable failures. I certainly don't know why he would assault a dying woman as his youngest children bore witness. God may have forgiven him, though my sister never will. No matter how many murders she solves, how many career criminals she helps put in prison, her fury, righteous and wholly justified, will be her solace.

I forgave our father because he became for me a paragon of all I do not wish to be, a self-deluded liar, a self-aggrandizer, a phony, a flimflam operator, a braggart, a swindler, a smarmy charmer, a bigot, a know-it-all, a man too proud to apologize, a man who, under different circumstances, may have risen to the presidency of the United States, indeed a man who may have earned my sister's vote. I forgave him because he was a flesh-and-blood cautionary tale, one I've managed in my better moments to heed.

Poets and other artists who deal in shadow currency, who exchange soul stuff in the spectral bazaar of intrinsic valuation, of prestige earned mistily elsewhere than through the relentless machinery of market imperatives, are parasites on the body politic, as are criminals, though to different effect.

There are two types of parasites, those that are good for you and the vast majority that are not, and though I mix my metaphors egregiously here, as I am wont to do, I will venture to put the poems being exchanged for shadow currency in Uncle Sam's gut as the work of benevolent intestinal parasites, of which I am one.

My father's job was crime, my sister's is facilitating justice, and if I must wonder whether my father experienced something like fun in the midst of a scam, I wonder, too, if dispensing justice, a no less liquid abstraction, might not be as recreational, in a fundamental sense, as "dumpster diving for body parts" implies.

My job, truth be told, is spotting and noting dangling participles, comma splices, subject-verb disagreements, logical fallacies, vague assertions, muddled constructions, superfluous verbiage, illogical progressions, dubious claims, awkwardly fulsome passive constructions (those last several being petty crimes I still dim-wittedly commit); it is also trumpeting the joys of English prosody, cobbling together something like a historical perspective regarding literary texts and imposing it on some impressionable, some cynical, young minds. My job is also to recognize when someone in my charge has a knack for storytelling and/or for making words sing and then to shepherd such a person through a process I find to this day utterly mystifying. It is my job to notice when a young person is roiling in a state of quietly hysterical desperation or when she or he is utterly deluded yet strong enough to process, possibly benefit from, unvarnished, measured, crystalline criticism.

It is my job not only to listen to but to hear inchoate, passionate voices and to celebrate, without irony or condescension, all innocent voices, even as I work diligently to skim innocence from the written manifestations of those voices.

It is my job to recognize my colleagues' emotional boundaries and to take them, and myself, not too seriously but just seriously enough. It is my job to recognize that all human organizations tend toward not only randomness but also absurdity, and we grown-ups just live with that fact, which is simply another way of saying that shitting the nest is bad form. It is my job to recognize that civilization is a gleaming veneer, that it is precious and under unceasing danger from the corrosive, aggregate effect of masculine ego, and that therefore my job, my tiny humble task, is not so much to suppress as tame my own ego in the enterprise of purchasing, then processing and selling dear, for shadow currency, the raw materials of the human heart.

Name-Dropping

When I entered the world of writers, in the early 1970s, creative writing was less a profession than a cultural insurgency. My teachers, at the time mostly poets, were in more or less unremitting conflict with scholarly colleagues, who viewed them as unworthy of wiggle room at the academic trough. Writers in the academy back then, and certainly even farther back, experienced a kind of camaraderie of Yahoos among the Houyhnhnms. Today creative writing is accepted as a legitimate, even necessary, component of a language arts or, more broadly speaking, humanities education. However, at moments I am grotesquely nostalgic for the outsider status of writers within the academy and from time to time reminisce to students about my formative years, which happened also to be the formative years of the profession, a time when creative writing was indeed becoming, alas, a profession. As a student, I relished the yarns my teachers would spin regarding other writers, other insurgents, they'd loved and loathed. I delighted in those occasions when my mentors, those glorious outlaws, dropped names.

Yet at its most banal, is there anything more boring, even loathsome, than name-dropping? It is an activity often parodied, almost always scorned, and rightfully so. The best, which is to say the worst, example I can recall is of a writer, stationed for years at an institution not far from Hollywood, who opened most conversations with strangers by informing them that he'd had carnal relations with not one but two Famous Movie Stars, and of course, he was never shy about naming those iconic women. But kissing and telling is one thing and hooking one's professional prestige to stars in one's field quite another. My own name-dropping opportunities were quite slim until 1976, when I received a "work scholarship" to the Bread Loaf Writers' Conference, a distinction so humble I'm now embarrassed by how lucky I felt to have received it, rather like being named third-alternate batboy for a winter league team in East Texas. But at the time, I was twenty-two and starstruck. I'd read the works of almost everyone at Bread Loaf that year, everyone except Richard Ford and John Irving. I recall an innocuous chat with the former, whom I'd get to know a little better a decade or so later when he moved to New Orleans, and spiking a volleyball into the face of the latter, who, for a nanosecond, acted as though he would traverse the net and wrestle me to the grass. It was pre-Garp, and Irving seemed to balance a gaudy chip on his shoulder; at the time, I thought it was just a short-guy thing. I recall him, Ford, and Stanley Elkin mulling together after a reading. Elkin and Ford seemed to tower over Irving, who, in the Fame Game, would tower over almost everyone in two or three years.

My mentor, that is, the writer to whom I was assigned, was Mark Strand, patrician, quintessentially handsome, acerbic. I'd devoured all of his published work and, like almost every young poet back then, was deeply affected by his iteration of the Plain Style. You either loved or hated it, but you couldn't ignore it. At Bread Loaf that summer, he ignored me quite regally, and for reasons too complicated to explain, I was probably lucky to have been ignored by him at that stage of my life. I'd have numerous contacts with Strand over the coming years, though none so memorable, indeed instructive, as when, at an after-reading reception at San Diego State University, where I was matriculating and at which Strand had nudged me to get him a reading, Mark Strand sighed and opined under his breath, as a clutch of admirers spun from his orbit, "Too many poets," and then, again, "Too many poets."

I pondered that judgment for years and eventually came to the conclusion that he was wrong; there are too many lawyers and too many soldiers and too, too many academic administrators, but there can never be too many poets.

Be that as it may, there were numerous poets at Bread Loaf that year, all of whose work I'd pondered at least cursorily. Marvin Bell was one of the Iowa workshop stalwarts about whom almost every older poet I knew had a story soaked in wary affection. I'd later not sign up for Marvin's classes at Iowa primarily because he seemed in no hurry to mentor me, though years later his terrific work in the Prague Summer Program would fill me with admiration and gratitude. David St. John, Carolyn Forché, and Carol Muske were among the Young Turks at Bread Loaf that year, and all three, too, would later work their magic as teachers in my program. Galway Kinnell was, in 1976, a demigod to me, though my most salient memory of him is bittersweet and human scale; in July 2006, he, Philip Levine, and my beloved colleague Herbert Scott read together in my program. Before the event, I told all three that though I asked most folks to read for no more than twenty minutes, because they were who they were, I wanted them each to read for half an hour. Kinnell performed with regal alacrity and abundant charm for fifty-seven minutes.

My interactions with two other giants, Denise Levertov and Adrienne Rich, were outside the confines of my modest authority as a program director. I managed to knock a glass of water into Levertov's lap in a New Orleans seafood restaurant on Lake Pontchartrain; the epitome of grace, she barely paused in telling whatever story with which she was regaling the table. When I met Rich, I was sitting at the middle of a long row of many long rows of chairs. The place was packed, and she was the star attraction. A colleague who had arranged her visit paused with her at my row and, across the bodies of at least a dozen other audience members above whom Rich's and my colleague's torsos seemed to float, introduced her to me. I waved and shouted over the din, "Break a leg!" Rich paused, two or three rows ahead, turned slightly toward me, and smiled wryly. As she progressed toward the podium, the fact that she was limping along with the aid of a cane became visible.

As a student, first an undergraduate at San Diego State University and then a graduate student at University of Virginia, University of Arkansas, and finally the University of Iowa, I loved it when my teachers told stories about writers living and dead. Gossip, I believe, is an integral aspect of a literary education, whether it is delivered by anecdotes over pitchers of beer or through formal works of literary biography and autobiography. By the time I was twenty-five, I'd heard, from several angles, including Levine's, about the time Phil Levine coldcocked John Berryman for drunkenly pawing Fran Levine at an Iowa after-reading party. I'd heard, from both Robert Mezey's and Philip Levine's mouths, the backstory to

Phil's "Silent in America." I'd heard stories too numerous to recount about Iowa workshop hijinks from the 1950s, 1960s, and 1970s and, of course, when and where and how many times who "did" whom and, alas, who couldn't rise to whatever occasion. The petty and salacious is irrepressible and oddly necessary to a literary life though antithetical to the ideal, if not the reality, of the academic profession.

Name-dropping is to gossip as invocation is to prayer: the saint, or deity, in question matters. As is also true of both cholesterol and ambiguity, there are good and bad forms of gossip: notwithstanding Empson's Seven Types, there are, for all practical purposes, two types of ambiguity, the kind that touches the question mark at the heart of existence and the kind that makes you scratch your head and say, "Huh?" Good gossip celebrates the foibles, the humanity, of those we love and/or admire; bad gossip seeks only to hurt.

There is one transcendent reason to attend the annual Associated Writing Programs (AWP) convention, and that is to gossip, once a year, with the same groups of friends with whom one is otherwise largely out of touch 363 days a year. When old friends gossip, name-dropping isn't an issue. When a teacher gossips, drops names, in the classroom and it is obvious that her or his reason for doing so is purely showing off, then that teacher has failed not only his students but the profession. If an anecdote (even if only half-true, and on such occasions, 50 percent often seems an abundance) serves to illuminate or genuinely contextualize a particular work or author's sensibility, then the student is reminded, at the very least, that literary art is produced by human beings who are subject to pimples and envies and rages and warts, people who may stink even, literally or otherwise, as often as not, and who likewise gossip and name-drop fluently.

That day I knocked a glass of water onto Denise Levertov's lap, I'd said in passing, over a dozen cold, raw oysters, something to the effect that since Levertov was considered a Black Mountain Poet, blah blah blah. Her response had been to state, evenly though emphatically, that she'd never visited Black Mountain College and that, quite simply, she had very little in common, besides mutually affable feelings, with Charles Olson et al.

A few years before that exchange, in the late 1970s, soon after *Self-Portrait in a Convex Mirror* earned everything but a kiss on the forehead from God, I'd met John Ashbery at University of California, San Diego.

On that occasion, it was someone other than myself vexing a great American poet with a glib assumption. An erudite, tweedy scholar, cocktail in hand, perfectly trimmed mustache atwitter, so self-consciously droll he seemed to ooze a honeyed urbanity, said to Ashbery, "Well, considering the obvious influence of Gertrude Stein on your earlier work, especially—"

"Gertrude Stein has nothing to do with my work," Ashbery shot back before the fellow could even finish his sentence.

Trust the tale and not the teller! D. H. Lawrence implored, and, frankly, in both instances here, the Major American Poets protested a bit too much. There are obvious aesthetic and philosophical ties between Levertov and Olson, Levertov and Creeley especially, and between Ashbery and Stein. All the same, there is a curious pleasure in knowing that Levertov and Ashbery resisted what many would consider common wisdom about their work.

To this point, I've mentioned Philip Levine a couple of times. I was introduced to him by the terrific poet-translator Robert L. Jones, who had been Levine's student years earlier. It was 1977, I think, an hour or so before Levine was to perform. Phil and Fran (a better half if ever one existed) were sitting on manicured grass near the venue. I'd read everything Levine had published to that point, memorized great chunks of it. I'd studied with another former student of Levine, Glover Davis, who had told many stories of Levine's adventures as a firebrand teacher in Fresno, California. I approached Levine, reached down to shake his hand; he barely glanced up and perfunctorily grasped mine. He was chewing on a grass stalk. I think he and Fran had cans of something they were drinking. Bob Jones, now dead more than twenty years, seemed in that moment filled with conflicted affection. His relation to Levine was, as we say, complicated, as mine was to become over the years. What Bob and Phil, what just about everyone and Phil, had in common, at the very least, was vast, rock-solid affection for Larry Levis. Truth be told, Levine didn't like me much, and I didn't like him much either, though my dislike of him is suspect even now in my own heart. Daddy issues? Of course. Unwillingness to kiss rings? Yeah, that too.

If a writer is of a certain age, no matter where she or he may place in the vaunted Pecking Order, that individual will have accumulated many, many names. Alan Levy is one of mine that most folks reading this will not likely recognize. He was a gadfly (in the Socratic sense), an American-born journalist who served as editor in chief of the *Prague Post* and wrote for it through the 1990s. Levy published the definitive eyewitness account, from an American perspective, of the Soviet invasion of Czechoslovakia (*Rowboat to Prague,* retitled *So Many Heroes*) and years later published *The Wiesenthal File,* about the great Austrian Nazi hunter. But between those stellar efforts, he published books that were centered on extended interviews with W. H. Auden, Ezra Pound, Vladimir Nabokov, and (no joke) Sophia Loren. Over the years, he also interviewed the Beatles, Fidel Castro, Graham Greene, Václav Havel, and Richard Nixon, among many others. Levy claimed to have coined the phrase "Prague is the Left Bank of the 90s," and though some dispute that the idea originated with him, I don't care. In my heart, that sentiment will always have originated with Alan Levy. He died in his beloved Prague in 2004, and the last article he published in the *Prague Post,* from his deathbed, railed cogently against the hospital to which he was confined. If, from the midst of that night at the end of his good life, Levy saw the proverbial light, he did not creep gently into it.

I see myself now as a living connection, among so many other living connections, an incredibly complex circuitry, to a past that is rapidly blinking out. If, as a young guy, I dropped names to impress, I now do so to mourn and celebrate.

Here are a few names of other writers who have graced my overseas program: Vance Bourjaily, Aleš Debeljak, Václav Havel, Arnošt Lustig, William Matthews, Grace Paley, Tomaž Šalamun.

Their names are scrawled upon my heart, as mine is written on water. For each, I have a story, an anecdote or two or three or more. I recall Vance tooting into a glorious cornet that he could not play, not really. It was Mardi Gras, and he wore a tux, and the horn was a prop, though I couldn't figure out whom he was impersonating and didn't ask. He stood on my balcony on St. Louis, between Bourbon and Dauphine, and sputtered into that glorious horn, wholly unaware that the great Al Hirt lived just across the narrow street and was home (I'd spied Jumbo entering his townhouse minutes earlier).

I met Šalamun when he visited New Orleans in the mid-1980s, and he introduced me to Aleš Debeljak in Ljubljana, Slovenia, in 1989. Aleš and his significant other stayed at my house during a visit to New Orleans in 1990, and I recall a young poet as charmingly intense as any I've ever known and as smart and quick-witted and deeply and widely read. I recall his holding forth, over shots at the Apple Barrel on Frenchmen Street, about being a poet in a language that barely two million people on the planet speak. And I recall commenting that the irony was that he had more readers, and enthusiastic ones at that, in his native tongue than just about any English-language poet I knew had in mine.

I met Grace Paley at the Fine Arts Work Center in Provincetown in December 1979. She ladled soup for me and a tiny, mighty sculptor. I can't recall the reason for our visit but recall vividly that as I spooned my soup, the sculptor, a blonde woman possessing Popeye-strong forearms, commented on my hoop earring, a bit of a guy novelty at the time, and Grace mentioned wistfully that she'd never had her ears pierced. The sculptor and I then gathered a potato, a sewing needle, a bottle of peroxide, a book of matches, and two ice cubes and pierced Grace Paley's earlobes.

When I think of Bill Matthews, I recall his numerous visits to New Orleans to troll the jazz clubs, and that once in New York, after a reading I gave at the 92nd Street Y with Deborah Digges, he led the group, which included Deborah, Stan Plumly, and a couple of other folks, to an expensive Italian restaurant, where he proceeded to order expensive bottle after expensive bottle of wine, and that at the end of the repast casually announced that we would split the check. I also recall the abundant wit and charm he poured into my program the summer before he passed.

Arnošt Lustig called me "Fighter"—an epithet more justly associated with himself. He himself had survived Terezín and Auschwitz and wrote some of the most original and agonizingly humane books about the Holocaust ever written. One day in the late 1990s, he and I found ourselves alone in the banquet room of a restaurant near the Center in Prague; we were waiting for the other faculty of the Prague Summer Seminars (originally the Prague Summer Writers' Workshop and finally the Prague Summer Program) to arrive for the annual dinner that opened the program. We chatted perfunctorily until a long moment of silence settled between us, and we both gazed out the window onto Dlouhá Street. Arnošt said, apropos of nothing about which we'd been chatting, "They fucked up a beautiful idea for a hundred years."

I knew the Beautiful Idea was communism and that Arnošt indeed had been an enthusiastic member of the Party for many years, right up until the Soviet Union's anti-Semitism became unpalatable and he fled into exile in Israel, then America.

Václav Havel, the Philosopher Prince, the Playwright President, inspired the Left Bank of the 1990s, and was the North Star of my Prague Summer Program. I didn't meet him until the day my university, through the offices of my program, granted him and Lustig honorary doctorates in 2007. The event, covered quite heavily by the press, was a surprising success, especially given that the ceremony itself had been a fly-by-the-seat-of-our-pants affair; that is, we pretty much made it up as we went along in the grand Karolinum, the ceremonial space of Charles University. My second ex-wife, Dominika Winterová—thank the gods—took charge at the last moment and made the event work as though I had thoughtfully planned the whole thing. At the reception following the makeshift ceremony, I chatted with the former president, the absurdist playwright, the unflappable former dissident and political essayist, and found him humble, charming, droll, and surprisingly diminutive. He was the only Great Man or Great Woman (besides, alas, George W. Bush, but that's another story entirely) with whom I've ever conversed, and I recall feeling sad that I didn't much like his plays.

Horace famously asserted that "we are the degenerate descendants of fathers who in their turn were degenerate from their forebears," and though I don't believe the sentiment to be objectively true, I do consider it quite healthy to live one's life as though it were true; that is, when name-dropping is cultivation of the relatively recent past, we reap a kind of folk history of life off the page, as it were, life in blood and breath rather than ink and letters, and that history by its very nature is an apotheosis of its subject. Name-dropping, done artfully, is humble celebration.

There will be writers, living and dead, who will be vexed that I *did not* drop their names herein, especially folks who have taught in the Prague Summer Program, so here are a few, and I won't even bother to alphabetize them if only because the muddle of memory is a divine disorder: Richard Jackson, Carolyn Kizer, William Gass, Josef Škvorecký, C. K. Williams, Mary Morris, Francine Prose, Gerald Stern, Gail Wronsky, Mark Jarman, Mark Doty, Al Young, Robert Eversz, Jaimy Gordon, Jayne Anne Phillips, Marvin Bell, Michael Waters, Carol Muske-Dukes, Stuart Dybek, Patricia Hampl, Petr Bílek, Helen Epstein, Alison Deming, Barbara Cully, Cynthia

Hogue, Brad Leithauser, Alicia Ostriker, David St. John, William Pitt Root, Gerald Costanzo, Rodger Kamenetz, Charles Baxter, Ludvík Vaculík, Willis Barnstone, Peter Cooley, Donald Hall, Edward Hirsch, Robin Hemley, Grace Paley, Garrett Hongo, Slavenka Drakulić, Tracy Kidder, Anne Marie Macari, Geronimo Johnson, Deborah Eisenberg, William Meredith, Amy Tan, Ann Beattie, Phillip Lopate, Mary Jo Salter, Jean Valentine, Andrei Codrescu, Moira Crone, Michael Collier, Melissa Pritchard, Robert Olen Butler, Linda Gregerson, Christopher Merrill, Bharati Mukherjee, Gregory Orr, Ivan Klíma, Colleen McElroy, Chuck Rosenthal, Mary Karr, Randy Fertel, Miroslav Holub, Helen Fremont, Pamula Uschuk, Maura Simon, Adam Zagajewski, Steve Stern, Jiří Stránský, Iva Pekárková, Joseph Parisi, Mark Slouka, Herb Scott, Jiří Pehe, Elizabeth McCracken, Valerie Martin, Eda Kriseová, Sidney Lea, Margo Livesey, Bret Lott, Philip Levine, Galway Kinnell, William Matthews, Václav Havel, Michael Blumenthal, Vance Bourjaily, Diane Johnson, Susan Richards-Shrive, Lynn Sharon Schwartz, Carol Smith, Galway Kinnell, Mihaela Moscaliuc, and Pavel Šrut.

In late March 1980, I found myself in a cramped Honda Civic with Carolyn Forché, Louise Glück, Tess Gallagher, and Gail Wronsky. The occasion was the Stanley Kunitz Festival at the University of Virginia in Charlottesville. I was hitching a ride from one festival venue to another and simply got lucky to have imposed myself onto such illustrious company. As the car engine turned over, someone ran up to the car and shouted through the open, passenger side window that James Wright had died.

I'd read and relished every published poem James Wright had written, but I'd never met him, never attended one of his readings. I'd heard that he was ill but was ignorant of specifics. I'm not certain how I felt about the news of his passing primarily because whatever I felt, whatever I was capable of feeling for a writer whose work I'd absorbed deeply into my psyche but whom I'd never encountered in the flesh, whose physical voice had never for me been tethered to his poems, was overwhelmed by the shock and sorrow of my fellow passengers. I felt myself an interloper to that small automobile; I felt unworthy to be in attendance, in that particular community of grief. Some names never stop falling from our grasp.

My Penchant for Violence

Poets and Physical Courage

My father persuaded me that he could beat the hell out of any other man. When he was nabbed in 1961 and carted off to the Harrisburg Federal Penitentiary, at six feet tall, he clocked in at maybe 160; when he got out—five-to-ten, paroled in three—he was 220, all muscle. And he was crazy, not just crazy like the larcenous fox who'd accrued, over six years, warrants in more than forty states as he dragged a growing family with him; but crazy-eyed, don't-fuck-with-me nuts.

I was proud of my criminal father's warrior prowess, though I'd only heard about it from his mouth and witnessed it only once. We were on the verge of a treacherous mountain pass in 1960, and he'd not been able to bounce a check in several days. We were broke in the midst of a blizzard, and he believed that our traversing the snow-clogged, two-lane mountain highway, alas without chains, would dissuade the cops from pursuing us. We were on the cusp of starvation. He entered a diner jacketless, exited grasping a white bag like a football, followed by a fat guy wearing an apron. Through the blur of flurries, I witnessed my young father wheel around and sucker punch the cook, splaying him out, before jumping into the Chrysler he'd finessed from a used-car dealer a couple of weeks earlier, dropping the bag of burgers on the infant in my mother's lap, and crunching away.

I learned early to seem tougher than I am. That seeming such is a lie didn't occur to me when I was a child, adolescent, and young man, or it was a character flaw that never rose from the murk of repressed self-regard. Perhaps seeming tough is a character flaw only when it is not a feature of self-defense in a psychological as well as physical sense. There are occasions when a boy or young man must puff up or be devoured, especially when he cannot escape the exclusive company of other males, and depending upon the persuasiveness of his acting, he may get gobbled anyway.

That I glommed onto poetry as an adolescent seems now, from the downward slope of life, a spectacularly incongruous plot element in a spectacularly weird life story. As life stories go, weird is neither a good nor bad defining feature, and if I may claim expert status at anything, it's being in the midst of a weird life for which I may claim no particular credit regarding its weirdness. Assuming the mantle of "poet," as an adolescent whose only source of the stuff that such humans produce were two books filched from a Salvation Army book sale, I stepped into a role I didn't even know existed; that is, I had no model, even a caricature, for guidance. In a nest of DC and Marvel Comics, in the bottom drawer of a nicked-up pine dresser in the bedroom I shared with my brother, were an anthology of poems, mostly by Brits, and Robert Frost's collected poems. I waded about in those tomes with perhaps 60 percent comprehension of the words on the pages but with miniscule understanding. I did not know what a poem was when I stole those books. I was drawn not to their wisdom but to their weirdness.

And as I attempted to imitate what I was reading, I did so with a sense of those books being as from another planet, as though they'd been tucked under Kal-El's red blanket in the space capsule, say; and though I had a sense of Robert Frost as a guy who lived in the country and wrote about trees and fences and that most of the guys in the anthology sounded "fancy," I was clueless as to what it meant to be a poet, except that such a person was exotic and being so suggested life outside the Chesterfield Heights projects, outside any aspect of life that I could claim. Robert Frost and those British guys (almost all guys) were nothing like superheroes. They didn't even seem much like guys. I didn't know how to formulate their difference, but if I'd known to call them sensitive, I would have. Poems seemed mostly what was going on inside their heads, the deep feelings of men who wrote down what they were feeling, what they were thinking about what they were feeling.

When my father was in prison for his second three-year sojourn from his family and any delusions regarding his warrior prowess, my mother and four siblings and I lived in the Chesterfield Heights Federal Housing Projects of Norfolk, Virginia. *The projects* invokes stock footage of urban decay and despair—sneakers laced together and heaved bolas-like over power-lines; intermittent gunshots, rampant graffiti, and the numerous other visual markers of "drug infestation," the most vivid tableau of which is a kid on a corner squatting to do business at the windows of a nightly parade of cars. But my projects were plagued neither by drugs nor guns, and the young men born and raised in projects over the subsequent two or three generations, since my occupancy of that world, seem from another world altogether. They are tougher than I, much tougher. Their lives have been on the proverbial line, the border between death and despair, to a degree and in a manner I cannot claim to understand intellectually or viscerally.

Yet I must try, and in trying, I must rise above the stock images from gritty cop shows to acknowledge that for every kid doing dangerous business, there's one dreaming of gridiron greatness or of dazzling huge crowds with his rhymes and glorious swagger. There is also one reading a book late into night, ruminating on big ideas, trying to figure out a fucked-up world. For every young guy in the projects living wholly in the moment because he cannot conceive a future worth occupying, there are two or three dreaming of a future worth living, dreaming with a fierceness as worthy of that grossly inflated term *hero* as that of any grunt on routine patrol. Such a dreamer must coexist with his hard-ass brother, who may murder him without compunction or provocation for seeming weak, for seeming a victim.

As a boy, I feared no one because there was no one in my universe to fear. I didn't think about guns because there were none, and when we wielded blades, we did so in shadow dances of mock manliness. The dreamer growing up in the projects through the seventies, eighties, nineties, two thousands, to the present, is "myself made otherwise by all his pain," given that my upward mobility has been on a staircase composed of the bones of his, and my, brothers.

The line is from Philip Levine's "Baby Villon," a dramatic lyric in which the poet encounters a long-lost cousin, a professional boxer, for the first time and takes the measure, over the course of the brief and intense meeting, of the light-years between them.

Villon is "116 pounds, five feet two," and has survived with dignity the world's brutalities. He's a prizefighter; at 116 pounds, he'd be a bantamweight, and the lower weight classes in boxing have always tended to be more culturally and racially diverse and more broadly representative in terms of nationality. Villon "holds up seven thick little fingers" to show the stranger, his American cousin, that "he's rated seventh in the world" (Levine should have written *ranked* rather than *rated*), and in the lower weight classes especially, such a high world ranking would have indicated a peripatetic life and numerous defeats against an albeit greater number of victories. Villon wants to know about Levine's father, about the American family of whom he'd no doubt heard but about whom he knows little and shares a story about life during the Second World War, the conflagration that took his own father and brother. We experience the little warrior's voice in a single, laconic statement: "Here they live, here they live and not die." The resolution of the poem is stunning:

> No bigger than a girl, he holds my shoulders,
> Kisses my lips, his eyes still open,
> My imaginary brother, my cousin,
> Myself made otherwise by all his pain.

Levine became my measure of how a man could be a poet. He was the teacher of my first teacher, Glover Davis, and he mentored, to one degree or another, the squad of Fresno poets who were my role models in San Diego through the 1970s. The Tough & Tender ethos of the Fresno School, I'll call it, appealed to me in my twenties, appeared a genuine synthesis of "man" and "poet," and such a being acted in and on the world in dynamic fashion, engaged others, not just an idealized "nature" and not just his own mind, and when he engaged his own mind, it was to judge the quality of his own engagements; according to the values of the Fresno School, every poem should be an occasion for Anubis, as in the Egyptian Book of the Dead, to weigh one's heart. I read Levine's "Silent in America" with inside skinny granted me by Glover Davis, who supplied the backstory of how Levine got roped into going to a biker party on a visit to Iowa City with Robert Mezey, where an altercation that Mezey instigated resulted in Levine getting his jaw broken, and hence the title. Of course, I found the poem immensely appealing for being grounded in a genuinely cool real-world context, one worthy of grade-A literary gossip. My father made clear that he'd won in spectacular fashion every battle he'd ever fought;

Levine wrote about the aftermath of a physical battle he'd lost in spectacular fashion (Whitman's "Vivas for those who have failed" chimed in my cranium as the poem's epigraph). He positioned himself not as a hero but as an antihero, a man fully aware of his weaknesses and inadequacies, a man who could laugh at himself, a man who, through poetry, could bear his weaknesses without shame and thereby achieve a measure of self-knowledge beyond my father's phony heroic status.

IV

And I, I am the silent
   riser in a house
of garrulous children.
   I am Fresno's

dumb bard, America's last
   hope, sheep in sheep's
clothing. Who names the past
   names me, who sleeps

by my side shall find despair
   and happiness,
a twi-night double header.
   He who loves less

than I, loves no one, who speaks
   more than I, speaks
too much. I am everything
   that is dishonest,

everything under the sun.
   And I say "balls,"
the time will never come
   nor ripeness be all.

I became a poet, or I committed in my heart to being whatever a poet is, as my mother was trying to disengage from my father through the mail and as she conducted an affair with a quite wonderful fellow who was kind, for a season, to her and to us kids. He'd visit us in our government-issued residence in the projects and was respectful of my position as the oldest male in the family unit, and he was respectful of all of us because he was a class act and not too good to be true but too wise to stay with us. He was a first-class petty officer. He sailed away with impeccable timing, just days before my father's release.

We lived on $169 a month in 1964, and that would be $1,400 today; out of the $169, we paid $40 for rent, the equivalent of $332. A grown woman and five kids, after rent, lived on the equivalent of about a thousand bucks a month. Pall Malls were a quarter a pack; my mother smoked a pack a day, less than $8 a month, or just over $200 in present dollars given that the price of cigs has soared well beyond the rate of inflation. We had few expenses other than utilities and food. We were pretty far below the poverty line, but we did okay, especially given that we didn't have to worry about getting shot dead, and Joan, our mother, didn't have to worry about her kids spiraling into drugged hopelessness, or more specifically, she didn't have to suppress the image of her oldest son's body traced in chalk on a Norfolk sidewalk. My family wasn't hopeless; the projects were not home; they were another motel, a temporary shelter. Our father would come back to us, eventually, and take us away.

My circumstances through adolescence did not render me a phony tough guy; my father did that, but it is simplistic to tag him as the sole cause. Actually, he was more the delivery system for the cause, which was a braiding of factors, some of which were grounded in nature and some in nurture. My toughness was a mask I wore negotiating male society, and there are few males, no matter the socioeconomic circumstances into which they were spawned, who cannot relate to masculinity as a mask they wore in adolescence, and beyond, among other males. The ones who can't relate either lack self-awareness or were born to be *the* toughest, *the* most aggressive, *the* most dominant, and as such, they should not be shunned but managed. Be that as it may, our primate natures impose upon us a penchant for determining rank within groups, and just as among gorillas, say, there is much posturing and faking, chest thumping, mock attacks and quick retreats, much noise in the dance of dominance among males.

Analogizing human to nonhuman behavior may lead to simplistic, inhumane assumptions, for example, the currency of the old-fashion term *breed-*

ing among the upper crust—the mixed metaphor here notwithstanding—being indicative of a classist process tending more toward actual idiocy than genetic improvement. Hominoids are singular, but within that singularity, defined, say, by a Venn diagram in which two modalities intersect so deeply that each contains most of the other, the human aspect outside the intersection is self-consciousness, pure and not-so-simple, the ghost in the meat machine, the realm of symbols, of "meaning" beyond the fact of animal urges. Primates seek self-esteem within social groups, human primates no less than nonhuman ones, but as much in the abstract as relative to access to sex and food.

My father had balls; I was told numerous times when I was a young man that I had them too. To have balls usually means that your fear quotient is less than for most others. Sometimes it simply indicates that a fellow has ignored social norms, has occasioned the ire of others by being impulsive, impolite, by transgressing in some manner a particular group's standard of social engagement, of decency. In such instances of indiscretion, to have balls is simply to be an oaf, but usually it connotes physical courage. As a boy and young man, I felt inordinate pressure to prove to other males, and thereby to myself, that I was not a pussy, even though I never doubted in my heart that I was indeed a pussy.

Betty White, the ageless TV star, famously effused: "Why do people say 'grow some balls'? Balls are weak and sensitive. If you wanna be tough, grow a vagina. Those things can take a pounding." Well, I wasn't a vagina; I was a pussy, a male who was like a female in not relishing danger, usually in the form of physical confrontation with other males. That I was a pussy was my biggest, really my only, secret and the molten core of my self-loathing. I therefore had to make my passage through the world never backing down from physical confrontations, never avoiding an opportunity to fight. The more fear I felt, the more tangled the tendrils it wrapped around my heart, the more powerfully I felt the simultaneous counter-urge to grind against the grain of fear, to repress the urge to flee any particular threat.

By the time I was adopted, in 1967, by my father's sister and her naval officer husband and transported, for three years, to Sasebo, Japan, I'd identified as a poet for at least three years, and to say one "identifies" with any condition fundamental to identity in a fundamental sense is to invoke an LGBTQ-like ethos; indeed, it is important to note that most more or less "straight" people don't identify as such—they just are. To identify, in this context, is to possess meta-awareness. It is to consider the nature of how one exists as a sexual and/or gendered biological and social being. As a poet, I was sensitive; I expressed my feelings unabashedly, if too often with hilariously unintended bathos, and that identification did not mediate so much as highlight the turmoil of a heart filled with fear and Rooseveltian fear of fear, in equal measure.

In Sasebo, even as my identity as a poet was coalescing in an aspic of fear, I discovered karate, had the incredible privilege of being trained by the late, great Yasozato-san, a ninth-degree black belt in Shobukan Okinawa-te (related to but not to be confused with Shodokan). Through an intensive study of karate, I discovered the beauty of brutality; during the years that, if I'd remained in the projects, I'd have witnessed the beginning of that community's demographic and cultural transformation, particularly regarding the influence of illegal drug economics, I discovered the aesthetic dimension of violence.

A mediocre athlete by almost any measure, I possessed one innate physical talent, what in boxing is called "heavy hands"; I had a hell of a punch. If I'd not so much hated getting hit, I might have been a professional fighter. That is, if I'd not been such a pussy, I might have followed my father into boxing because, according to my father, he'd one year knocked out everyone in the Norfolk Golden Gloves competition; he'd missed being middleweight champion because the knockout punch in the final match had arrived as the bell ending the third and final round gonged. Of course, he'd been robbed. I believed this until I was eleven. I'd believed everything, all of his stories, and, needless to say, wanted desperately to be as fearless as he.

I had forty-seven matches, lost eleven, not a bad record, but in karate tournaments and in the intramural competitions within our dojos—both the one on the base and the one downtown to which an American had to be invited to attend—we wore pads and were prohibited from striking above the chest or below the flap protecting the groin, and transgressions below occurred much more often than blows to the head. I'd many times rolled on the mat clutching my Bad Boys and groaning.

But the violence of the dojo possessed a veneer of civility, and though I was an above-average fighter, at least within the formal, mitigating parameters of the rules of karate as a sport—the aspect called *kumite* (**koo**/mi/tae)—I most loved the kata, the often intricate choreography the formal efficacy of which Yasozato-san and his acolytes enforced righteously, absolutely. My sensei often carried a bamboo pole composed of strips bound at both ends and wielded it mercilessly on our forearms, bellies, thighs, asses, when any parts of our bodies were misaligned by even a centimeter. My sensei enforced precision as though it were a religious tenet, and I worked constantly to achieve absolute precision, an impossibility, of course, but I didn't know that. I wanted to be perfect, but being perfect performing a dance, even when it celebrates a warrior's demeanor, is just that, the ideal of perfection in the service of celebrating a thing, not the thing itself.

For better or worse, when I composed poems, I was a formalist probably most notable for addressing subjects not usually associated with the formality of rhyme and meter, and doing so in a range of tones, in rhetorical registers, many would consider incongruous with formal verse, and I doubt I'd have veered quite so dramatically, and so early in my apprenticeship, toward couching the nitty-gritty and ugly in traditional verse forms if I'd not located "the imperishable quiet at the heart of form" that Theodore Roethke espoused in "Meditation at Oyster River," though I discovered that place most saliently in the kata, not in the poetry I was reading. The kata indeed taught me to read verse in ways that I'd never have considered had I not absorbed those structures of stylized violence into both my nervous system and my psyche.

I've been arrested thrice, thrown in jail twice, for physical altercations, though those events are, if barely, far enough in my past that I feel a certain nostalgia for that state of ignorance, that state of being profoundly unaware of how poorly I was prepared to manage my cowardice. In two of the three instances, I engaged other men whom I perceived to be threatening women, and there have been at least four or five other occasions I've managed not to get arrested after altercations occasioned by my perception of threats to women. It is dubious to assign the cause of serial behavior to a single event, but if I had to choose such a defining event from my childhood, it would be the day my father got out of prison the second time.

My mother was pregnant by that very nice sailor, Joey, who'd been smart enough to vacate our lives just days before Dick's arrival to our cinder block hovel in the projects, and that evening I heard Joan screaming as I'd never heard any living thing protest the horror of life on earth. I tried to get past the door, against which Dick had hooked a chair on the knob, jammed my skinny, twelve-year-old shoulder into it again and again. He was punching her in the stomach, I would later realize, to force a miscarriage.

Basking in his success, Dick sat at the kitchen table all night swilling Four Roses and bragging to no one, to the ghost of his father, to himself, and my golden, childish adoration collapsed into leaden, adolescent fury.

I assumed the role of poet within months of my father's transformation from hero to monster. Of course, he was neither, just a sick young man possessing more chutzpah than self-awareness, more confidence, than intelligence. My hatred of him oscillated over those months between his release and his driving my brother Chuck and me to San Diego to be adopted into his sister's family. I loathed him one moment and retreated into my former state of adoration the next. So it would be for years, though each year the periods of loathing elongated as the remnants of adoration scattered across the landscape of my passage into adulthood. In that chamber of my soul in which I hated my father, I hated all men and, by extension, myself.

I remember laughing my ass off when I first caught wind of Robert Bly's "men's movement." I appreciated the sentiments, found the Jungian underpinnings charming, attractive. But it resonated, in a (post)feminist context, as primitive not in the anthropological but, rather, in the broadly intellectual sense and certainly in terms of both the ideological debates as well as Realpolitik within the academy, where the range of feminist critiques of patriarchy were grinding the rhetorical bones of such quaint formulations as "Iron John" to dust.

I wish I had a Rosebud, a repressed memory of an object from my earliest years; it would have to be a memory that bobs to the surface as the objective correlative of my Daddy Issues, though of course, I would want to have it revealed not on my deathbed but while I am still vital.

Perhaps it has already been revealed to me.

I have nine tattoos; my father, Dick Harris, had one, a skull and crossbones on the top of his right forearm. I never asked where or why he got it; it was as indelible a feature of his physical presence as the color of his eyes or his irrepressible smirk. He was a pathological liar. I know this even though I am not qualified to make such a clinical judgment. I know that he was a pathological liar the way I know, even though I'm not trained in the science, that climate change is real and catastrophic. The anecdotal evidence is overwhelming.

He lied about almost everything; it would be easier to list what he didn't lie about. If it was raining, he wouldn't say that it wasn't. If the car in which he transported his family from motel to motel, bounced check to bounced check, was green, he wouldn't insist that it was blue. If the day we slid past the local authorities of a midsize midwestern town was a Tuesday, he wouldn't assert that it was in fact Friday. But that's about it.

That skull and crossbones, in the lime mist of a speedometer's glow at night, from my station overlooking his right shoulder, my cheek pressed against the top of the front seat, was not a lie. Perhaps it is too easy, too schmaltzy even, to say that it was the truth of his heart, the emblem of his pirate nature, a frank declaration that he could only be trusted to steal, cheat, and lie. It was the symbol of the ultimate truth, and even as a child, I processed that symbol as an indication that manhood is an endless encounter with death.

In the world of poets and writers, I've had numerous fathers. Philip Levine, though we never liked each other much, was chief among my surrogate fathers when I was a young poet, though I have felt closest to Gerald Stern, who was the father of my middle years. The Czech novelist and Holocaust survivor Arnošt Lustig was a father of my more recent life, and one anecdote from his sorrowful and beautiful hoard of memories has been instructive.

Notwithstanding Theodor Adorno's famous formulation regarding the efficacy of lyric poetry after Auschwitz (and I believe it extends to all literary art, all writing that is not mere reportage), the moral imperative to bear witness is indisputable, and over the course of his sixty-plus-year writing career, Lustig wrote about nothing that he had not witnessed by the age of nineteen. The Nazis sent him first to Theresienstadt (Terezín to the Czechs), then to Auschwitz, then to Buchenwald, but then, in transit to Dachau, he escaped when the train's engine was hit by an American fighter-bomber. Why did he survive Theresienstadt? Why did he survive Auschwitz? Why did he survive Buchenwald?

He was strong. He could work. He pounded the ties of tracks out of Terezín in the direction of Auschwitz. Dachau would certainly have been the end of the line. In Lustig's *Darkness Casts No Shadow* (English title), two boys who escape slave labor and death under similar circumstances die before reaching Prague. I once asked Arnošt why the boys in the novel died when he and his companion, in reality, did not. He answered, "Because they had to."

I'll not presume to unpack that cryptic yet profoundly resonant response, though I'll say that it was not uttered with meanness or contempt. Arnošt Lustig, who passed in Prague in 2011, was the most joyful, most mischievously happy man I've ever known. It always seemed as though his fictions were the receptacles of his sorrows, that by putting them there, he freed space in his heart for its more natural inclination.

As my brother writer Robert Eversz, who loved Arnošt Lustig no less than I, recently reminded me, Arnošt never wanted to talk about the horror of his youth; he preferred to talk about women and always with love and respect, though also a hint of concupiscent charm. However, I recall an anecdote he told me, in the nineties, as we awaited the rest of our dinner party in a restaurant on Dlouhá in Prague. I don't recall the context or whether the event is chronicled in any of his books, but the memory he shared with me is burned into my life.

After his tenure pounding spikes into rails in Terezín, the Nazi "show camp," Arnošt Lustig was relocated to Auschwitz. Upon arrival, he was ordered to strip and stand naked in the freezing cold with a clutch of naked older men. Those men who had lost everything but their humanity, including their own children, seeing the skinny boy shivering, crowded around him, surrounded him, pressed warmth into him.

Their Fathers' Queer Sons

The Apotheosis of Larry Levis

An inordinate number of (mostly male) poets sprouted in the San Joaquin Valley in the 1940s and were cultivated before being shipped off for processing in the graduate writing programs around the country, most in the Iowa Writers' Workshop. I'm thinking of the students of Philip Levine, Robert Mezey, Peter Everwine, and Charles Hanzlicek at Fresno State University through the 1960s, talents such as Bruce H. Boston, Glover Davis, Sherley Anne Williams, Robert L. Jones, Greg Pape, Herbert Scott, Gary Soto, Roberta Spear, Omar Salinas, David St. John, and of course, Larry Levis. If there is something we may legitimately tag "the Fresno School," it has already entered the Misty Flats of American Poetry; and a later generation or two for whom Philip Levine was already a famous geezer, a patriarch who not long ago entered the Mist as all must but is now a name and body of work still being digested by history, has germinated in the fields and hothouses of creative writing around the country. I recall Stanley Kunitz years ago pronouncing that we may live in a time of great poems but one in which, despite (or maybe because of) a glorious and swelling glut of the creatures, there are no great poets. Let's assume we live in a post-greatness era, at least regarding makers, if not the stuff they make, and let's assume that the reason for this breach has to do with the twenty-four-hour news cycle and all that it represents, the ubiquity and surfeit of mostly worthless information, and the general (we can only hope temporary) diminution of the human spirit resulting from an ass clown ascending to the apex of political power and martial authority. Oh, and there's the dimming from casual and constant overuse of honorifics such as *heroic, genius, best* (especially *best American*), and yes, *great.* In other words, *great poet* resonates as shallowly as *great flick* or *great burger.* Be that as it may, "greatness" usually, at least in the arts, happens outside the usual causeways of moderate "success," and those paths, for almost all American poets, lead to and from universities and their creative writing programs. I would argue that there was a time when poets in the academy could be both "institutionalized" and oppositional irritants within an institution (conjure McMurphy in *One Flew Over the Cuckoo's Nest*), and here I'm thinking of the generation of poets born in the twenties and into the thirties (Ashbery, Kizer, Kinnell, Bly, et al.). By the time creative writing became more or less professionalized, from the midseventies to the present, professor poets, most anyway, became, alas, professors first and poets second. Larry Levis may have been one of the last terrific poets who was a poet first, a card-carrying member of the professorate only incidentally. He possessed the charm, the aura, to pull it off; whether that aura was residue of something like greatness, the transcendent quality and visionary nature of his poetry, only Stanley Kunitz, surely a full-fledged angel by now, would be qualified to proclaim from Heaven into the hearts of the next generation's poets and scholars. That Larry Levis was special—another adulterated term—seems starkly clear from the commentaries of the many good people, good poets who loved him, some of them dear friends of mine. As kingship is what the kings of a rich land and a poor land, respectively, hold in common, the identity of poet is one thing Larry and I held in common. However, also like Larry, I am the son of two fathers (yes, I, too, hear Charlie Sheen in *Platoon*) who represented two very different life paths. Like him, I've led a life that is different from most, though that difference, that special charm, which emanated no less from Levis's poetry than from his life, in my life has been more bizarre, perhaps, a cascade of odd occurrences. Like Larry Levis, I became a poet, at least in some small part, because of my desire not to be like one of my fathers and was encouraged and empowered, at least indirectly, by the other father to regard poetry as a dynamic cluster of moral choices. Larry's biological father was a successful rancher whose success was rooted in a rigged and racist system; mine was an unsuccessful criminal, unsuccessful inasmuch as he spent more than twenty years over three decades in state and federal prisons. Larry's second father was the important American poet Philip Levine, mine a low-ranking naval officer, Lt. Cdr. Raymond Johnson. My strong intuition is that poetry, the world of poets, saved Larry's life for its duration, and I know it saved mine.

In late spring of 1982, I phoned Larry Levis and asked a favor. Though it had been out for a few years, I'd just read *Lucky Life* by Gerald Stern, and though I'd thought I'd read the work of every good poet of the generation of Levine, Ashbery, Rich, Wright, Kizer, Kinnell, Merwin, Levertov, et al., Stern was a revelation. I was faking it as a haughty waiter in a high-class tourist trap in the French Quarter of New Orleans, on hiatus from the University of Arkansas. I'd heard that Stern would join the faculty of the Iowa Writers' Workshop, where Larry had a visiting position. I asked Larry, point-blank, to expedite my transferring from Arkansas, an excellent graduate program, to Iowa, a storied one, even though he, Larry, would be long gone by the time I got there the following autumn. I wanted to know that lucky life, that older poet who seemed to appear as suddenly as morning fog on the Lake Pontchartrain Causeway. Larry in fact expedited my acceptance to Iowa; he was exceedingly dependable in such matters.

Going through my email queue, I recently came across an advertisement for a documentary about Larry. Among the blurbs was one declaring him one of the greatest poets of the twentieth century. Though I didn't know Larry Levis as well as the folks interviewed in that charming and thoughtfully rendered documentary had known him, I think I knew him, and his work, well enough to judge that Larry himself would have dismissed such praise with no hint of false humility. After viewing Michelle Poulos's quiet and thoughtful *A Late Style of Fire: Larry Levis, American Poet,* I recalled a poem Larry wrote about his one and only visit to New Orleans, in the mid-1980s; it's addressed to his guardian angel, whom he imagines in the poem to be the soul of a two-year-old entombed in St. Louis Cemetery, on the other side of Rampart from the Quarter. I remembered that he and Jerry Stern had driven down together from dual readings at LSU. I recently phoned Jerry so that his scarily sharp ninety-three-year-old memory could calibrate my fuzzy recollection of that time, and he told me an anecdote about his excellent adventure in a rented car from Baton Rouge to my apartment in New Orleans, and he recharged my memory of

Larry Levis exploring the Big Nasty. I recall trying to figure out which of that pair, in a non-impaired way, would have been Hunter S. Thompson and which the Samoan lawyer.

But that's Jerry's story, and I know that he's written about it in an essay and a poem. If we did not live in a post-greatness era, at least by the great Stanley Kunitz's reckoning, Gerald Stern would be a great poet; he is something like a pure voice. His poems, essays, and conversations are singular: the Voice of Gerald Stern. And that singularity is wise, original, funny, mournful, at once iconoclastic and respectful of institutions, at least the ones that manage not to piss him off, though I can't think of any offhand that fall into that category. Jerry visited me numerous times in New Orleans through the eighties and into the nineties, in part, I'm sure, because he had a crush on Lynn, the mother of my first (and second) wife, Betty.

With me quietly bemused, in tow, he escorted Larry through the French Quarter with the casual authority of a local. Larry was wide-eyed joyful; I recall Larry Levis happy in New Orleans.

Levine said somewhere that though Larry grew up in sumptuous Fresno County in Selma, California, in a well-off household, his heart was with the men and women who worked the land, the migrants who facilitated his family's wealth. Well, Phil adored Larry; I recall him saying, years after Larry's death, that Larry had been more like a brother to him than a son, though the years between them would have suggested a relationship of the latter kind. He and Larry were often each other's first readers of new poems. I'm sure there are boxes of their correspondence in Phil's archives; Phil was an inveterate letter writer, and I've heard Larry was too. My correspondence with Larry was minimal, though always thoughtful and entertaining from his end, and my exchanges with Levine also minimal, though finally poisonous; I must admit that I deserved Levine's venom if only because I should have known not to tread that particular rhetorical ground: I confessed in a letter that I had reservations about his book *A Walk with Tom Jefferson* and, in the same missive, raised the issue of Larry Levis's addiction to cocaine. In the mid-1980s, Levine was either in denial or simply didn't think it was my place to bring up the issue of Larry's exceedingly self-destructive behavior. In either case, he lashed out because he loved Larry and was fiercely loyal to him. It was bad form for me to critique, unsolicited, Philip Levine's newest book and to cast shade, no matter how indirectly, on his spiritual son.

In his interview for the Larry Levis documentary, Levine spoke of Levis working beside the seasonal laborers on the family ranch, and I would never dispute that Larry Levis's heart was with the migrant workers his family exploited to achieve and maintain their privileged lives. The divergence of one's heart from one's material interests may be pronounced in a poet's life, though that righteous gap is likely nonexistent in his father's, and it's often the sins of a father that subsidize a poet's righteousness.

In 1985, a few months before Larry and Jerry's visit to New Orleans, Betty and I, Carolyn Forché and her husband, Harry Mattison, Bruce and Marsha Boston, Robert Jones, and Barbara Cully caravanned in three cars from San Diego to Fresno. We were on a kind of pilgrimage "to see Larry." Bruce and Marsha and Robert were returning to their origins to celebrate life with an old friend. Carolyn and Larry had recently become friends and were at similar phases of their stellar poetry-academic careers. Harry was a part-time Renaissance Man and full-time top-notch photojournalist. Barbara and Betty and I had returned, from Iowa City and New Orleans, respectively, to San Diego to visit families.

As much time has passed since then as I'd lived until that event, so I recall nothing of the journey and little of the sojourn at Larry's ancestral home, though what I remember resonates with a mild, sweet dissonance.

I thought I knew Larry better than I did; I'd actually been in his presence only a few times: I viewed him chiefly through the anecdotes with which other Fresno poets had regaled me for years, the aggregate myth of a 1960s antihero who possessed a preternatural capacity for ingesting drugs, especially hallucinogens, a Rimbaudesque Mr. Natural who read voraciously and lived hard, a late-night talker and stalker of beauty. The salient detail that had not shone through the membrane of that myth, at least for me, was that Larry was a rich kid, if only by the standards of my own origins.

I was mildly stunned sitting by his pool, overlooking an undulating green valley laced by a sprawling orchard. His solicitous, white-haired mother was the essence of grace, flitting from house to pool and back, committed to our comfort.

I can't recall what we drank, though I'm fairly certain it was nothing plucked, squashed, and distilled or fermented from that particular landscape. I didn't drink as much, generally, as the Fresno poets—Bruce, Bob, and Larry—did back then, and Harry and Carolyn were moderate drinkers, as were Barbara and Betty. The old Fresno friends, Bruce and Marsha, Robert and Larry, were particularly festive that evening by the pool on the Levis estate.

It was sunset much longer than it should have been. I mean, when the sun descended the other side of the farthest, highest hill, the sky remained dully illumed for what seemed hours, though that's just a trick of memory, the time warp distortions of events protruding from the muck of nostalgia like old tires. Everyone was lovely in that protracted twilight. Everyone was charming in proportion to their loveliness.

I am inside, just off the pool. I am smoking a joint with Larry, and he is showing me the galleys of *Winter Stars*. I sit on a couch and page through the poems as Larry breezes in and out, then back in. The only light in the room is twilight through a window. I can barely read the pages, but to flip a switch feels inappropriate. I place the galleys on a coffee table and rise to engage Larry, who is pinching another joint. I comment casually upon what I have thus far perused; he listens, smiling, then begins to monologue, looking past my head at a wall. He is smiling as he chatters, his back to the door, the pool, the backlit vineyards and hills. I've no idea what he's talking about. He is effervescent, his voice matching the muted light. Our faces are two feet apart. I would smell his breath if not for the pot and the cigarettes, which is all that I can smell.

I have a revelation, a small, odd one: Larry Levis is in a trance. I take a half-step to the side. He doesn't move, doesn't acknowledge that I have moved. He talks, staring at the wall his full view of which I have enabled by shuffling sideways. He is telling a story, a charming anecdote, but I am clueless as to its context. He chuckles as he chatters. I walk around him, turn, stare at the back of his head. He is regaling the wall or a ghost that stands before it. I walk outside, slouch by the pool, bemused. Everyone is engaged or staring off toward the hill beyond which the ocean is endlessly rocking miles away, and the sun, suspended just above the horizon, reclines. I turn and reenter the house. Larry is standing where I left him, chattering, chuckling, still facing the wall.

As I grow less unlikable over time, I am still not a particularly likable person, though I've never begrudged others their likability. Everyone else at that gathering was eminently likable, especially Larry, the rich kid who had slummed with his father's workers, who even, from time to time, had worked beside them, though not quite in the same spirit as Philip Levine had occupied the factory floor beside Detroit's postwar workingmen; Levine's father had died when Phil and his twin brother, Eddie, were little boys and had certainly not owned the factory where his son would someday labor. Whereas Philip Levine—and this is wild speculation—had been fairly certain he'd not spend the rest of his working life on a production line, Larry certainly had never considered daily, body-snatching labor as a potential necessity; Levine probably regarded the grinding redundancy of factory work a powerful incentive to rise out of that world he would someday by turns damn and memorialize. Beyond what is revealed in the documentary about his life, I've no idea what daddy issues Larry may have addressed, or encountered, sweating among the vines, not daily but time to time, beside the men his father paid, legally or not, fairly or not.

Before rap, before hip-hop, creative writing workshops rendered the role of poet available to the progeny of the working class, the working poor, and even the nonworking welfare poor, of which I was a statistic during most of my childhood. This is simply to say that the postwar proliferation of higher ed opportunities, fueled by the GI Bill and a collective desire to cover the offal of war with the sands of accelerated time that flowed through the body politic post-victory, accommodated even the miscreant artsy types across the least advantaged end of the economic spectrum.

Yet though I think that class figures into any poet's profile, is one determinant of her or his or their relation to language and the ideas of beauty and freedom and all other glorious abstractions—to an extent and in a manner commensurate with a child's sense of placement within the social order—I don't think that class identity is immutable, especially for poets.

I was adopted into the middle class by a dyspeptic paternal aunt and her naval officer husband; I lived with them for four years. As I exited their home on my eighteenth birthday, they must have felt that they had reaped the whirlwind of their generosity; I certainly carried with me out the door to my '67 Mercury station wagon, in addition to brown paper bags in which I'd stuffed my worldly possessions, their crushed hope that I would ever develop into a proper Republican.

However, after living with them first in Sasebo, Japan, just a few months after I'd arrived on their doorstep, and then on affluent Coronado, just across the arching blue bridge from San Diego, I'd absorbed a sense of entitlement I'd never have had purchase on living in the federal housing projects in Norfolk, Virginia. When my very dear, deeply decent uncle-stepfather got home on November 4, 1971, from the North Island Naval Air Station, he wore his dress whites I know not why; he stood in the middle of the living room, obviously befuddled, as I hugged grocery bags out the door again and again. I'm certain he was certain I was doomed, but he honored my spanking-new adulthood with silence. He didn't know that he'd gifted me a speck of his decency, if not his politics, though I will never be as decent, as modestly decent and honorable, as he. When I left his house, I carried not only grocery bags stuffed with clothes, books, and adolescent male stuff as well as an iota of decency he'd gifted me; I also carried in my heart, or whatever one wishes to call it, a sense of expanded possibilities afloat on foamy white, bourgeois entitlement.

I understand that sense of entitlement as someone who—certainly didn't earn but—acquired rather than was born into it; that is, I have murky recollections of a childhood void of expectations beyond my enlisting in the navy or shipping out with the merchant marines. Having barely made it out of sixth grade, I'd not been wired to consider college an option. However, as I prepared to crank up my '67 Mercury station wagon, which I'd just purchased with four hundred dollars I'd saved at my janitorial job on the Coronado Amphibious Base, I didn't doubt that I would attend college, right after I'd racked up a fortune writing hit songs in LA with my musician buddies Bruce and Bob.

The sky was the fucking limit, such that on those occasions, over the next couple of years, I was homeless, I could always find someone with whom I could crash, and she was always likewise entitled, Daddy's little girl, a white, middle- to upper-middle-class kid who wore puka shells and would inherit something. I knew I'd never inherit anything from my step-parents, or, I should say, anything else, for they'd already bequeathed me privilege on which I'd otherwise not have had purchase: white, middle-class access to blonde young women who wore puka shells and to an over-powering sense that higher education was inevitable.

My stepfather is the reason that, though I hate late-capitalist conservatism, I feel affection and respect for so many of its adherents, though only those from my stepfather's demographic, men and women whose values were forged in the Great Depression and who believed that sacrifice is the essence of adulthood. He stood in the middle of his living room on November 4, 1971, clad in his dress whites, probably home from a change-of-command ceremony on North Island Naval Air Station, and watched, silently, as I shuttled in and out of the house hauling my worldly posses-sions—single-season, Southern Cal wardrobe wadded up; my karate gee; thirty or forty paperbacks; a folder containing my "important papers" (birth certificate, Shobukan Okinawa-te black belt certificate); and several spiral notebooks containing the ragged effusions of my inchoate genius.

Lt. Cdr. Raymond Johnson held his shiny black-billed white hat in both hands. His left breast pocket dripped the primary colors of service ribbons he'd earned mostly as a noncom. He watched me through several trips from my brother's and my bedroom to my new used car, and when I entered his house for the last time as a resident, he finally turned and walked toward the kitchen. I thought I heard him say, "Good luck," as he turned, but that was probably wishful thinking.

My stepfather was a year or two too young to have fought in World War II, and there was no mention in the Levis documentary as to whether Larry's father had fought in that war. Larry's father was probably a decade older than my stepfather, but they were both in the wheelhouse of that era in which Americans defined themselves by the common purpose of overcoming unambiguous evil.

But the older guys my seventeen-year-old stepfather found himself among scant months after the end of the war had nearly all been "in the shit," as the Vietnam generation of servicemen later designated battle in

the jungles and rice paddies of Southeast Asia; that boy-man was accultur-
ated into a fraternity of victors, servicemen and officers who had traversed
oceans to enter the maw of doom and survived.

Each generation of men, for better and for worse, is defined by who was
in the shit and who wasn't, and this goes for poets no less than for truck-
ers, scholars, and insurance adjustors. One of the first things I note upon
meeting a male contemporary is whether he was in the service during
the Vietnam War and, if so, whether he'd been in the shit. One of the first
things I note about men born in the 1920s is whether they'd fought in
World War II or Korea.

Larry and I did not fight in Vietnam; Lt. Cdr. Raymond Johnson,
commanding officer of a wooden-hulled coastal minesweeper, the USS
Phoebe, traced the coast of Vietnam trolling for mines, among other tasks
about which my stepfather never spoke. He'd been on the edge of the shit,
close enough to have been forced to stave off many consecutive hours of
unrelenting fear. I've no idea how Larry managed not to be drafted, how
he avoided going either to war or prison, though I do wish that the documentary celebrating his life and work had addressed that issue, given that
it's among the most important, indeed one of the defining issues of our
generation, as it is, alas, of every generation.

Oh . . . I was in the lottery. My number was 339 in 1972, a golden ticket
to Not in the Shit.

Larry Levis's father, it seems from the documentary honoring Larry,
was taciturn, a tough, quiet man who neither discouraged nor much encouraged Larry's artistic tendencies.

My stepfather was loquacious. Even after I vacated his home, I'd return
fairly often to cadge meals and bask in his low-key, dinner table diatribes
about the degradation of the republic. Sometimes I'd get stoned before
visiting my stepfamily for dinner, and I've no idea if Lt. Cdr. Raymond
Johnson knew I was stoned, though I now have to think that he did. But
whether he did or not, he'd sit with me for an hour or more, drinking
coffee, smoking cigarettes, and holding forth.

I was clueless, when I was nineteen, twenty, twenty-one, and twenty-
two, as to how important those moments were. I didn't understand that
my stepfather was making me a better human being than I otherwise
would have been, though that may not be saying much. My stomach full

of pork chops and mashed potatoes and something green or yellow, my buzz mellowed by calories and caffeine, I'd listen to him drone on and on and on about the pros and cons of aluminum siding or the vagaries of professional sports or the death of common sense or the clear and present danger posed by the goddamned Democratic Party and sometimes pressed back on what I considered his reactionary evaluations of social reality but usually just listened. It didn't matter what he was saying, only that he talked to me, that he seemed to want to talk to me, that he cared for me enough to want me to know what he thought and felt.

Those hours at the table after dinner, after I'd vacated his and my aunt's house and become a wearisome chronic guest, were when and where Lt. Cdr. Raymond Johnson infused me with a modicum of his decency by droning amicably about the withering of the American Spirit and degradation of the American Dream. I came to take for granted that he cared for me enough to want to persuade me away from my radical commie perspective and that he indeed cared enough to continue his mission of persuasion well beyond the point when it was obvious that I was unpersuadable, that I was a goner, that the forces of evil, led by Senator George McGovern and his Fifth Column of bleeding-heart losers, had already assumed control of my mind.

Poets, male and female and every gradation between and beyond, exist because and in spite of their fathers, even on those rare occasions when the fathers are amenable to their progeny flitting about in Never Land and even, I suppose, when the fathers themselves are poets (James and Franz Wright, Peter and Nicole Cooley, Willis Barnstone, and Tony and Aliki, etc.). In the Levis documentary, it is proposed that Larry Levis fairly early on regarded his life's prospects as binary: he would take over the ranch-vineyard, I suppose with his older brother, or he would become a poet. There seems not to have been a psychic space in which a rancher-poet could flourish, a situation in which vocation and avocation might be blended like a Black and White at Tastee Freez. This is a forgivable failure of imagination; young people, especially budding poets, are drawn to the melodrama of either-or life decisions. Larry Levis could not imagine himself occupying his laconic father's role as overseer of laborers and cultivator of vast expanses of dirt, on the one hand, and his own dreamy life's role as cultivator of language and the heart's boon, on the other. Perhaps he early on noted the farce that Robert Frost's farmer-poet persona promulgated, or more likely, he simply wished to escape his father's judgment, probably never spoken, that physical labor is the only honest, unadulterated thing that a person can do. The fathers constituting the greatest generation (Tom Brokaw's dubious though powerfully adhesive appellation is deployed here with only a sliver of irony) were the last in a line of mostly white American men who accepted as axiomatic that reality is one thing and everything else beautiful horseshit, somehow feminine, a feminine chimera called culture. Work is necessary activity, and productive work is cultivation of natural resources, rendering them the artificial fruits of exploitation. Culture is cultivation as play, as both sex (the fun rather than the procreative aspect) and religion (sitting, kneeling, praying, singing: ritual rather than practical activity), and as such isn't serious, not really. church (its not-work-ness) and sex (the fun part) were auxiliary to reality, perhaps important but not quite necessary, and reality to the greatest generation and those preceding them was what is necessary, all things pertaining to what will suffice regarding each day's fulfillment, each day's grinding upon the next.

I never had to announce to my stepfather, that right-wing, thoroughly decent, warmongering deeply principled man, that I was a poet because he knew, the way some fathers just know that their sons are gay, that I read and tried to write the stuff. I suppose that his coming upon library books of poetry or un-balling balled-up scraps that had lines of mostly illegible adolescent abstractions scrawled upon them was similar to a father, pre-internet, coming across gay porn at the bottom of his son's closet.

And what I'm getting at is probably the most obvious yet least explored aspect of poetry's place in American culture, that it occupies a realm outside of necessity, like church and (non-procreative) sex, like all activity that isn't work, that isn't, therefore, real. It is the bifurcation of what is real (necessary, stark, potentially satisfying without being fun) and what is culture (playful, frivolous, feminine, edifying, fun). Ye ol' Puritan work ethic, yes, though this bifurcation is the conceptual bedrock of all agrarian social constructs, all subsistence-driven units of human activity. An assumption of the unreality of culture is a defining feature of masculinity generally and of American masculinity most prominently.

No adolescent male, and especially no adolescent American male, regardless of his sexuality, escapes the ramifications of such a fundamental bifurcation, of one in which masculinity is a province of reality, and therefore of truth, and is as such a condition to which a male ascends or becomes mired in mere culture: nonproductive, nonexploitative, yet also wholly unnecessary cultivation, play for its own sake, and in the case of poetry, and unlike even strumming a guitar and belting out original songs, there is absolutely no legitimate dream of a living wage available to poets, outside of academe, who do not set their words to tunes and emote them in a groove.

My stepfather didn't talk much about my artistic tendencies, but he talked about everything else ad nauseam, and I relished, as a young man, his droning voice, his tortured locutions, his willingness to sit across a table from me and sip his coffee, drag on his cigarettes, and hold forth about the world, his by turns reasonable and militaristically aggressive sense of how America should guide it, whether the world wants to be guided or not. I relished my sessions with that man I'd only known for a few years but who had taken me on as a project. I thought I didn't want to be like him, though now I am enough like him to look back and know that he loved me, that his talk, his tone, his time, not his beliefs or judgments, were the manifestations of his love for a damaged kid who was becoming a dubious man before his eyes.

Male poets—straight, gay, bi, trans—no matter how butch or butch-seeming, are queer, or might as well be. As straight guys obsessed with the relation of language and emotion, of nuanced feeling and the music of verbal expression, as exponents of an activity in direct contradiction to the basic tenet of manhood—that only work is real or true and culture not—Larry Levis, the entire Fresno tribe, indeed every white male American poet including myself, straight or not, entered queerdom on the day and at the hour he began to contemplate not *how different* he was but *how he was different* from his father. Yes, this is generally true of males drawn to theater, music, visual and even culinary arts, almost any identity-granting activity that has an aesthetic dimension, but no such identity runs counter to the ideal of American manhood as gaudily, as flamingly, as that of poet.

Larry Levis was a cross between American poetry's Arthur Herbert Fonzarelli, "the Fonz," and its Lord Byron. Like the Fonz, he had the cool factor and daddy issues out the wazoo. Unlike the Fonz, however, but very much in the Byronic spirit, Larry was a romantic; as Glover Davis recently quoted Philip Levine, over brunch when Glover and Maryanne were passing through Kalamazoo, "Larry could fall in love with a glass of water," though I can attest to the fact that none of the women, mostly poets, who own up in the documentary to having cavorted with Larry resemble by any overt feature a glass of water.

And Larry's Byronic panache was mitigated by a kind of wholesomeness at odds with both the English poet's profligate galumphing across early-nineteenth-century Europe and his own libertine path through the twilight of twentieth-century America. That wholesomeness was the vortex of his likability and seemed in no sense contrived. It was, perhaps, a quality endemic to an agrarian childhood at its best, a quality born of clean air and fecund dirt and green stuff, of time apart from family yet in the midst of it by virtue of a deep sense of shared ownership. I'm reminded of Dylan Thomas's "Fern Hill," though without the dreamy music of a dead language playing in the background. I'm reminded, too, of how deeply entrenched is the sense of "other" in a child's heart. Those men and women who worked the land of the Levis estate, beyond the Levis swimming pool overlooking the rolling hills laced with orchard rows, those Hispanic laborers whose language he certainly could not understand when he was young and easy under not apple boughs but grapevines, *as other* were not alien any more than the air and the dirt and the vines; those people were other in the same sense that the air and the dirt and the vines were other: they were owned. *That* Larry Levis, as he matured, grew genuinely to empathize with his father's workers, even to venerate them in that sticky-sweet way that white privilege incurs, which is testimony not only to his fundamental decency but also to his queerness, his own sense of unmanly otherness within the family unit.

If idle hands are the devil's workshop and idle lips his mouthpiece, poets are his acolytes, as are all performers and artists and preachers and motivational speakers, though poets, at their best more edifying than entertaining and, when entertaining, usually in the same manner as otherwise staid office party drunks are so, are the queerest of his acolytes if only because they are farthest removed from meaningful, remunerative labor. Larry Levis, my big brother from another mother, as the saying goes, navigated between his fathers, the Rancher and the Poet, with a languid grace that informed his later exquisite meditations on death and death's mediation of life. I have navigated between my criminal progenitor and warrior philosopher with far less grace but a tad healthier skepticism regarding the value and relevance of my own queer nature. Larry was, in poker parlance, *all in* as the best at any endeavor must be and as only the best are. Did he produce great poetry? Only time will tell. I do not doubt, however, that he was, queerly speaking, a great poet.

My Gorgons

Our true teachers educate us only incidentally, particularly if we are destined to become painters or poets, gangsters or politicians, athletes or chefs, stand-up comics or astronauts, any category of social being composed of individuals who, compelled by mysterious and inexorable forces, must challenge the laws of conduct or nature or both. A true teacher knows that such humans are largely uneducable and that her task regarding such as they is less to impart information and knowledge than simply to protect them at the most vulnerable stages of their development, their careening progress toward sometimes glorious, often dubious fates.

I should have flunked sixth grade. My mother was dying of multiple sclerosis, and my father was poised to get out of prison and was angry, if my mother's nightly weeping over his letters was any indication. She was pregnant by a sailor who had been kind to her and the five of us kids but who was smart enough to sail away from the event horizon of our doom. He apologized to me, the oldest, before he left, and I accepted his apology. Just diagnosed, my mother was still, as we now say, processing her inescapable predicament. I was distracted in my sixth grade classroom, at Chesterfield Heights Elementary, in Norfolk, Virginia, on the edge of the government housing projects where my mother and the five of us kids were sustained by a $169 a month from welfare.

I was failing because I couldn't concentrate. All I could think about was my father's messianic return, an event I'd anticipated, before the sailor's gentle presence, with pubescent intensity, but in the wake of my mother's sorrow and in anticipation of my father's wrath, I couldn't focus on Mrs. Tunstall's voice or what her chalk screeched on the blackboard in perfect cursive. I was indifferent to any speck of the future but the date of my father's return. That season was the only period in my life when failure had no meaning.

One day, when Mrs. Tunstall asked me a question that I couldn't answer because I hadn't heard her and didn't even know the subject the class was discussing, she paused, stared me into stone. Then she wiggle-wormed her finger for me to leave my seat and approach. The class, mostly Black kids only a few years after desegregation, sat stupefied. Mrs. Tunstall grabbed her green spiral book, in which she noted everything, led me out the door, into the hall, and closed it behind us.

She was tall, thin, severe. Her voice was deep and raspy, and her breath stank of coffee and cigarettes. Kids feared "getting" her, beginning as early as third grade. Having got her, I'd resigned myself to the scholastic torture for which she was infamous.

And yet, earlier in the school year, before my mother's diagnosis, before the sailor, before the pregnancy and rage-filled letters that arrived daily like a bird of prey to peck and slash all joy from my mother's soul and body, I'd been fully engaged at school. Mrs. Tunstall, a pedagogic force of nature, had set the class the task of composing, collectively, a play set in ancient Egypt, one that we would subsequently stage.

She'd stand at the board and elicit ideas, plot points, dialogue. There were at least thirty children in the class, and I practically wrote the whole script. I was that kid who jumps from his chair and waves his raised hand, and if not called upon immediately, both hands, and if still not recognized will semaphore as though guiding a jet onto a carrier. Mrs. Tunstall tried to get the others involved in that communal composition but usually, wearing a mask of reluctance, would point at me, tentatively, as though at a mug in a lineup she wasn't quite certain was that of the perpetrator. We constructed costumes from tinfoil and pillowcases. I was a nobleman and remember that before the first of two performances in the gymatorium, Mrs. Tunstall, in her introduction, informed the audience of first through sixth graders and their teachers that the play they were about to experience had been composed by her entire class, and in that moment I felt cheated.

In the hall Mrs. Tunstall opened her grade book and told me to read down one of the rows. Then she pointed at a number by Tony's name, then the one by mine. She explained that they were scores we'd received on the day-long aptitude test we'd taken earlier in the year. Tony, a beautiful, gentle Filipino boy, was the smartest kid in the class. He was a gifted drawer and was efficient and got everything right. My number was higher than Tony's. She stabbed with her finger my number again and again and yelled at me without raising her voice, her breath so rank it made me nauseous.

Mrs. Tunstall probably broke some rule passing me, considering that I did almost nothing through that spring of my father's return. More catatonic with dread than obdurate, I began to write down prayers that had nothing, except perhaps obliquely, to do with God, and when Mrs. Tunstall caught me scribbling one instead of adding columns of numbers from the board, she informed me it was a poem and ordered me to stand, once more dishonored, with my nose pressed into the rear left corner of the room, below the portrait of Lincoln.

I did not love that foul-breathed, dyspeptic hag until years later and then only through the gauze of nostalgia, and when I landed my first job, age sixteen, at the "geedunk" cafeteria on the Amphibious Base in Coronado, California, across the elegantly arcing blue bridge from San Diego, I entered servitude to another hag, another benign Gorgon who protected me without my even knowing she sheltered me under her invisible, magnificent wing.

Ester Hale stood six feet, weighed perhaps 115. She'd held the position of manager of the geedunk since before the Second World War. Her hair was white and short and permed. Her arms were blotched and bruised from work she shouldn't have been doing given her status. Her beige face skin seemed chamois rag soft and was webbed with wrinkles within wrinkles within wrinkles. Her lipstick was Red Cross red and her voice as soft as lard, actual remnants of which it was my fortnight task to scrape and scrub from beneath the evil deep fryers and in which were embedded cockroaches that had expired, legs up, in the throes of what must have been something like ecstasy.

My daily duty, for five years, was to arrive at three fifteen, after the cafeteria had closed its doors to famished sailors. Ester would unlock the door to let me in, then return to her calculator and logs in the rear of the single-story, square building.

I stacked 120 chairs on thirty tables, swept the linoleum with a push broom, mopped it, waxed it, then shined it with an electric buffer, before unstacking the chairs. Ester always left me change to play the jukebox, though she expressed muted disdain for my playlist, the heart of which was Rod Stewart crooning "Maggie May," Mick Jagger "Satisfaction," Otis Redding "(Sittin' on) The Dock of the Bay," and best of all, Eric Burdon belting out "House of the Rising Sun." I had it timed so that I was setting the last chair on the shined linoleum as the Animals' organ player squeezed out the final chords. Then I'd clean the mop and bucket, secure the buffer, and wait by the side door for Ester Hale to finish the books.

Some Fridays, she'd inform me I'd be coming in the next day to perform auxiliary duties such as clearing the muck and corpses from under the deep fryer; scrubbing the seeming miles of molding with Ajax, water, and a toothbrush; or washing the four glass doors and fourteen windows of the building. There was no refusing her, no begging off, no lame or legitimate excuses. For a buck seventy an hour and for whatever task she required my elbow grease and, often, marijuana-mellowed stick-to-itiveness, she owned me.

At twenty-one, I sauntered into a classroom at San Diego State. I was a junior, only two years from graduating, from actually completing successfully the gen ed courses one needed to garner a humanities degree. Installed in the seat of power at the front of the classroom was a gorgeous young woman.

My hair was shoulder-length and wild. I was barefoot. I went everywhere barefoot back then. I all but slithered into the second desk in the row nearest the wall, propped my filthy feet on the chair in front of me, lit a cigarette, winked. Unflustered, the new, young professor smiled at my insolence, even, I seem to recall, shook her head and blinked back mirth.

Three and a half years older than I, Carolyn Forché became my mentor. When we were young, I was much more her muse than she mine, if only because a muse cannot be a mentor, merely a catalyst for the heart's more combustible reactions to the pith of life's sorrows and joys.

It seems I was fated to accept the authority of one such as she, mercurial, flamboyant, abuzz with life force so intense whole rooms of smart people succumbed, gobsmacked, to her allure, a potion part medicine show elixir, part magical stuff.

She didn't know much back then, and lucky for her, I knew less, though what she knew she wielded like a perfect weapon for cutting the Gordian knots of rarified discourse, the horseshit of intellectual intrigue. I was along for the ride of my life, and she drove me in her brown Honda Civic to the end of the 1970s, where I jumped out, the car still rolling, and made it, barely, to the train called the Crescent, via Atlanta, to New Orleans.

Ester Hale unlocked to let me out and followed, locking the double doors behind. She wore an all-white uniform every day, the skirt catching her four inches below her knees, and some winter evenings, as we departed, a thin, sky-blue knit sweater. "Do you need a ride, Rick?" she'd ask, knowing I'd answer yes, as I did every other 6:45 p.m.

The image of her hand—her thin arm nicked, bruised, and covered in age spots, slowly, faintly, quivering from the strain of extending to the passenger side lock—pulling up the button, day after day after day, to let me enter her immaculate, mid-'60s Buick Skylark, is an image inexplicably tattooed on my heart. We didn't talk much on the half-mile ride through the security gate guarded by marines, onto the Silver Strand, past the marina and the Chart House restaurant, past the Victorian Hotel Del Coronado, into tony downtown, where she pulled over on Orange Avenue and let me out in front of Joey's Pizza.

The day our father returned, the five of us kids performed for him, like a traveling troupe for a king, though he was the interloper within the painted cinder block walls of *our* dingy domain. I played my tuba, requisitioned from the Chesterfield Heights Elementary School band, and he drank whiskey through the evening.

I awoke to my mother screaming, ran to her door blocked by a chair wedged under the knob, and heard my father, that stranger, punching her, again and again, in her fifth month.

Our true teachers are disseminators of skills and information only secondarily; they're primarily guides to the dragon's den, where the smoldering monster of comparative identity sleeps fitfully on a horde of the world's glittering indifference, where each student has her individuality locked to the multiplicity of soul-grinding and soul-sustaining competition, and love, alas, becomes a matter of gradations.

Ester Hale's pedagogic modus operandi was to shame. On those weekends she compelled me to assume auxiliary duties, she would emerge from her office off the enormous, dark pantry, her crisp white uniform that of a militant angel, and inspect my work. She would actually *tsk* as she surveyed, run her immaculate finger over whatever surface she had charged me with emancipating from the grime and corporeal petulance of sailors' shoes and hands, the nasty, often misogynistic treatises they carved and scrawled on toilet stalls and on the surfaces of tables. Then she would take the brush or cloth from my hand and begin to rub where I had rubbed or scrub where I had scrubbed, and filth, actual and symbolic, that I had found indelible, beneath her scrawny withered hand would begin to disappear.

When one apprentices to a chronological peer, sibling-like complications and qualities of intimacy are endemic to the power relation. Carolyn was the oldest of seven, I of five. At first, I didn't know how to be the younger brother of a strong older sister, but I adapted to her strength of will, her need to lead. Once, at a Provincetown Fine Arts Work Center potluck, attended by writers who, in a few years, would be household names in hundreds, in a couple of cases thousands, of homes across America (such is the numerical valence of most writers' fame), everyone at the long picnic table was arguing amicably in pairs. I found the tableau, and the ruckus, hilarious and had an epiphany. I yelled and made the time-out sign; when everyone had piped down, I asked, "How many here are oldest kids?" There were more than a dozen poets and novelists, sculptors and painters; everyone looked around, bemused, and raised her or his hand. Absolutely everyone at that long picnic table, everyone seated at that groaning board of makeshift abundance, had been trying to dominate, with no malice and no *conscious* sense of entitlement, someone else at the table, as only an oldest child can.

Peer mentors, in sports, crime, and the arts, wield only the authority of example. On the field, the teammate who can't perform what he demands is an object of disdain. On the streets, the buddy not willing to chance getting popped is no reliable partner in larceny or any other miscreant enterprise. In the arts, as in sports and in crime, the peer mentor's authority often has more to do with courage than wisdom; indeed, the peer mentor's example is to exhibit the courage of flying in the face of common wisdom.

When Carolyn Forché, barely out of her twenties, riding the success of one little book of poems, began her shuttle between El Salvador and San Diego, and then Salvador and wherever else in America served as her temporary home base during those years, few of her friends and fewer of her own mentors offered unqualified support. My oldest daughter is now roughly the age that Carolyn Forché was then, and if my adult baby informed me that she would be visiting, regularly, a civil war zone over the course of a couple of years, I certainly would not be enthusiastically supportive.

Mrs. Tunstall knew something was wrong in my home life, but something was wrong in almost every kid's home life in that community. She had no compunction about failing kids, keeping them back, as the euphemism still characterizes scholastic failure, though it was a time when the proverbial bar was higher and, consequently, failure more frequent and F not the scarlet letter it is today. Though I can't help wondering how different my life would have been had she failed me, had she compelled me to repeat sixth grade. I can't imagine the cascade of missed opportunities that would have followed, especially given that I attended hardly any of the following school year due to my father's criminal machinations and my mother's physical, and emotional, deterioration.

Ester Hale was my embodiment of the Greatest Generation, a designation I loathe when I consider Jim Crow, Hiroshima, internment camps, and Rosie the Riveter's forced postwar domestication, and yet one I, well, hail when I recall Ester Hale's gentle yet fierce loyalty to her job, her regal humility and Jobian patience with the likes of my boy-man self. She did not so much teach as condition me to scrub until all filth is gone, and if I have not always adhered to that principle, I've at least felt guilt for each failure to do so.

The Gorgons were so dreadful that their images were chiseled onto public spaces for the purpose of civic protection. Of the three sisters, Medusa, the single beauty, was also the mortal one, and an issue of her severed head was Pegasus. The truth in myth must be distilled from millennia of patriarchal, serpentine agendas and is often the essence of a power as elemental as any female mammal's protective urge regarding its young, some males' primal fear of the castrating mother notwithstanding.

That young woman who was my mentor and my friend, the older sister I'd not had and didn't want or need, was by turns an artful dodger of the slings and arrows shot by the pious agents of institutional conservatism in the arts and an embodiment of the righteous-shading-to-self-righteous progressive critique that is the bedrock of poetry's implicit moral agenda. As is true of most transcendent talents in the arts when they are young, her acute instincts compensated for her inchoate intellect, and her courage, both physical and artistic, was a curative for American poetry's smug sensitivities.

Freud connected Medusa to fear of castration, and of course he would. Academic feminists have reduced her to the purest expression of female rage, and that certainly makes sense, but I prefer to contemplate the protective role of all three sisters, particularly Medusa. Perseus used her visage as a defensive weapon, eventually gifting her to the ultimate female protector, Athena, who installed that powerful head—out of whose detached body had issued Poseidon's offspring, a giant and a winged horse—upon her shield.

It is not an exaggeration to assert that my Gorgons saved my life. Mrs. Tunstall rescued me from the stupor of adolescent despair, in the sense that instead of simply watching me sink below the churning waves of Poseidon's jealous rage, she tossed me a plank; it wasn't much, but I hung on, and it was all I needed. Ester Hale instilled in me the duty to rub against the grain of entropy. All things may tend toward filth and decay, but everyone owes life a little elbow grease, everyone is duty-bound to sweep and scrub and buff and squeegee and rub and scrape all surfaces, exposed and not, and to empty the grease traps, change the grease in the deep fryers of the world.

Carolyn taught my young-man self a kind of humility, and certainly not by example and certainly not deliberately. She taught me, without knowing or much caring, the humility that a person must feel in the presence of female power and that that power is everywhere and at all times, and not to see and feel it is to be any Somali warlord, any NRA ass clown, any Russian oligarch, any Freedom Caucus congressional crusader, any economic nationalist, any sexual predator, any offshore banker, any man or woman who opposes a woman's right to terminate a pregnancy on her own terms, any orange narcissistic meat puppet presuming to lead the Free World, any pedophile lacking restraint, any homophobe, any bully, anyone who harms for an abstract cause, any state senator who conspires to gerrymander districts and pass racist voter ID laws, any internet troll, any subprime lender, almost any health care or insurance executive, and every goddamned petroleum executive, hedge fund manager, and climate change denier on the planet . . . to name a few.

Mrs. Tunstall and Ester Hale are long dead, and Carolyn Forché and I are old friends who rarely reconnect. Once in a while on Facebook, where she is active and I am nearly dormant, and once or twice every other year at this or that conference, we cross paths, and I am always delighted to see and hear her for an hour here, twelve minutes there. We are not now what we were when we were young, for, like all who survive and manage, even modestly, to thrive, we are both more and less.

My youngest daughter, Ella, lives each year half in Prague and the other with me in Kalamazoo, Michigan. She attended the first half of the sixth grade with me and is attending the second half in Prague, living with her Czech mother. For her twelfth birthday last month, I sent her a gift card to purchase books. She immediately acquired the *Complete Works of Shakespeare,* without prodding, and called me this morning, which was her Central European afternoon, and said she'd purchased *Lord of the Flies* and *A Clockwork Orange.* She'd chosen those particular books without being directed, influenced, and we chatted about them, about power and violence, about males when they are left to their own devices. The father of three females, I feel sufficiently protected from my own worst tendencies.

Local Poets

I find the term *local poet,* the very idea, oddly unsettling. I've seen it deployed thousands of times in announcements for readings: "Local poets Bob Roberts and Dick Richards will share from their new books, both published by Funkville's own Hangnail Press, on Friday, April 33," or worse, "Beloved local poet Anna Anderson passed away on Thursday," or worst of all, "Local poet Ben Benjamin has won honorable mention in the *Carbuncular Quarterly*'s annual 'Why I Love Southwest North Dakota' haiku competition."

Local accountants, local plumbers, local restaurateurs, are rooted in place. Local artists, comedians, actors, and singers may be propelled to New York, Chicago, or LA, dragging behind them the quaint charms and Big City dreams of their neighbors, but local poets are like supine dogs chained to trees, beside pickup trucks on cinder blocks. Just like that.

Local politicians are another matter; most are like local poets, though at least they may harbor the dream of statewide or national office. No such pipe dreams are available to local poets and tethered K9s, no matter the length of their chains.

Are poets living in New York or San Francisco, say, local poets? Well, not necessarily. Frank O'Hara lived in New York, but I don't consider him a local poet, the New York School moniker notwithstanding. Philip Levine, in his last couple of decades, lived between Brooklyn and Fresno, though I wouldn't consider him local to either location, not regarding his identity as a poet, and though we associate him with Detroit, that place in his poems is more akin to a factory-centric Brigadoon than to the blighted urban "bitch" Madonna famously implored Michiganders to resuscitate: "Let's bring that bitch back!" When I gave a reading in Detroit recently, local poets clued me that neither Levine's nor Madonna's Detroit will ever return, though something more dynamic and interesting is already shimmering into view. Local poets are often prescient.

More to the point, is any poet, any writer, who teaches in a "college town" a member of that municipality's literary community? If so, at what phase in the individual's absorption into that burg's cultural bloodstream does she or he become, psychically and according to the collective identity of that network of poets and writers, "local," that is, one of them? Does she become local upon earning tenure? Does he become local when the concrete particulars of that place's identity, names of streets, local hangouts—bars and coffee shops—seep into his published work? Is a local identity simply a matter of time?

Local poets are itinerant composition instructors, abysmally remunerated hired guns galloping between classrooms. They are bartenders who also work on cars and junior high drama teachers who coach volleyball. They are trust-funded raconteurs waiting for their parents to die so that they may move into the master bedrooms. They are subcontractors staring officiously into exposed wires and poised to screw you on the estimate and ministers torn between Sunday morning's sacred pulpit and Saturday night's profane open mic. They are doctors and lawyers, bakers and janitors. They own bookstores and antique shops. They are homemakers. They are usually "progressive." Many are hipsters, or weekend hipsters. They listen to NPR and join causes. They are readers and movie aficionados too hip ever to utter the word *cinema*. They watch TV without guilt but mainly cable news. They are disproportionately vegan, which means roughly 13 percent. Each has approximately two thousand Facebook friends, almost exclusively other local writers all over the country, indeed, all over the world; they are therefore paradoxically local. Tip O'Neill, one of the more prosaically lyrical statesmen ever to nurture the body politic, famously declared all politics local, and though it is unlikely he had "unacknowledged legislators" in mind, the spirit of his bromide resonates through the coffee shops and independent bookstores of this great land, through the farmers' markets and college auditoriums, anywhere local writers, local poets, cavort with local pot dealers who restore, by day, neighborhoods ripe for gentrification. Local poets are salt of the earth that never loses its savor, to paraphrase the Sermon on the Mount, and they tend to be the best and brightest of their (larger) communities.

William Carlos Williams was a local poet who dived into a black hole of provinciality and emerged oddly urbane, though this is just to say that white chickens and cold plums may placate the most discerning palate. Robert Frost, purveyor of cagey pastoral allegories, as our first (perhaps only, Whitman excepted) professional poet, was no more local to the hardscrabble New England farmlands than any twelve-term, agribusiness-owned congressman. Expatriation was the Modernist rule, not the exception, and as movable feasts follow celestial rather than fixed calendrical patterns, Paris was less a clockwork banquet than an ephemeral trough to America's self-loathing early-century geniuses, Hemingway's self-aggrandizing notwithstanding. Iowa City may be to Paris what Deadwood Tavern is to Maxim's, but culinary fame is probably a lagging indicator of a community's literary relevance.

Hand-wringing over what fine arts grads will "do" with their degrees is both hilarious and disingenuous. What did I ever do with the three years I studied karate in Sasebo, Japan? Well, actually, I taught it, in part, to put myself through college, but more to the point, it was a rite of passage by which I gained skills and self-knowledge that cascaded through every other aspect of my life. Could I have sustained a living teaching it? Probably not. I wasn't *that* good, but when I applied for my first *real* teaching job, a four-and-four, all-composition, Sisyphean grind I indeed garnered, I was later informed that the committee had been impressed, and amused, when my letter of intention likened the teaching of composition to that of the kata, those intricate dances that are the aesthetic, and pedagogic, heart of Shobukan Okinawa-te.

That was my karate-callused foot in the door to the Ivory Tower, but given how relatively few who attend graduate writing programs make careers of college teaching, how may we justify their (pick your pronoun reference) proliferation and maintenance? How many local poets and writers may any city or town or village sustain?

Employment and quality of life are intricately, but not inexorably, connected. Somewhere between Silicon Valley and the Rust Belt is a sweet spot where vocation and avocation become as our two eyes making one sight, to paraphrase our great and phony farmer poet. But as difficult as it may be to get the news from poetry, or skewed left or right from MSNBC or Fox, no one really dies miserably for lack of what may be found in verse, free or formal. One may die horribly, though, for lack of fellowship, lack of community, and the greatest local poet of recent years, I submit, was a beloved lush from New Orleans named Everette Maddox, who seems to have died horribly yet happily. He certainly did not lack friends, lack community. Indeed, he was the epicenter of the 1980s New Orleans literary scene.

Raging alcoholic poets are *so* last century, and Everette was every inch a poet of that century's twilight. I really didn't like him, and as was true of so many of my personal judgments in the 1980s, I was singular in my evaluation of Everette Maddox and kept it to myself. He was the beloved miscreant poetry saint of the Maple Leaf Bar, the barfly impresario of its famous reading series, "famous" in the sense that such long-standing and sloppily organized venues may benefit from the faint luster of nostalgia.

His fingernails were long and crusted with filth. His frayed suit hung from him as from a Halloween skeleton. His brown hair dangled past his frayed, dingy collar in greasy strings. He was shabbily genteel, a southern gentleman Faulkner would have recognized and with whom the great writer would have felt comfortable sharing a bottle. Everyone loved Everette, found him authentic. I got along with him just fine; it was almost impossible not to. His collegiality was constant, and he hid nothing. His presence on *that* barstool at *that* bar—the sour odor of any previous night's blues quartet or zydeco-jazz mash-up hanging on the Maple Leaf air, a mix of tobacco and stale beer, clinging to that suit he'd no doubt slept in—was haunting in a way not usually associated with the living. Indeed, he seemed, through the eighties, a man freed from the exigencies of mortality. He'd decided to drink himself to death and went about his merry way doing so.

I was in my thirties, publishing books with a hotshot university press and in "national" literary journals. I loved New Orleans, but as a resident tourist. I was no "local poet," though I wrote poems, anecdotal lyrics set primarily in the French Quarter.

And I got so many things wrong, in my verse and my life, regarding that storied city. Did *real* New Orleanians resent me, my poems set in 1970s and 1980s New Orleans? The wiser ones of that tribe of insiders probably just didn't care. I was innocuous, by turns a cultural carpetbagger and scallywag but, youthful bluster aside, harmless.

I sometimes couldn't even look into Everette's face when chatting with him; I'd avert my gaze as he drawled, with exquisite, slow, wry, deep southern elocution, a humorous story in which a mutual acquaintance's minuscule misprision resulted in a bartender being late for her shift. He was a cursed soul who harbored no bitterness, no meanness, and who saw good in everyone, even me.

I recall sitting around with local writers, local poets, at private gatherings or in bars other than the Maple Leaf, when Everette Maddox's hallowed name would be invoked. More than once, I'd opined that there should be some sort of intervention; the concept I don't think was current then, but that's what I'd meant. Someone should intervene, should take Everette somewhere disinfected, safe, and, most indubitably, healthy, somewhere he could spend some months drying out, putting on some weight, cleaning up his filthy yet elegant act.

The local poets of New Orleans, the *real* local poets, didn't exactly scoff at my suggestion though seemed to regard it, usually without much comment, as a call for betrayal, as though to intervene in Everette Maddox's slow-motion suicide would have been to betray precisely that which was the source of his greatness.

Yes, I'll call it that. In every neighborhood dive of every American city, there are people committing suicide in similar fashion, but none that I've known has done so with such beatific panache.

There are many Maddox admirers, mostly other local poets, who loved him on his own terms and who no doubt hoard precious stories about him. It is their tributes that should be run up the metaphysical flagpole. They were invigorated, quickened, somehow affirmed, by how Everette Maddox was killing himself, and I offer this with no malice and only in the humblest judgment of their apotheosis of his—oh, let's call them—lifestyle choices.

Whitman ruined us, not just poets, local and otherwise, but the entire culture, with sweetness and optimism that militate against our creature survival unto the final American twilight. Of course, Whitman was the vessel, in both senses, of our transcendence, the best container and dispenser of American exceptionalism and the means by which we traverse the ocean of our despair. Whitman was the antithesis of a local poet, though a humble number of the multitudes he contained were indeed local bards chained to trees and howling at the moon.

Born in Montgomery, Alabama, Everette Maddox attended the University of Alabama when it was still Bear Bryant's plantation, and published early in such venues as the *New Yorker* and *Paris Review*. He arrived in New Orleans in the mid-1970s to be poet-in-residence at Xavier University, a very good, predominantly Black, school. By the time I met him, that plum gig had been long over, and how he lived, financially, from day to day I've no idea, though gainful employment never seemed an option. Other local poets lead dual lives, one, jury-rigged and belching smoke, that sustains the other, the *real* life of making and sharing language constructs among like-minded folks doing the same. Everette, as far as I could ever discern, and I certainly didn't pry or relish gossip that might have revealed answers, never had duties beyond sitting in the Maple Leaf Bar and presiding over a more or less weekly poetry reading series. Was there family money? Did family or friends marshal resources for his subsistence? Did he collect disability? Was he in any sense on the dole? Every local New Orleans poet with memories of that time may know the answer to the question as to how Everette Maddox subsisted, but it really doesn't matter. He was a conduit for the kindness of strangers and admirers alike, and I certainly never recall him without a glass of amber liquid in his emaciated hand or on the bar before him as he slowly gesticulated through a story worth hearing if only for the kindness and sincerity in his voice.

In one of my favorite photographs of Whitman, his hand is extended rather daintily, and a butterfly has lighted upon his finger; on close examination, one sees that a minuscule wire, or a ring of some sort, tethers the bug to the bard, his preternatural connection to all things wild and beautiful a mere tableau and therefore a ruse, an advertisement for his persona. We are conditioned in our time to explore images produced by mechanical means for such incongruities; we are vigilant for tricks to an extent that Whitman's contemporaries could not be.

One of the tricks of greatness, in the arts especially, is to construct a persona that is itself interesting largely independent of the texts, the products that are its issue. Yes, Charles Bukowski (whose column "Notes of a Dirty Old Man" appeared in New Orleans's underground *NOLA Express* at the end of the 1960s) had deployed his randy, alcoholic golem across the landscape of urban hippiedom; that beloved monster protected, in its fashion, the cultural ghettos of mimeographic effusion, the already decades-old bohemian communities teeming with the best minds of a generation not so much destroyed by madness as numbed by dubious relevance. Bukowski tended to his persona no less deliberately and judiciously than had Whitman, than had Whitman's other progeny who had gathered primarily in the Bay Area, local poets and artists who, collectively, raised local status to national prominence.

In some sense, every contemporary local writers' scene is an echo of the San Francisco Renaissance and the Harlem Renaissance. With rare exception, every dog has its day when the tree to which it is chained acquires a golden fleece of national relevance and that rusted truck becomes a gloriously restored '57 Chevy.

Everette Maddox was not simply a more genteel, southern-fried Charles Bukowski if only because the latter had been fiercely ambitious, as had been Kenneth Rexroth, one of the Dutch uncles of the San Francisco Renaissance, and as had been Ginsberg et al., who celebrated an earlier generation of poets who produced towering edifices whose foundations had been laid in ideologies, paradoxically, anathema to the radical egalitarianism of the Beats. Maddox actually wrote relatively little, and if a young man's high-octane ambition had fueled his sending poems to the *New Yorker,* by the time I knew him he was running on empty but more like a mystic sage, a Zen Buddhist monk, than an internal combustion engine. Some of the Beats and their precursors talked a mean Eastern game, but Everette Maddox lived it. He seemed amused by ambition, all ambition, not only that which motivates a reaching for the stars but also the reaching for a glass on a bar top or even the drawing of another breath. I recall how, in the midst of a chat, he'd slowly turn and tilt his head, stare at his glass; he'd seem in the throes of deliberation: *Shall I reach out my hand and grasp that glass? Shall I draw a breath and then lift that glass to my lips and drink? Okay. This time . . . ,* which became another and another and another.

If, as Randall Jarrell famously asserted, more poets fail for lack of character than lack of talent, Everette Maddox's greatness was that he not only eschewed but wholly transcended the very distinction not only between character and talent but between success and failure. He was a rare human creature whose self-destruction was *self*-destruction. If his life was a testimony to Bacchanalian abandon, it was reverie not revelry he sought from the wild god's dominion. His significance as a poet had less to do with his poetry, which I still judge to be but two or three notches above mediocre, than with his integrity, a quality indicated by the fact that he contrived no persona yet was a caricature of himself, a man in pain for reasons he seemed unmoved to broadcast beyond the borders of his own predicament, his own calculations of not life's but his own life's value.

Everette Maddox didn't love poetry as much as he loved being a poet, and though this distinction in so many others is the essence of folly, in the context of Maddox's life, in a New Orleans now delegated to the ash bin of pre-storm nostalgia, the distinction achieves postapocalyptic status. The New Orleans in which he was unofficial laureate of local poets was not transformed by disaster so much as transferred from the realms of mythos to logos, from the anticipation of doom to its material realization. Everette Maddox embodied the anticipation of doom. His New Orleans was a mother's lap in which he laid his head, never to sit upright again.

I believe that poetry is a living art form as long as fourteen-year-old boys and girls hide poems of love under their underwear and socks or sequester those tattered fragments of libidinal gibberish in the cyber equivalent of that drawer containing what the more prudish of a previous generation called "unmentionables." It dies minute by minute, again and again, in the hearts and on the lips of all for whom its making and consumption is a matter of prestige. And yet how can it not be?

The lyric impulse is toward loneliness, its tableau a shepherd whose audience is composed only of indifferent sheep, but its moral authority is the pedestal on which private troubles and public issues embrace. That tension between primal impulse and social imperative is located in the adolescent loins but migrates, over time, to a rag-and-bone shop whose commerce is subsidized by the bankrupt state of shared memory.

Everette Maddox's posthumous destiny will have been fulfilled when everyone on the planet is a poet or when poets outnumber those who are not, when the chain has been broken and the dog roams free, which is to say that it can never be fulfilled.

Kafka's "Hunger Artist" is hardly a how-to for career success in the arts, though it is something of a cautionary tale regarding career development: *Don't engage in anything that can be considered career development.* Local poets may jockey for the inside rail toward the homestretch, but the other side of the finish line is oblivion, not a gaudy wreath of roses. Pegasus flies off the track, his jockey, yet another hungry artist, broken on the turf. "Provide, Provide" for desolation's smug purring or simply unchain the dog and sic it on that feline nightmare of irrelevance. The only real poets are local poets; all others are mere professionals.

Shakespeare, on Acid

For her twelfth birthday, among other things, I gave my Czech American youngest daughter, Ella, a book gift card. With it, she procured, quite unprompted, from one of three English-language independent bookstores in Prague, *The Complete Works of Shakespeare.* That the store, on the Vltava and near Charles Bridge, is named Shakespeare and Sons, I shall assume, had no bearing on her choice.

As best I can recall, the first time I heard *Shakespeare,* I was in the sixth grade, as Ella was then, and the name was uttered by Mrs. Tunstall, who said that William Shakespeare was the greatest writer ever and that he'd written plays.

"What's a play?" I asked. The question was a non sequitur, later in the day and as the cigarettes and coffee–reeking pedagogue breathed on my cheek and checked my long division; no one laughed. We hadn't yet begun to compose, as a class, our play set in ancient Egypt; perhaps my clueless query inspired the assignment.

Most of the other kids lived, as did I, in the federal housing projects in Norfolk, Virginia. It was 1965. The Cuban missile crisis and JFK assassination were at our backs. Mostly African American, we were children not of the corn but of the Great Society: wards of the welfare state, recipients of postwar American largesse, at least enough to survive day to day. Play was what you ran outside to do, screen door slamming behind you, or what you drew up in a huddle, on one knee, in the dirt.

Of course, Ella would think it funny that I'd not heard of plays, except the sports kind. She and her sisters take perverse delight in stories centered on their father's past, particularly my childhood lack of sophistication. My daughters, bilingual and bicultural, solidly upper-middle-class, worldly, and even a little patrician, celebrate my hardscrabble past but with a faint measure of condescension as well as pride.

As I was figuring out why Williams's glistening red wheelbarrow was no less worthy a subject for poetic expression than Milton's Lucifer (whose own white chickens, Sin and Death, served as a less benign frame), what I could assume was that both Milton and Williams had had Shakespeare at the back of their minds as they composed. How the Shakespeare opus occupied both mental spaces, one modern yet rustic, grounded in empiricism and contemptuous of literariness, the other Platonic and resplendent with the vestiges of "high culture," is the key to something, perhaps the efficacy of poetry itself. Shakespeare is the neon-pink rhinoceros occupying a hall of mirrors—Poetic Ambition—that many traverse, squeezing past the beast, but few should occupy with more alacrity than humility, even Ezra Pound, whose "make it new" injunction, filched from the inscription on a Chinese emperor's two thousand–year–old washbasin, rings hollow when measured against the immeasurable, atemporal influence of "the Bard."

As difficult as it is to un-ring the bell of Progress—the idea of it loud and unremitting—condescension to the past, the false consciousness for which such condescension is a marker, is the consequence of failing to do so. No one in an Elizabethan audience was aware that evolution underpins all organic stuff or that spacetime lends the lie to space and time or that modernity, its economic essence as such, is rooted in the lie of planned obsolescence. The Renaissance idea of Progress, by definition, was rooted in an idealized past; modernity is tethered to an idea of progress that idealizes the future. That the former is (more or less) knowable and the latter inscrutable has little bearing on how the complexities of identity and value get marshaled through literary art; we learn that whether we conceive of the future guided by remnants of a golden age or by a more or less unique design grounded in pure speculation and in the assumption that manipulating the exigencies of daily life—improving it by making it more comfortable and laden with glittering distractions—people continue to experience often debilitating, sometimes lethal, conflict. Essential humanity resists improvement, which is to say, change. We un-ring the bell simply by recognizing that though we may not be, as Horace famously asserted, the degenerate descendants of fathers who in their turn were degenerate from their forebears, nor are we an improvement over those who lived before us.

I read *King Lear* and *Hamlet,* over the course of many nights, aloud at bedtime to my oldest daughter, Ema, when she was nine and ten. Now a professional opera singer in middle Europe, she is comfortable with all things elevated, rarified, alas, elite. I recall her asking, after one of my bedtime performances, the same question Ella recently asked: "Why is he the greatest?"

"Why is he the greatest?" I asked my mother as she stirred a can of water into Campbell's Beans and Bacon or peeled potatoes into the sink. She was dying of multiple sclerosis but hadn't yet been diagnosed. Over the past few months, she'd had seizures; her arm, the same one each time though I can't recall which, would jerk into a curl, her hand toward her chin, and freeze there. She stumbled, and fell, often. She also fetched stacks of books, in a wagon, from the library while I was in school, peered into them each night, and wrote reams of letters to my jailbird father.

I don't recall her answer, but once she speculated that everything—I; she; my four younger siblings; our ratty, cinder block apartment; the sun; moon; stars; grass; Elizabeth River; streets; cars; trees; clouds; and our battered Motorola—could be the projection of one of the many eyes of "that fly on the wall over there."

I would recall that dreamy speculation years later as I contemplated Hamlet's assertion to Horatio that there's more stuff in the universe "than are dreamt of in your philosophy." Dr. Ted Barnake had quoted the passage in passing, and I immediately took issue with the formulation. Dreaming doesn't occur as any aspect of philosophical speculation, I insisted.

Watergate was percolating, and I was in my first semester at San Diego City Community College, where my Monday, Wednesday, and Friday mornings began in Dr. Young's Intro to Philosophy, followed by Dr. Barnake's Intro to Shakespeare. A Brooklyn Jew, Barnake was older than starlight and very entertaining. The first day of class he asked if we wanted to know the secret of life. He actually asked, "Who wants to know the secret of life?" Everyone, that early fall of 1973, wanted to know the secret of life. Some of us actually raised our hands.

"Fighting and fucking," he said, and an uncomfortably long silence followed. "And nothing on earth affirms this more powerfully than Shakespeare's plays," he finished. Over the course of the semester, there was no homework, no reading outside the classroom. We attended three fifty-minute sessions each week and took turns reading first *A Midsummer Night's Dream,* then *The Merchant of Venice,* aloud. Dr. Barnake was funny and wise and very lazy. He was a terrible teacher and exactly what I needed at that time.

"Interesting point, Richard," he said, "but don't you think that Shakespeare, by equating dreams with rational speculation, is offering a judgment of philosophy?"

"Huh?" I can vouch for the absolute accuracy of this utterance, even as I must admit that the question to which it was a response is reconstructed. Ted Barnake found it amusing that I was questioning the rhetorical efficacy of a line of verse dialogue composed by the greatest writer who has ever lived. I know this because he grinned sardonically at my incomprehension, as did God and everyone else over the age of forty, it seemed back then.

My next MWF course was Intro to Greek Mythology, and my classmate buddy was seventeen-year-old Cameron Crowe, who was already writing cover stories for *Rolling Stone;* he invited me to his interview of Jimmy Page and Robert Plant, and I declined because I couldn't get off work—swabbing linoleum on the Coronado Amphibious Base—thus perpetrating one of the great missed opportunities of this life or any that may have preceded it (Cameron's mom was my counselor at City and a champion of all things New Age, especially past-life exploration).

My final MWF class was American History, team-taught by Larry and Harry. There was no homework in that class either. They didn't even assign a textbook. We met at a bar across the street from the campus and watched the Watergate hearings. Larry and Harry bought us pitchers—even those of us too young to drink legally—and explained institutional precedents and political nuances; in this, they were our MSNBC. But they also explained historical contexts and generally critiqued the whole shit show, as Harry called it, including the loyal opposition, whom they grudgingly cheered on with New Left irony and panache. They, too, were terrible teachers and precisely what I needed at that time. Larry said the whole thing was like Kabuki.

Having been adopted into a navy family in my early teens, not long after my stint in the projects, I'd lived in Sasebo, Japan, for almost three years, and so had a rough idea what Kabuki was; I shyly suggested to Larry, as he roared at John Dean hoisted above the bar, that in Kabuki there isn't much drama; everyone knows how things will turn out. Larry Swartz flicked a glance at me, quaffed, wiped his hand across his mouth, grinned, and called me a smartass. It was a compliment I relished for weeks.

But as smartasses go, I wasn't that sharp because, of course, all dramatic presentations are, broadly speaking, predictable. Hamlet dies. Oedipus probably one-upped every other hero for all time by consigning himself to a life worse than death. But Lear dies. Othello dies. In tragedies, almost everybody dies: the hubris-infected hero takes a false step, yada yada yada. In comedy, no one dies, and there are weddings after everything gets wacky then fixed (kind of).

My first Shakespeare play, sometime in the mid-1970s, was *King Lear,* at the Old Globe in San Diego's Balboa Park. A facsimile of the storied London theater, the charming structure is juxtaposed to Cassius Carter, a theater-in-the-round. I'd read *King Lear* at least twice, though I'm not certain why I'd been drawn to that particular play at that phase of my life. I was much too young to identify with Lear, as I now do. I suppose I identified with Edgar but probably a little with Edmund too (having been adopted, I, also, was a bastard, kind of). But my attraction to the play had less to do with identification than fascination. I was fascinated with Lear's moral status, his being a man more sinned against than sinning. I considered myself deeply insightful for recognizing that *that,* indeed, was the human condition.

I dropped acid, a tab of Mr. Natural, to heighten the experience of attending my first Shakespeare play. That's the sort of thing we did back then. We dropped acid to see certain movies, certain concerts. We dropped acid to do just about anything we wanted to render more memorable. My second daughter, Annie, says things haven't changed much in that regard, and I am loath to press my wild child for details on the matter. Suffice it to say that a very good live performance of *King Lear,* experienced on a two-way hit of Mr. Natural, is transformative the way staring into a sunset at La Jolla Cove, on acid, is transformative, though more expensive, especially on a part-time janitor's hourly wage of $1.67.

I attended the performance with Sally, who was sometimes into chicks, as she put it, but who also liked guys and liked me just fine. A beneficiary of

Title IX, she was at San Diego State on a volleyball scholarship, if memory serves, and majored in biology or sports medicine or something else well outside the humanities' bailiwick.

That evening, Sally jabbed the second hole in my left earlobe; few guys had piercings back then, and Sally thought I was cool to have one and suggested a second hole in the same lobe would set me even further apart. We sucked on the tabs of acid and sipped quarts of Coors as Sally held the needle over the match flame. When she was certain it was sterile, she squeezed my left lobe between two ice cubes, placed a potato behind the numb flap of skin, and then poked the needle through the popping cartridge and into the spud.

Sally had heard of Shakespeare in the same sense that other non-artsy civilians had heard of him but wasn't particularly keen on attending a play, especially given that she'd heard they went on and on much longer than movies or concerts. She was amused, however, at the prospect of attending a Shakespeare play on acid.

There are no bad seats in the Old Globe Theater. We sat in the second row, slightly to the right of center stage. Sally told me to stop fidgeting with my earlobe, but it stung, and I had to keep pulling the string she'd tied off in the new hole so it wouldn't get clogged up in the gunky healing. We'd started to come on to the acid on the bus to the park, and as we sat, an hour or two before sundown, the first wave peaked, receded, then washed over us again. Sally and I looked at each other often, smiling idiotically; she was magenta in the fading light. Her straight blonde, sun-lightened pageboy smelled of the ocean. She wore puka shells and blew Bazooka bubbles. I asked her, as nicely as I could, not to blow bubbles when the play began.

Cordelia was hot. Sally whispered that she looked like Stevie Nicks, and I knew that Sally fancied Stevie Nicks, as did I. Everybody fancied Stevie Nicks because she just looked, well, moist, and the actor playing Cordelia was sexy that way. Sally joked in a whisper what she'd like to do to Cordelia, and I shushed her. I was into the play, feeling sad for the old king. Was I a thankless child? I was twenty-one, a grown man, but did my stepparents think me thankless? Was their displeasure with me born of pain sharper than a serpent's tooth?

I could barely contain my sorrow, my remorse. Sally found the spectacles, on the stage and seated beside her, hysterically funny. She plugged her mirth with wads of Bazooka, seemed on the verge of exploding with laughter. She was rosy in the dying light, held her fingers to her mouth to suppress giggles. "I can't understand a thing they're saying," she whispered, sputtering.

"Please shut up," I whispered back. Edgar, as crazy Tom, had led his father to the white cliffs of Dover and tricked him into living. I was filled with terror at the prospect of a crazy man leading a blind man and concentrated hard on who was who in that equation: Nixon was Gloucester or Edgar? Who was the blind one, who the crazy? Surely Nixon was the crazy; we, the people, were the blind. And "'Tis the time's plague," which means that when the people are blind to their leaders' insanity, it's as though a biblical plague has ravished the earth. But Edgar was only pretending to be crazy; Nixon, clearly, was cuckoo for Cocoa Puffs.

I had to squeeze Sally's knee, she was working so hard not to laugh out loud. She was red, grunting and sputtering; people around us wanted us dead.

The hair of the woman in the seat in front of me was blue spun glass; it glowed a little, and when she turned to shush us, I was certain she was in league with Goneril; she was as old as the witches in *Macbeth*, though more regal, I thought; however, I immediately wondered if "regal" is like "pregnant," a condition that may indeed have phases but not degrees, like life and death and impeachment. I could tell that Blue Hair had voted for Nixon, would vote for Ford, and therefore was viewing a different story than I.

I scanned the audience; they were all dressed casually and had lots of money. Blue Hair's husband might as well have been the Duke of Albany. The two of them were not to be trusted, and I squeezed Sally's knee before she could say anything smartass.

When the Duke of Albany turned in his seat to castigate Sally, I was certain we were doomed, but he only gave Sally a hard look before turning back to the stage, to Regan conspiring with hubby, the Duke of Cornwall.

"That guy's a real ass licker," Sally remarked of Goneril's lackey, Oswald, "and he killed Kennedy!"

"Shakespeare's like the sun," I mumbled as twilight deepened, meaning that in the moment I fully *understood, got, comprehended, assumed, was enlightened to the fact,* that Shakespeare was the greatest poet who had ever lived, that poetry is language organized against despair, even when it interrogates all shades and configurations of hopelessness.

"Who's your favorite?" Sally asked. "Bet it's the Fool," she said before I could answer.

"Yeah," I answered, or think I did. I was peaking, the term for that intense second phase of an acid trip: first you came on, then you peaked, then you came down. Sometimes, when you peaked, you thought you were talking but weren't or thought you weren't when you were. On acid, soliloquies, as such, seemed quite normal.

"Think Shakespeare dropped acid?" Sally asked as fifth-act carnage ramped up. It was a sophomoric question, even for Sally on acid.

"Come on, Sally, you know there wasn't any acid back then," I admonished, though years later I'd read that clay pipes tainted with marijuana and cocaine have been discovered in what had been Shakespeare's garden and that he might have smoked myristic acid, a hallucinogen derived from nutmeg. Of course, drug references abound throughout the plays, from Puck's potion to the spectacular concoction the good friar slips Juliet.

The cast received a standing ovation; Sally remained seated because she was contrary that way, and as I stood and clapped, I watched bugs flit in and out of the footlights and thought of electrons and Speedy Gonzales, and as the actors took their bows and the crowd applauded, I thought about madness, whether I'd know if I were nuts. Can someone be crazy if he knows he is?

"Yeah, that's what evil is," I said as we jostled from the theater, though I wasn't sure if I was responding to something Sally had said or to my own inner voice, and it didn't matter because Sally was studying the crowd.

Or maybe it was one kind of evil.

"Who you talking to?" Sally asked. I'd never dropped acid with her before and was deeply impressed by her equanimity. The crowd was white, mostly middle-aged, and a breezy affluence wafted from them; Sally breathed it, seemed quite comfortable enveloped by it.

During those years, I didn't realize that I looked "a little ethnic," as a friend later characterized my appearance. I didn't realize that I looked a little Hispanic, even a little Asian, and that as a consequence, not all other white people considered me unambiguously white. I was, indeed, ambiguously white in 1973 San Diego, California.

"I'm not talking to anyone," I assured her, and immediately felt the full profundity of that assertion. Monterey cypress, cork oak, camphor, acacias, and eucalyptus grace Balboa Park, like most of San Diego a reclaimed desert butting up to the Pacific Ocean. I was struck, back then, by the fact that it wasn't natural. I'd worked the previous summer, in addition to my gig on the Amphibious Base, with a crew of landscape gardeners, three older blond surfer guys who labored hard and partied harder and who'd told me I was their obligatory Mexican. I cheerfully accepted the role, though only years later would I realize they'd been insulting me. Most trees didn't belong in San Diego, wouldn't exist there without intervention, and the same was true of white people. We'd used jackhammers to make holes in the hardpan to plant shrubs in the affluent, dusty yards of Point Loma and La Jolla.

Like trees and white people, Shakespeare was a forced fit in San Diego. In 1978, the year I'd depart that phony paradise except for visits, an asshole would burn down the Old Globe, but it would be reconstructed because everybody loves Shakespeare, or the idea of Shakespeare, especially upper-middle-class white people who have constructed a paradise for themselves and their progeny, who have planted trees on a desert, right up to a beach that extends endlessly in both directions, in the sense that human folly is endless and the desire to distract from it a likewise endless sunset.

I've met Martin Hilský, the renowned translator of Shakespeare into Czech, several times in passing. Most memorably, in the late 1990s, on the third floor of the Philosophical Faculty, I asked him on what floor I'd find the office of one of his colleagues but have never asked him anything about Shakespeare or why he has centered his life on steering the bard into a language that only ten million people on earth speak and understand. He has also translated Joyce, Lawrence, Woolf, and Eliot, among others, and my guess is that translating Modernists might be aided by having translated the greatest writer who has ever lived. In 2001, Hilský was named an honorary holder of the Order of the British Empire, and not because I know him, because I don't, but because I know something about Czechs, especially inasmuch as I've raised three, I'm fairly certain that he found the honorific at least as humorous as flattering. "British Empire," except for its lingering and dubious effects, is a joke, and Czechs are sardonic to the core regarding all claims to power, as such claims may solicit anything like genuine prestige.

But they (the ones who are not the cultural equivalents of our nasty Red State yahoos, a much smaller percentage of the whole population, I should add) revere Shakespeare as the pinnacle of human expression. Whether poetry is that which is lost in translation, as Robert Frost famously insisted, or rather is that retained in good faith translation, as Mark Strand and Charles Simic (Simić) asserted in the introduction to their 1970s anthology, *Another Republic,* the Czechs, and most of the non-English-speaking world, take on faith, even if grudgingly, that Shakespeare was the greatest writer of all time. It is faith distilled from generations of cultural diffusion and colonialism, of imperial hijinks, of rape, exploitation, and conquest, none of which was Shakespeare's fault or Nixon's or Ford's or Dr. Ted Barnake's or Harry's and Larry's or Cameron Crowe's or his hippie mama's. It certainly wasn't my fault, though perhaps it was Sally's, for chomping on seven wads of Bazooka bubble gum as she critiqued, on acid, a better-than-mediocre production of *King Lear* and found my sincere engagement hilarious and who I'm certain eventually met someone and had kids, one way or another, and who has lived heartbreak and failure but I hope a little triumph, too, some happiness. Alas, she was an Angel of Truth, like Cordelia, but perhaps more like the Fool and therefore may be blamed for everything yet should be punished for nothing.

A few years ago, the hole that Sally poked through the cartilage in my left lobe broke from the awkward weight of a dangling earring I shouldn't have worn to bed. I awoke to a bloody pillow. Of course, I thought of Sally.

Since that minuscule catastrophe, which occurred when my youngest was maybe four years old, Ella, my youngest Cordelia (all three of my girls are Cordelia), following her sister Annie, who actually began the practice, will reach up, apropos of nothing in particular, to my ear with both hands and make the broken hole "talk"; she says it looks like a fish, and she calls it a talking fish and gives the talking fish a silly voice, and I'll tell her, the next time she does that, that she's tapping into her inner Shakespeare.

My Wicked Thirties

Men at forty
Learn to close softly
The doors to rooms they will not be
Coming back to.
　　—DONALD JUSTICE, "Men at Forty"

A sixteen-year-old kid jacked on meth who shoots another dead should get incarcerated for how long? A twenty-five-year-old man who succumbs to gendered rage and kills his mate should be locked away for how long? Those are different questions, I think, from that of how long a forty-year-old who murders a cubicle-trapped colleague should be put away. A sixteen-year-old, a twenty-five-year-old, and a forty-year-old are very different creatures and, arguably, deserve different manners of consideration in the matter of punishment.

The easy, and perhaps appropriate, answer is that all three, things being equal, should be put away for the rest of their lives. But things are never equal. I don't support the death penalty, but no one I've loved has been murdered. I'm dubious about punishment in general, but I know that I'd attack with my hands or any handy blunt object anyone who sought to harm any member of my family.

I hope it's true that in a letter to his father, from college, young Sigmund Freud wrote: "You needn't punish me anymore, Father. I shall punish myself now."

I'm much quicker to forgive my boy-self than the man I was at forty and fifty. But that guy in his thirties . . . I don't know what to do about him.

None of the individuals I've been has committed a serious crime, though they, especially that thirty-year-old, have committed innumerable petty, comical ones, the kind that piss off victims of verbal slights, say, for lifetimes, the kind for which one is not incarcerated but, rather, enshrined in a community's Cavalcade of Assholes.

"Reputation is an idle and most false imposition; oft got without merit, and lost without deserving," and of course we consider the source of that judgment, issuing as it does from Iago, one of the supreme assholes in all of literature, though not all villains are assholes. Milton's Lucifer isn't, nor is Melville's Ahab or Doyle's Moriarty or Conrad's Kurtz or Nabokov's Humbert or Orwell's O'Brien or even Grendel's mom, for that matter. Joining Iago are the likes of Dickens's Fagin, du Maurier's Svengali, Jay Ward's Snidely Whiplash, Andrew Dice Clay's Dice Man, and Steve Bannon's Steve Bannon.

I once angered a department chair so thoroughly he ordered me to stay off of the North American continent, contrary to any civic law or university rule or other statutory power determining his authority. He was a bright and decent fellow who passed from this world a few years ago and much too soon, and I gaze back now upon our multiple conflicts with wary affection and muted glee. I'd been teaching online from Prague and decided to return to New Orleans for personal reasons, among them an illicit affair (are there any other kind?), in full knowledge that I could perform my duties from there, or from anywhere, as effectively as from transatlantic Prague. It was the late 1990s, and online instruction, especially of graduate students, was a novel arrangement he allowed in my case precisely because he wanted me exiled. By this time, I was in my midforties, but my precipitous slide on the slippery slope of his managerial regard had begun, alas, in the previous decade.

I was in my thirties for most of the 1980s, the first decade of my professional development (we'll call it). I was a poet and had spiffy thin volumes to prove it. I was hired to teach freshman composition, four courses a semester, but I managed to publish enough, verse and prose, that the department had to promote and eventually tenure me.

The University of New Orleans English department was split along ideological lines regarding how freshman composition was constituted and delivered; there were other points of conflict, but those all unfurled from that contention, a sword I giddily fell upon again and again. Indeed, in my wicked thirties, I relished department politics, enjoyed the give-and-take, the molten gossip and petty intrigue. In the beginning, my team and the opposing unit were fairly equal in numbers, though through the eighties and into the nineties, my side retired and died and found other employment until, by the time of my exile, I was practically, and vulnerably, alone.

Preceding me at the University of New Orleans were the likes of David Wojahn and Yusef Komunyakaa, and there were numerous other terrific writers employed at UNO, teaching at other local institutions, and scattered throughout that mythical, sumptuous, evil, glorious city. Beyond the department, my relation to the New Orleans literary community was that of a giant intoxicated gadfly in a china shop.

My signature sin was publishing a mediocre poem titled "Meeting Yevtushenko," in which I dissed not only the smarmy Russian poet but the New Orleanian who hosted him, the matronly boss of a local organization of poets, not to be confused with a confederacy of dunces or a battalion of mimes. I didn't piss in the punch or molest the family dog; I didn't rip off my clothes and croon "What a Wonderful World." I didn't punch the Soviet poet, though I wanted to, just because he was such a pretentious asshole and hit on every female at the soiree regardless of availability.

I enjoyed my thirties probably more than I deserved. The 1980s were the decade of Reagan, and I should have been terrified and despondent, but I was too stupid and self-absorbed. I routinely insulted people, sometimes meaning to, often not. I assumed I was immune to the ill regard of those more tender, more inwardly directed, than I.

I must have glittered with some charm back then. I didn't crash and burn or even crash-land and stumble from the wreckage of my folly damaged and despondent. My daily joy was that I'd survived my peripatetic, often despairing childhood, survived my treacherous adolescence, somehow surfaced from my picaresque twenties dripping from that ocean of my dead mother's tears, to gaze upon a glorious island, my thirties. I lived tethered, no matter how loosely, to a gorgeous human being, at first in the heart of the French Quarter, later on its cool and funky outskirts. I was gainfully employed not swabbing floors, digging holes, or busing tables but holding forth in classrooms and red-penciling muddled constructions.

I had no fathers back then, not in my heart. As a child, I'd longed for one; as an adolescent, I'd searched for one; in my twenties, I'd latched onto several in succession only to reject them before they could reject me. My wicked thirties were for hunting down and killing them, though, with one exception, I didn't.

I mean, Gerald Stern, whom I'd "worked with" at Iowa, visited often to give readings and troll the Greek bars on Decatur with me and Betty and Betty's mother, Lynn, whom he fancied. Why did we camp in those bars where Greek sailors from merchant ships, docked on the river, drank and danced? Because Lynn, from whom Betty had inherited extraordinary physical beauty, loved to sit and sip and watch men dance among themselves. Once, when a sailor ripped off his shirt and jumped upon a table and danced his grief toward something like joy as the tinny, unremitting live music blared so loudly conversation was impossible, I pounded my chest and declared with derisive affection, "My people!" Jerry grasped my shoulder, bent toward my ear, and said, "That dance is thousands of years old," which was simply his suggestion that I show some respect. I recall glancing, that moment, beyond Betty's beautiful face to that of her mother, her best friend, a woman barely out of her forties; Lynn's eyes, in the muted light of that enormous room whose margin we occupied like four abstracted judges, glistened.

Another father I did not kill, Rayburn Miller, was a UNO "founder"; that is, he was hired out of Iowa into an inchoate institution that was little more, in the early 1960s, than Quonset huts on the shore of Lake Pontchartrain. An autodidact of enormous classical erudition, he put his queer shoulder to the wheel and participated, soulfully and with stoical patience and Pythagorean practicality, in the building of an honest-to-god university primarily for working-class white people randy, year-round, with the Mardi-Gras ethos.

One day, soon after I'd been hired, I casually suggested he show me "some of [his] work." Within hours, my cubby was engorged with a four hundred plus–page manuscript of lyrics so fine, so refined, so heartbreakingly crafty and smart, they filled me with shame. He'd published most of them in journals so small and marginalized those typed pages might as well have been shredded and flushed. He'd helped build and sustain a university, a complex social structure, and over the two decades when he'd labored with his fellow founders to do so, he'd also spun exquisite lyrics he'd husbanded rather than flaunted. I secured a grant, gleaned sixty pages or so from his hefty tome, and helped Maxine Cassin (owner and editor of the *New Orleans Poetry Journal* and the New Orleans Poetry Journal Press) publish Rayburn's first book.

I might as well have bludgeoned a kitten and impaled it for display in the faculty lounge, though now, almost forty years later, Rayburn long dead, how a few colleagues, most of them long dead, responded to Rayburn's and my oddly warm collegiality is irrelevant. He was my gay father, one I did not know particularly well except from his measured and wise commentary at department meetings and through his poems of spiritual weariness and physical yearning.

I murdered only one father in my thirties. *A Walk with Tom Jefferson* had just been published, and Philip Levine was in town to read at Tulane. Peter Cooley, bless his heart, invited Betty and me to dinner with Fran and Phil, him and Jacqueline, at the Chart House, across from the Cabildo and overlooking Jackson Square in the French Quarter, where Betty had served cocktails for years and where I'd met her in the summer of 1976, days after hitchhiking to the Big Nasty from San Diego. For all the times I'd delivered platters to and then bused those tables or tonged sirloin at the exhibition broiler, for all the thousands of drinks Betty had delivered to those tables on which intricate maps of the Caribbean were lacquered into the oak, we'd never dined there, not together. Phil and Peter, both born in Detroit, reminisced. Betty was still friends with many of the waitstaff and chatted with them as they tended to our table. Fran and Jackie were serene, amicable.

I'd just read Levine's new book and hated it, though I was alone, it seemed, in that evaluation and kept it to myself among my national tribe of poets. At some point in that evening, though, I piped up and complimented him for yet another stellar performance, earlier that evening, of yet another powerful book of profound and profoundly beautiful verse, or some such horseshit. Levine casually accepted my fulsome praise with typically jaundiced humility.

Oh, had I been wise enough in my wicked thirties, had my sense of self-preservation been strong enough, I'd not have written Philip Levine a letter apologizing for my lack of authenticity that evening in the Chart House restaurant, on an enchanting spring evening in the French Quarter of New Orleans, and I wouldn't have proceeded to enumerate the reasons why, even though I was an inveterate fan of his work, I'd found that most recent effort, well, lacking.

Philip Levine wrote, not on a sheet of paper but on the envelope in which I'd sent the letter, a scathing response that pointed out, among other infelicities, two misspellings.

Reading his rant, again and again, I felt neither chastened nor enraged. I slipped that missive, composed on the envelope in which I'd sent my confession, into a larger envelope and tapped it back to him. Days later, I received that unopened envelope in an envelope. I placed the mess into a larger envelope and mailed it back to him. A week or so later . . . I can't recall how many times we tapped that shuttlecock of ire back and forth, but eventually one of us, probably he, lost interest, and I shuffled out of the shadow not of the great American poet but of my colossal regard for him.

The Don't-Soil-the-Nest Rule is sacrosanct, and yet my wicked thirties were conducted, as I told myself, in a workplace unique in academe and therefore exempt, I was convinced, from that otherwise Mosaic directive. That institution's youth was its uniqueness, along with its location in the softly corrupt Deep South. Its third decade overlapped, in a Venn diagram kind of way, my own wicked thirties. It didn't bend academic conventions so much as adjust them to a ruling coterie's rational, by turns noble and ignoble, agenda. If individuals who never earned terminal degrees rose like petroleum, they did so displaying exceptional native intelligence and political acumen, not to mention a delightfully vicious sense of entitlement issuing from the fact that most of them were independently wealthy and locally connected. If most of the department's professorate had been hired sans national searches, an objective judge would have to take into account the enormous effort it requires to staff a university from scratch. If a service department like English was forced to hire hordes of overqualified, bottom-feeding instructors and if many of those instructors subsequently staffed courses that should have been taught by tenured and tenure-track faculty, at least they were then encouraged to compete, like Roman gladiators, for tenure-track positions that had not been advertised nationally. Crusted in blood and gore, maimed for life, we who stood at the end, holding high the severed heads of the vanquished, were showered not with cheers or jeers but with amused indifference. For those who could not compete in the arena because they were not even remotely qualified to do so or simply because of bad timing but who had curried favor with the ruling cabal or simply managed to attract its sanguine regard, a status dubbed "retained instructor" was made available, a professional Phantom Zone of which other departments across this great land have cobbled versions, but few have such dense populations. Because New Orleans is New Orleans, because the best never want to leave, too many beautiful souls, superior minds, settled, for entire careers, into the academic equivalent of sweatshop labor.

But I digress. In my wicked thirties, the psychic distance between my professional and personal lives was several light years, though the wormhole of my wickedness, my unfettered enthusiasm for intrigue and melodrama, brought my classroom into my French Quarter bedroom (in an apartment my landlord swore was the original House of the Rising Sun): I would lie awake for hours, too many nights, replaying lectures and class discussions but also rehearsing what I should have said to this peer or that senior colleague, improving, sharpening, my contribution to the previous post-department meeting's hallway repartee.

I'd grown up on the highways of America, my parents fleeing innumerable crimes, and in federal housing projects on welfare. I'd been homeless much of my childhood, some of my adolescence, even intermittently in my twenties. In my wicked thirties, I craved and feared institutional acceptance in equal measure, and in the deepest part of me, that wacky collection of artists and intellectuals at UNO, that pirate ship of academic outliers (our sports teams were "the Privateers"!), was the only stable family, the only stable home, as dysfunctional as we were, I'd ever known, as pathetic as that confession is now to my own ears.

I've been a walker all of my life, and in my wicked thirties, I was peripatetic to a fault. When I lived in the House of the Rising Sun, on St. Louis between Bourbon and Dauphine, I'd turn left from my gate and walk to Rampart. Sometimes I'd mosey into St. Louis Cemetery II (back then, anyone could get in at any time before sundown) and leave a cigarette at the shrine the world had made of Marie Laveau's tomb, then head up to Canal, then toward the river to Decatur, and downriver past Jackson

Square and Café du Monde, past the French Market to Esplanade, sometimes onto Frenchmen and back around through the Faubourg Marigny, toward St. Claude, back onto Esplanade and usually up Burgundy, all the way back to St. Louis and the House of the Rising Sun.

I smoked cigarettes until late into my wicked thirties and would ash at least half a pack on my almost daily circuit. I was not faithful to her to whom I was tethered, but Betty didn't require my carnal loyalty, only my predictable presence. She occupied a perfumed haze of linked moments, each extraordinary unto itself, and regarded the future as something feline, stray, and self-sufficient.

A ballet friend of hers, an anorexic uptown woman who volunteered at the Audubon Zoo's Bird Rehabilitation Center, would bring me nestlings, mostly mockers and jays, that had fallen from trees. It was my task to raise them, teach them to fly, then set them free. At the appropriate time—when they were obviously ready to fledge, hopping around and chirping crazily in their padded box—I'd toss each one a few feet into the air, watch it flap and fall, flap and fall, flap and fall. By degrees, they'd remain in the air for longer and longer durations, until, eventually, they'd circle the living room, crapping joyfully on the furniture and the windowsills, crashing like cream puffs into our floor-to-ceiling windows overlooking Rue St. Louis. After two or three weeks, I'd throw a batch of three to seven off our second-story balcony overlooking a lush courtyard. They'd flit away but return, the whole batch of them, every day for a couple of weeks, at exactly 6:15 a.m.; they'd line up on the balcony railing and squawk until I'd pad out, puffy eyed, scratching my privates through my drawers, to drop a pinch of moist cat food down each squawker's gullet. Eventually, they'd cease returning, but by then, another batch would have graduated from the University of Flap and Fall, and I would toss *them* off the balcony to be eaten by cats or to live long and productive avian lives.

In my wicked thirties, I yelled and screamed and blustered some but not inordinately, though I once invited a colleague, a large novelist with administrative ambitions, to stroll with me across the levee behind the college to settle our dispute. And once, at three in the morning, four hulking college boys verbally abused drag queens promenading from the Roundup across St. Louis. I took umbrage at their noise—not, alas, their bullying—and stomped onto the balcony to request they push on toward Bourbon.

The biggest and drunkest questioned my manhood, and his mates howled. I descended to the street and beat him bloody before the shocked eyes of his posse, then climbed back to the apartment, painted my knuckles with iodine, and slipped back into bed.

In my wicked thirties, I was called once for jury duty. I tried mightily to get thrown off a murder one case. During voir dire, I insulted the defense, openly made fun of both lawyers. One of them looked a little like Robin Williams. "Well, Mork," I began, when asked my opinion of the death penalty.

I condescended to the lead prosecutor because he was a stupid, inarticulate good ol' boy, and my fellow potential jurors, all Black, clearly loathed him. I did everything but declare myself an emissary from the planet Woodstock here on Earth to eat the brains of all litigators as a gesture of my people's desire for peace.

We were sequestered, I and the other eleven, for the week's duration of the trial. Three Vietnamese kids were accused of murdering a Vietnamese shop owner, ordering him on his knees and blowing his brains out for no particular reason other than the fact that they were evil little pricks.

The prosecution's star witness was a fourteen-year-old child who'd occupied a cell with those three sixteen-year-olds. He testified to hearing the three brag about the murder. Oh, he had an IQ that hovered around seventy, the defense was able to get into the record through expert testimony, before dicing the poor kid, clearly an ambulatory eggplant, into tiny cubes.

After we were led, at the end of the trial, to the official room of our deliberations, within seconds of our assuming our official chairs around the official table, we elected a foreman whose first official utterance was to query as to whether the decision should be guilty of murder one or murder two.

I recall that we were serious folks who took our task seriously, and the fact that I was the only white face at the table seemed incidental. The fact that I was a teacher, kind of, also seemed incidental. So, when I piped up and pointed out what seemed quite obvious, that the prosecution had mounted an insultingly stupid case (I didn't have to suggest that the defendants' and the victim's ethnicity might have contributed to the prosecution's lackluster presentation) and enumerated the ways in which that had been so, my colleagues all immediately agreed. We filed back out literally within ten minutes of beginning our deliberations and reassumed our public seats.

After the three had hugged each other and their lawyers and the courtroom briefly went a little fuzzy-buzzy with incredulity, the judge, a handsome guy with a very Italian name I can't recall, poked his head into the jury room where we were gathering our stuff to go home. He informed us that he thought we'd made the correct decision given what we'd heard but that we should know the murderers' confessions had been thrown out for procedural reasons.

In my wicked thirties, I judged others, particularly writers whose talent I didn't immediately recognize, too quickly, flippantly even, though I was respectful toward those I admired. Some of that local 1980s New Orleans cohort have scattered, and I've no desire to gather that tribe anywhere but here and in cursory fashion: Valerie Martin, Domenic Stansberry, Steven Schwartz, Andrei Codrescu, Carolyn Wright, Ellen Gilchrist, David Wojahn, Yusef Komunyakaa, Gillian Conoley, Carolyn Maisel; and among those who did not scatter, Peter Cooley, Moira Crone, Rodger Kamenetz, Ralph Adamo, Maxine Cassin, John Biguenet, Kay Murphy, Everette Maddox, Frederick Barton, John Gery. The last two were prime enemies of my wicked thirties and even a decade beyond, and I list them here less in the spirit of forgiveness than as a final, wicked act, in this case simply to scoff not at them but at the three of us, in the 1980s in New Orleans, in the midst of so much absurd treachery, so much energy and beauty, so much realized and squandered potential.

Fresno, California
"Armpit of America" and Breeding Ground
of American Poets

A few years ago, the Hawai'i football broadcaster Robert Kekaula inti-
mated over a hot mic that Fresno, California, is the armpit of America,
unintentionally insulting the good citizens of Bakersfield, California, and
those of the entire state of New Jersey, who may relish that distinction
as their own. New Jersey may have Walt Whitman, Stephen Crane, William Carlos Williams, Marianne Moore, Allen Ginsberg, Amiri Baraka, X.
J. Kennedy, and Stephen Dunn; and Bakersfield may have Kern County
National Poetry Month; but Fresno has Fresno State University, an institution that, through the 1960s and into the 1970s, gave America more
than a dozen significant poets. Let's face it: New Jersey is an entire state
with a large population, much of which slushed over from culture-clogged
New York, and Bakersfield, well, is a little piece of the Texas Panhandle
that somehow snapped off and floated northwest and got lodged in the
San Joaquin Valley. Both may legitimately vie for the distinction of being
American armpits, though I think the fairest resolution to any conflict over
the matter is to grant New Jersey the distinction of being the East Coast
pit and then simply to acknowledge that the 109 dry dusty miles between
Fresno to the north and Bakersfield to the south practically renders them
twin cities, especially given how distant both are from the ocean and,
therefore, from the La-La Lands of the coast.

Though it seems at first a rather noxious mixed metaphor, regarding
Fresno as both a breeding ground for poets and a national armpit is actually a twin-headed honorific: armpits are, if nothing else, fecund, espe-

cially in the arid California valley, and the notion of working-class poets sprouting from such fecundity seems somehow, well, perfect.

Bruce H. Boston, Glover Davis, and Robert L. Jones attended Fresno State University in the early 1960s and studied with Philip Levine et al. Through the 1970s, and even into the 1980s, they were my big-brother poets. Bruce was Scarecrow, Bob was Cowardly Lion, and Glover was Tin Man.

I was Toto, and poetry was our Dorothy. I guess the Emerald City was our Sublime, and Fresno . . . Fresno was Kansas, Kansas as a Podunk state school, a third-rate institution in the second-tier of a "multiversity" system.

But no, Fresno is nothing like Kansas; it is the other armpit of America and a breeding ground for poets, and Bruce Boston, Bob Jones, and Glover Davis were older poets, men in their thirties, living in San Diego when I was there in my twenties. Glover was my first poetry teacher, at San Diego State; Bruce taught at La Jolla Country Day; and Bob was an itinerant composition instructor shuttling between community colleges. The three were wary friends of one another, with whom I interacted pretty much separately; they didn't get along particularly well, though they told the same stories about Fresno, about the poets of Fresno, the likes of Philip Levine, Larry Levis, Greg Pape, David St. John, Gary Soto, Robert Mezey, Charles Hanzlicek, Peter Everwine, Luis Omar Salinas, Herbert Scott, and (sigh) Sherley Anne Williams and Roberta Spear.

Fresno was a mythical place for me, a city everyone who'd grown up there hated and couldn't wait to exit and yet also a hardscrabble place where poets were born in disproportionate numbers and with dirt under their tiny fingernails. The terrific Sherley Anne Williams and Roberta Spear notwithstanding, it was a boys' club, a tribe of tough, sensitive guys mentored by tough, sensitive guys, young working-class Christian white men guided primarily by older transplanted working-class Jewish white men.

Whether they meant to or not, though they probably just didn't care, Glover, Bob, and Bruce turned me into—in my own heart—a Fresno poet; that is, through my identifying with them, and through their poetry and guidance of my reading and critical discourse, I identified with that place of their origin, which wasn't Bakersfield or New Jersey or Kansas but, rather, the other armpit of this great nation, a city of sweat and longing, of a grounded, grouchy eloquence, of chipped front teeth and smoggy dreams, where the muses are biker ballerinas and class clowns become lyric poets.

I've only passed through Fresno on three occasions, once to visit Larry Levis at his ancestral home, once to give a reading at Fresno State, and once, actually my first time there, in the mid-1970s, while running kilos of pot to a dentist in Marin County; I think I took an inland route from San Diego because I had to pick up a girlfriend's sister there. That first visit I explored the Forestiere underground house on acid, and would have stayed forever if I'd been allowed. Having done landscape gardening in San Diego, that is, having had to crack open the California hardpan literally with a jack-hammer, I could only marvel at the labor that had gone into digging out, over the course of forty years, that enormous subterranean abode. As it happened, it was into subterranean Fresno that I put down metaphysical roots as a young guy.

Years ago, the diaspora of Fresno poets created a network across America. Some settled relatively close, remaining in California, but several took academic positions across the continent. The pipeline between Fresno and Iowa City poured some of the tough and tender Fresno ethos, the Fresno swagger, into Paul Engle's fiefdom; Glover Davis attended the Iowa Workshop and apprenticed, primarily, to Donald Justice, but both Robert L. Jones and Bruce H. Boston attended the MFA program at University of California, Irvine. The three had different reasons for settling in San Diego, reasons grounded in, though also existing beyond, expediency, reasons I needn't explain here beyond noting that Bob's San Diego bordered Bob's Mexico, Glover scored a tenure-track gig at San Diego State in his late twenties, and Bruce and Marsha's daughter Denise had special needs that were uniquely and gloriously met by a beatific institution in San Diego.

The beginning of my friendships with Glover, Bob, and Bruce pretty much tracked Carolyn Forché's entrance upon the San Diego literary scene in 1975, and that twenty-five-year-old woman's influence on that scene should not be downplayed. She oozed charisma, native intelligence, undeniable talent, and street smarts. She was clearly on a fast track to a kind of poetry stardom that was possible back then. However, beyond noting her local, and national, sizzle and the fact that she developed different relationships with Glover, Bruce, Bob, and me, I'm going to avoid, respectfully and with abundant affection and respect, further mention of her.

Glover, Bob, and Bruce wrote very different kinds of lyrics. Glover was a macho formalist for whom thought was grounded in physicality. Bob composed understated though deeply emotional elegiac verse informed by a Jungian model of the unconscious and of the value of dreams. Acerbic, witty, fiercely smart, and honed to an essential shine, Bruce's poems assumed the authority of what will suffice and nothing more. What all three had in common, as artists, critics, and social beings, was a deep, abiding, utterly Fresnoian aversion to horseshit.

The term is at the core of the Fresno ethos. Statements of feeling and of judgment are horseshit, or they are not. Yes, there are gray areas, but gray areas are all horseshit when they are invoked for the sake of justifying assertions of institutional authority or of justifying any boorish, bullying, condescending behavior. It is the watchword of a Panzaic chivalry; indeed, it is that un-slayable dragon any Fresno knight must battle.

Would there have been a Fresno had Philip Levine not taken a job at California State University, Fresno, in 1958? The place on the map, the arid inland California city, of course would be there; the Forestiere underground house would be there. The question is whether Glover, Bruce, Bob, and the others in the band of Fresno brothers (and one, maybe two or three, sisters) would still be there.

Probably not. They were destined to be intellectuals, artists, and as such would have escaped from a Levine-less Fresno, but they would not have escaped as, for better or worse, *Fresno poets* because there would not have been a "Fresno poet" had Levine not been exiled to that glorious, sweaty, culture-free zone in 1958.

In *Lives of the Most Eminent Poets,* Samuel Johnson jostled and cajoled the dead singers of English verse. Alas, I am not Samuel Johnson, and Levine has not been dead long enough for anyone to jostle and cajole him with much historical perspective, but I'm certain that, Michael Schmidt's excellent (and charmingly fanciful) *Lives of the Poets* notwithstanding, a discussion of post-modern—as well as postmodern—poetry that does not contextualize individual careers relative to institutional affiliations, and, indeed, that does not attempt to contextualize the distinction between the production of literature and the pedagogy of creative writing, not only misses the forest for the trees but implicitly denies the existence of the forest.

Levine's was the first generation of professor poets. The previous generation had held academic gigs, but with the exception of Theodore Roethke, Yvor Winters, the Fugitives, and a bevy of other trained scholars who dabbled in verse, poets of the generation previous to Levine's were, in the academy, exotic flora. Of course, Robert Frost, for example, taught at colleges and universities for much of his protracted, stellar twilight but always as "poet in residence," as an exalted interloper. It was the generation of poets–creative writers that hammered out academic careers in the midst of the tumultuous ascent of the counterculture that created, if serendipitously, the cottage industry of creative writing.

Plop. That was me falling off my high horse, or what Jones, and Levine, would designate as horseshit hitting the trail behind me, though I think Bob would have smiled saying it and Phil would have sneered. Both would have been wholly justified, from a Fresno perspective, in such a judgment. Levine studied with Ivor Winters and credited the great curmudgeon with little more than turning him on to syllabics. Bob studied with Phil and credited him with little. That is to say, Bob, curiously, unlike every other Levine acolyte I've known, hardly ever mentioned Levine as a mentor. The fact that both relationships, Levine to Winters and Jones to Levine, were mediated by institutions is one that neither Jones nor Levine seemed willing to acknowledge. The Fresno Panzaic chivalric code sacralizes an aesthetic centered on authenticity and begs the question as to whether beauty and truth are, indeed, the same. Keats's equation, its very reflexivity, dogs the institutional dimension of the role of poet in the academy; "horseshit!" is what the (institutionalized) poet designates all that is inauthentic, including his own station within the academic order. Philip Levine and most other academic poets (not to be confused with Academic Poets such as, say, Justice, Nemerov, and Wilbur, though including them) saw themselves as insurgents, as somehow getting over on academia. When Levine punched the clock and took his place on the academic line, the prevailing assumption was that there can be no such thing as an academic poet any more than there can an academic warrior or an academic zucchini. Almost to a poet, Levine's generation felt itself to be getting over, and God bless them, they were.

Of course, Fresno poets are essentially Romantic and, as institutionalized Romantics, don't so much sing in their chains as keep erratic office hours.

An institutionalized Romantic poet not in a straitjacket or a padded room is a falling off from Romantic decorum. A poet obliged to participate on a department subcommittee digging into the troubling diminution of junior college transfers is fit for stratagems and spoils rather than holy degradation.

Philip Levine's primary subject was work, that is, labor, specifically factory labor of the sort that was necessary before hyper-automation. As a bottom-feeding academic artist patrolling the fetid pond behind one of the satanic mills of American higher ed, one established in the swampier of the two armpits of America, Levine cranked out anecdotal lyrics extolling a postwar Detroit that hummed and sparked at full employment. That Levine worked in factories is undeniable. That Levine was ever a factory worker is utter horseshit. I offer this judgment as one who worked off and on for years in several of the fine dining establishments of New Orleans. I was a waiter, for three to six months at a time, at Court of Two Sisters, Chart House, the Royal Sonesta's Begay's, and Broussard's; several of the guys I worked with were like me, biding time and making money to get through graduate school. Most of our colleagues were "lifers," to borrow a self-explanatory term from the military. The lifers tolerated us, found us amusing. Philip Levine was a Detroit factory worker in the same sense that I was a New Orleans waiter. In reality, he spent fifty years on the academic line punching out working-class poems and, incidentally, working-class poets; he assumed, meticulously cultivated, the persona of America's Factory Poet, and alas, his product was poems and poets rather than car parts.

Literary ambition is the ultimate horseshit, though horseshit may be pressed into the service ("Eeuu," my youngest daughter would say) of a higher purpose for which ends justify means. I'll leave it to others to tease out of the particulars of Levine's stellar career whether his (largely, ambiguously) horseshit persona attained something like a Higher Truth in his roles as poet and mentor of poets. Suffice it to say that Levine inspired deep and abiding, fierce loyalty in his acolytes, even the ones, such as Bruce, Bob, and Glover, who did not benefit much from the fact that Levine ascended beyond the role of mere floor boss to that of a majority-stockholding owner of American Poetry.

I love Bruce, Bob, and Glover. I feel blessed to have latched onto them at a time in my life when I could have ended up in prison like my father. Their tolerance for my horseshit was, it seems now in retrospect, beyond the call of duty. The point of this essay, beyond its being an exercise in mixing metaphors and beyond its left-handed apotheosis of a nondescript American city, is to thank my spiritual brothers for tolerating the mess that I was.

Robert L. Jones ("Honez," because he spoke Spanish fluently and adored all things Mexican, especially women and poetry) has been dead for more than twenty years. I could pick up the telephone and talk to Bruce or Glover but never do. Once in a while, I drop an email to Bruce but only if I know I'll be in San Diego. We've done brunch at the Naked Café in Solana Beach a couple of times this decade, once with Marsha, his one and only for more than fifty years now, and Krista, my then wife. The four of us dined pleasantly, cursorily. We spoke of Honez a little, though not enough. We spoke of poetry and gossiped about poets a little, though probably too much. Levine was alive on that occasion, and his name didn't come up once. Hallelujah.

When I learned that Leonard Cohen had died, I recalled Krista and me having attended his concert a few years earlier in Louisville, Kentucky, particularly how many lesbian couples slow danced in the aisles to "I'm Your Man" and, of course, "Hallelujah." My second daughter, Annie, was with us, and she missed her own girlfriend, who was pining for her back in Prague. The three of us delighted in women slow dancing to Leonard Cohen, especially to "I'm Your Man."

Recalling that concert, I thought also of Bob. I thought of dead poets in general but of Robert L. Jones, Honez in particular. I recalled him passing out, seated upright, on the couch in his apartment in Hillcrest, how I would nudge him over, cover him with an orange-and-blue Mexican blanket, clear the coffee table of the bottle and glasses, and how the commercial jets would begin their descent into San Diego at six in the morning, clearing Bob's roof, literally, by only fifty yards. As Honez slept off the cheap vodka with which he kept his freezer stocked, I'd read through the hundreds and hundreds of first-edition poetry books that filled the techno-metal shelves around his apartment, and when Honez house-sat for Glover one sabbatical semester, mainly attending to Glover's three German shepherds, I apartment-sat for him and finished off that entire collection. The building shook when the jets curled over the Pacific to approach from the south, and more than one overnight guest expressed foggy-headed terror when the conveyor of jets began at dawn.

"How can you live with that?" a visitor asked.

"One gets used to it," I assured her, though she never tested that assurance.

Bob didn't have any animals; I don't even recall plants, only books. I wasn't taking care of anything. Bob was taking care of me. I'd been sleeping on floors and couches and in the beds of young women, and Honez gave me a permanent place to sleep for four months, but most importantly, he gave me access to his books, a collection of poetry books of which he was humbly proud and that to this day is the nucleus of what I know about American poetry.

Sometime in the mid-1990s, someone—Elise Miller, I think—phoned me in New Orleans from San Diego. She was trying to cobble together a monthly stipend for Bob. I'm sure I contributed something, though I can't remember how long it was before I received yet another call, this time from Eduardo Moctezuma, informing me that Honez was dead.

I'd disconnected from the San Diego community years previously. I'd not spoken either to Elise or Eduardo in about a decade, and though I'd connect with Bruce and Glover whenever I passed through San Diego, I'd lost track of Bob.

He'd been homeless, living in his car. Why didn't he go home? I mean, why didn't he return to Fresno? It was a stupid question, but I asked it anyway. Where would *you* rather die, I asked myself, Fresno or San Diego? Actually, he'd rallied, found work, stopped drinking, got another apartment in Hillcrest. He'd applied for some kind of grant and, as the story goes, was literally a few steps from his mailbox when he dropped dead. In that box had been a letter informing him that he'd been granted thousands of dollars, enough money for him to live comfortably in Mexico for two or three years.

The other major theme of Levine's writing was the Spanish Civil War; recalling the older boys from his Detroit neighborhood who shipped out (only half of whom returned) to fight Franco's trolls, he took his family to Barcelona a couple of times. Levine learned some basic facts about the Spanish Civil War and got a few of them into excellent poems, though he never learned to speak Spanish, not really. Bob would chuckle when the subject of Phil's "translations" from the Spanish came up.

Glover and Bruce continue to pan the ore-rich stream of their golden years; Glover has never written better, more soulfully, than now, and I hope the same is true for Bruce. Glover has settled in, of all places, San Antonio, Texas, a place oddly similar to Fresno, demographically speaking, and makes spring forays to a property in central Michigan with his new wife. Because Kalamazoo, Michigan, is pretty much on his and Mariana's way to the property in central Michigan, they've stopped, going and coming, in Kalamazoo. We have lunch, laugh and reminisce, do what old friends do on brief, casual, yet intense visits, before the visitors hit the road again.

All that I knew about Kalamazoo, Michigan, before taking a job here, was what I'd heard from Honez, who'd taught here briefly in the early 1970s just before I met him. When I'd hear Bob mention Kalamazoo, Michigan, in passing, in the mid-1970s, I'd think very little of it. I could have no idea that fate, and career expediency, would deposit me in a college town two hours equidistant between Chicago and Detroit.

When Levine visited Kalamazoo several years ago, he looked old and tired, wizened even, but then he assumed the stage, and I remember thinking, "Oh, there he is," there's the great Philip Levine, that voice, that acidic, spontaneous humor, that edgy charisma, that ironic masculine tenderness and vulnerability, that essential humanity. There before me was the great American poet declaiming on a stage just two hours west of where he'd been born, where he'd fought other—Jew-hating—boys, run the wartime streets of a great American city in which he would later toil in factories and matriculate at a quintessentially urban, working-class university not unlike the one where he would spend more than fifty years as a professor poet.

Earlier, before Levine's glorious performance, I'd sat next to him at dinner, and I'd tried to figure out, in the midst of table chatter, why I didn't much like him. At some point, responding to an innocuous, polite question, I mumbled, "Yes, sir," and he gently castigated me for sirring him. We had some history. We had many mutual friends and acquaintances. We'd had a decades-long conflict that had resolved when he back-channeled to me a desire to visit Prague and I made that visit happen. I was in my fifties.

It had somehow slipped out. He'd asked me if I liked living in Kalamazoo, Michigan, or perhaps he'd asked if I often made it to Detroit or if I was enjoying my ratatouille. Whatever the question, I answered, "Yes, sir."

I realized the moment Levine chastised me, gently, with wit and no malice, that that inadvertent *sir* had shot like a molten spark from the lava muck of my unconscious, particularly that sector where my father junk lay submerged. After dinner, as the party dispersed in the Food Dance parking lot at twilight, headed to the reading venue, Phil and Fran walked ahead of Krista and me. Probably unaware that someone could hear him, Phil pointed at the sky. "Look, Pussy, the moon!" he half-whispered to his mate of almost sixty years.

Krista loved telling that story, the story of that moment. She'd point at the Kalamazoo sky and exclaim to me at twilight, when the immensity is dark blue and the moon translucent, "Look, Pussy, the moon!"

There was once a man named Robert L. Jones. He'd been born in Fresno, California, one of the two armpits of America. He learned Spanish and studied poetry writing with a great American poet no one yet knew was a great American poet except the great American poet himself. Then Robert L. Jones, Honez, earned an advanced degree and taught for a while at a university in Kalamazoo, Michigan, and eventually migrated back to California, settling in San Diego, where he wrote exquisite poems very, very slowly and translated poems by Mexican poets very, very slowly and taught, mostly Freshman Composition, with an abundance of wit and grace and compassion for a number of years. He drank alcohol, every night, very, very slowly.

One night, under a full moon, when the grunion were running, Honez and some friends (Bruce and Marsha Boston, Barbara Cully and I) got drunk and went swimming on Moonlight Beach near Cardiff. We chased grunion in the tide, laughing and stumbling, diving into the staccato waves.

Honez went missing for a full minute. Shocked sober, we scanned the foam for him and then spotted his white back in the moonlight; Bruce and I gripped him under his armpits and dragged him onto dry sand.

The breeding grunion did not care. The moon did not care. Alas, America does not care, nor should it, but on that beach, inebriated, passed out, crusted with primordial salt, lay a poet.

Poetry Is a Dead Art

Though I sang in my chains like the sea.
—DYLAN THOMAS, "Fern Hill"

In recent years, I've been horrified by the efforts of poets laureate of the United States to encourage more people to read verse for pleasure's sake. I've been equally horrified by a spate of books that would instruct us how to read poems and actually enjoy doing so. I mistrust anyone who enjoys reading poetry, as I do those who advocate for it. Poetry love is a form of necrophilia.

Most good poems are about death; dying; fear of death; courage in the face of death; the death of love; the inexorable passing of time unto death; the death of passion; the death of civilizations; the death of the world; and they are about eternity, which is everything after death. Good poems can also be about love, but as everyone intellectually and emotionally capable of appreciating (not to be confused with loving) a good poem knows, love is what we do most fervently and authentically in the shadow of our own mortality. Oh yeah, and some poems are about the death of meaning.

I recall a Poets in the Schools gig in 1980; I was goosed out of Fayetteville, Arkansas, the big city in the area, down to Hope, Arkansas, before anyone who'd never screamed "Sou-eeee pig!" had heard of Bill Clinton. Upon arrival, we stopped in a gas station for directions to the high school; we were greeted by a postcard rack, all of its dozens of slots filled with the same card touting that municipality as "The Watermelon Capital of the World!" Above the caption, a naked boy baby lolled in a giant, gutted watermelon.

I've puzzled over the iconography of that image for more than a quarter-century. Of course, I at first found it hilarious, but by the time we arrived at the high school, I was deeply troubled by the image of that infant, no more than three or four months old, steeped in watermelon sugar water.

What did the composer of that image think she or he was conveying? The watermelon did not appear neatly cut, but was jaggedly split, smashed open with a blunt instrument or by being dropped. Did the infant belong to the composer of that image? Did she or he borrow the baby? And did the maker of that image take pains in the decision to place the baby in the melon naked?

What does a naked infant have to do with watermelons? I suppose I should mention that he was a white baby; if he had been a Black baby, the image would have been merely hideous, not troubling. Would the image have resonated any differently had the infant been female? I think not.

As I stood before a class of thirty juniors and seniors, reciting "Fern Hill" in my baritone almost as resonant as Thomas's but of course not as beautiful (and I wouldn't have dared to attempt a Welsh accent), I was suddenly overcome by the image of that baby boy ensconced in melon. Even as, through my inferior voice, Thomas was singing in his chains, I stared upon those kids, most a decade younger than I, and did not wonder what they were making of my shtick. Those were the sons and daughters of Hope, each baptized in watermelon sugar, each profoundly at ease in fields of melon. What could such lovely gibberish as I was spouting mean to them?

I explicated the poem deftly, in an audience-appropriate manner; I drew parallels to their lives, or at least to what I imagined their lives to be. I talked about innocence and experience, about Blake, about the Dionysian and Apollonian, about ecstasy and wonder, but they weren't buying it, for they knew, I could tell from their postures they knew, that the whole thing was about death, about a crazy Welshman drinking himself to death, about his not being able to get an erection maybe but definitely about his wanting to die, to be released from the lie of his life, the torment of his own egotism.

What could such a poem mean to those who had rocked in cradles of melon? I imagined all thirty of them in a patch unto themselves, swaddled in sweet juice, fated thus to be together on that particular day to hear a hippie prattle about a farm some guy goes a little nuts remembering, some guy who says he was happy when he was a kid running all over the farm, but that now he's chained up but sings anyway, like the ocean. But the ocean's not chained up, so the last line of the poem doesn't make sense, especially to the children of Hope, the children of the Watermelon Capital of the World.

When the time came to get them to try their hands at writing poems, I told them to "free write" for ten minutes about the earliest childhood experiences they could recall, the earliest experiences they could recall having to do with watermelons.

There were bemused looks, wrinkled brows, a low rumble of discontent. I'd struck a nerve.

I told them that when I was a boy living in Elizabeth City, North Carolina, sometimes an aunt would bring over a watermelon and that such occasions were glorious to my family. My father, I explained, had been in prison, and we five kids and our mother lived on welfare, so we depended heavily upon the kindness of strange aunts, our mother's mother's sisters, for fresh produce from their farms, and watermelons in summer were a rare treat, an occasion for celebration. I told them how we'd spread newspaper on the table and our mother would carve the melon into many wedges, and we kids would sit half- or fully naked around the battered aluminum table gorging on melon, not even bothering to spit out the seeds, and I could see that the children of Hope were a little mystified but also *with* me in a way, that I was on familiar ground with them. I wanted desperately for one of them to break into rhapsody about being rocked to sleep in a gutted melon, but that was too much to wish for. I wanted one of them to shout, "When is a poem not about death?" so that I could answer, "Never," and perhaps there was a brilliant one among them who would then ask, "But what about joy?"

I am old enough to be the father of who I was then, and I have three young daughters, one of them almost the age of the children of Hope. Every time she sighs, every time she gazes over a book, every time she switches on the bathroom light and leaves her bedroom door slightly ajar so that the small glow will reach her, it is as though she is asking me, "But what about joy?"

No one who feels joy should want to write or read a poem about it, I would tell her, unless death is a wall, joy a lamp, and poems of joy the silly shadows we make with our hands.

Poetry is a dead art form; it has been dead since contagion magic became passé, sometime toward the end of the Stone Age. The only succor it offers is an assurance that others through the ages have been no less terrified than we, no less ridiculously, paradoxically hopeful in the midst of terror, but I suppose that's something.

What Poets Know

Dry and Wet Knowing

> Humankind cannot bear very much reality.
> —T. S. ELIOT, *The Four Quartets*

I awoke this past Tuesday astonished that I am sixty-six. I'd been sixty-six on the previous Monday, too, but had not been astonished. Indeed, I had been, last Monday, sixty-six for almost a 150 days but had not been astonished until I awoke that otherwise innocuous early-spring day, a Tuesday, and realized, even as I drew my first conscious breath, that I am no longer middle-aged, that I am light-years from my youth and consequently don't have very long to live. As sudden realizations go, that was a humdinger.

But how could I have not known before last Tuesday that I am old? This question is located in that blurry epistemological space in which there are two kinds of knowing, dry and wet. Dry knowing is the apprehension of information that has not been dragged through the blood-soaked rag-and-bone shop of the heart; wet knowing is drenched in the fear of extinction. In a state of dry knowing, I'd dovetailed my personal mortality with mortality generally. This past Tuesday, at 6:28 a.m., my death came a-knockin' on my dream-soaked noggin.

History squats on our chests as we lie awake in the dark, grows heavier and, over time, oddly, more bearable. Existential dread is born of the mere possibility that life, as such, is *nothing but* a "disease of matter," as Mann is credited with first noting in *The Magic Mountain*. Yet "nothing but" is my Am'r'can rhetorical imposition upon Teutonic perspicacity; no one who truly believes that life is *nothing but* a disease of matter would even bother getting out of bed to do anything but jump out a high window or chug a Drāno-Clorox cocktail. Stipulating that all life is a disease of matter, one posits that its origin is meaningless, not that it is meaningless as such, and "nothing but" is only the unpersuasively punkish swagger with which one may whistle past the contagion ward on one's stroll to the cemetery. Existential dread is nothing but "nothing but," a knee-jerk howl at the new moon of our ravenous need to fill the universe with our singularity, to subsume It All.

Lest I drift on the jet stream of my fancy into a neo-hippie stupor, I'll stipulate that life is a disease of matter *but* that it is not just that. It is as meaningful as the biological imperative to survive and as the urge to self-expression beyond creature needs but in relation to those needs in similar fashion as is posited between two quantum entities displaying Spooky Action at a Distance.

My biological imperative to survive is my link to all that lives, from the shiest amoeba to the most lugubrious pachyderm (or vice versa); my link to my fellow humans is the urge to self-expression, which is a manifestation of the fact that, as Ernest Becker pronounced in his wise and beautiful *The Denial of Death* (1973), we are "angels with anuses." That is, we are biological entities, but we are also symbol-consuming and symbol-making creatures, each fully aware that she or he arrives among the living stamped with an indeterminant yet circumscribed shelf date but is also imbued with an irrational desire not only to live forever but to do so while filling the entire universe as a singular awareness. I submit that how we manage that fundamental paradox of human consciousness is the essence of what we call wisdom and that this wisdom is the essence of art.

I proceed on the quaint belief that there are three kinds of wisdom corresponding to the three stages of life. There is a wisdom of youth, a wisdom of midlife, and a wisdom of old age, and each is discrete. The first does not necessarily segue into the second as one transitions, the second into the third; additionally, the potency of the first diminishes whether one transitions into the second or not, and the potency of the second diminishes whether one segues into the third or not. Indeed, the foolishness of one's youth may be shed as she or he transitions into a wiser midlife, and the foolishness of midlife may evaporate as one assumes the wisdom endemic to decrepitude.

My generation—at the lower end on the verge and on the higher end in the midst of geriatric bliss—is defined in infantile terms and, coincidentally, was the first generation to define itself primarily in opposition to the previous generation's parental authority. At the heart of the 1960s and 1970s counterculture ethos is a radical egalitarianism that sprayed plumes of Any-Boy-and-Girl-Can-Make-Art in similar fashion to the DDT trucks' spraying of neighborhood streets in the 1950s, many of us galumphing ecstatically behind those toxic beasts as our loving parents looked on in ignorant approval. The Neverland of creative writing shimmers in the mist several miles offshore and down the road, into the highlands, from Brigadoon. Transit from the former to the latter is from treacherous innocence to idyllic indeterminacy. Implicit in pedagogy is generational authority, subset of parental authority, and the *Wanderung* from Neverland to Brigadoon is subcontracted to the Pied Piper of Hamelin, the first tenured poet.

The arc of my career would be the arc of my self-esteem, my sense of social value, if I were deeply traumatized by poor potty training or a too abrupt transition from breastmilk. But I am one Baby Boomer who, I was told when I was too young to appreciate the humor, stood in my crib at ten months and smeared my own feces on a wall, pre-articulating the egocentric predicament in a soporific state of blissful self-expression. For better or worse, I do not require much tribal affirmation, and though I delight in my little career successes, I regard them as incidental to the intrinsic value of what has garnered me those successes, as humble as such efforts have been. The fact is that I feel I am just hitting my proverbial stride at the tender age of sixty-six, that though I found my voice in my twenties, I just didn't know, for the most part, what to do with it. The wisdom of youth, coiled in my loins, struck my frontal lobe a few times but otherwise relished the dark. Now I trace the contours of my ignorance as unabashedly as I once traced the contours of the gods' faces on a wall with my shit and in a state of jubilation no less potent.

According to actuary tables, the world may stick a fork in me. According to my own hoary heart, I am neither raw nor done; yet I feel a force trying to pull me too soon from the fire, a force that is the collective will of those younger than I wishing for a place not at but on the banquet table— that they, too, may be joyfully consumed. By what? By whom? Perhaps by ambition, a condition pertaining to career status and tethered to practical lifestyle considerations.

This is no country for old poets, and it isn't amenable to young or midlife poets either. Poets, literary artists generally (those whose products with rare exception do not sell in airport bookstores), exist in a more or less hermetic loop, as though the exclusive audience for stand-up comedians were stand-up comedians. But stand-up comedy exists in the brutal context of market imperatives, and poetry is wholly subsumed by academe (poetry slam culture and its auxiliary activities notwithstanding) such that it tends to duplicate academic publication and dissemination; something like peer review replaces, at least augments, market dynamics, though, alas, it is peer review more akin to gang initiation than to academic assessment, and the plethora of high-sounding awards and distinctions that has accrued over the past fifty years or so has everything to do with the incursion of creative writing, particularly poetry, into academe. The Bum Schmuck Award doled out semiannually by *Your Dirty Drawers Quarterly* could indeed be the clincher for a hiring committee at MLA, and the lucky putz thus welcomed into the Valhalla of Full Employment will seek to garner other such distinctions in pursuit of tenure, a state in which she or he exists as the Po Biz rep at the High Table graced by roasted magic boar flesh and mead that issues from the ut(d)t(d)ers of a magic goat. And thus ensconced, she or he will, consciously or unconsciously, advocate for the general interests of the Po Biz as those interests seem coterminous with the interests of students who likewise seek admittance to the Hall of Valor and who relish the battle, the competition, for a vaunted seat at the table (or to grace a silver platter on it).

But unlike the magical groaning board in Valhalla, there are only so many seats at this glorious table, and to the more ambitious, and more socially adept or charismatic regardless of talent or commitment to the art, the table at which they belly up is rounded not exclusively by other warrior poets but also by scholars of the various categories of literary history, genre, theory, and pedagogy. This is no country for old poets from the POV of young poets seeking steady, protected gigs, places at the table (or on it).

I love my job. I love academe. I love the life that I've been afforded. I don't love poetry any more than I love the Earth's molten core, but I love the role of poet, often too much, sometimes not enough. I hate that the Founders of Creative Writing, the (mostly American) poets and writers born anytime from the outbreak of the First World War to the end of the second, are largely fading from the collective memory of Millennials. I hate that the process of professionalization that the Founders initiated and husbanded has ossified into a cottage industry more dedicated to blind expansion than to cultural enrichment. I despair, just a little, that poets have been tamed, have been admitted, if incrementally and with Kafkaesque caveats, into the polis.

The Baby Boomer poets were mentored by a parent generation for whom the role of poet still afforded exquisite outsider status. The "Greatest Generation" of poets suffered from an enormous shared sense of inferiority relative to their own progenitors, the High Moderns, those who resuscitated, in a manner of speaking, "the dead art of poetry" and in so doing determined, inadvertently, a course toward professionalization.

It is the nature of lyric discourse to shuttle between dry and wet knowing and to comb, by virtue of its redundant route, from the velvety threads of imagination, the grit of the quotidian. And I am free to make poems and essays about poets and stories and novels and memoirs and any other damned thing I may wish to make, but if I haven't, by this stage of my life, achieved something like a first-tier career status, however that may be judged, will I be allowed—or, to put it more fairly, encouraged—to change, to advance in career status by virtue of present and future creative efforts?

Life expectancy in the United States is seventy-eight and seven-tenths years; it's probably higher in my demographic. I bench press over three hundred pounds on a good day. I power walk or jog three miles most days. I do a karate workout intermittently. I'm type 2 diabetic but control the condition with exercise and metformin. I feel consistently better, having quit alcohol several years ago, than I felt for the previous decade or so. All things being equal, I may have at least a good decade of productivity ahead of me.

And my relation to the profession—and yes, my relation to art is one thing and my relation to the profession quite another—is like that of the persona of Robert Frost's "Two Tramps in Mud Time" to manual labor. The two indigent fellows are thirty or more years younger than I and need the work. But I relish chopping wood in the way that one relishes activity that is not required of him but must get done all the same.

My parent generation of poets, which included Pied Pipers such as Allen Ginsberg and Robert Bly ("tenure" was incidental for both, though both suckled academe for their entire adult lives), conjured careers from the generational breach; to jumble the trope, they were Pied Pipers who led a Children's Crusade, and that holy invasion has settled into a protracted occupation of the unholy but fecund Land of Opportunity, Am'rica, Amerika, Om-erica. They proceeded, at least superficially, from a sense of radical purpose, or radical *repurposing,* to deploy a current popular term, regarding lyric art.

I read Stanley Kunitz's poem "The Layers" when I was in my late twenties, when I was, at least somewhat, on the make for something like a career. I *got* it—the poem, but the career too—but in a dry knowing kind of way. Now I cannot help but consider it as I am drenched in the exquisite terror issuing from the simple math of my mortality:

THE LAYERS

I have walked through many lives,
some of them my own,
and I am not who I was,
though some principle of being
abides, from which I struggle
not to stray.
When I look behind,
as I am compelled to look
before I can gather strength
to proceed on my journey,
I see the milestones dwindling
toward the horizon
and the slow fires trailing
from the abandoned camp-sites,
over which scavenger angels
wheel on heavy wings.
Oh, I have made myself a tribe
out of my true affections,
and my tribe is scattered!

How shall the heart be reconciled
to its feast of losses?
In a rising wind
the manic dust of my friends,
those who fell along the way,
bitterly stings my face.
Yet I turn, I turn,
exulting somewhat,
with my will intact to go
wherever I need to go,
and every stone on the road
precious to me.
In my darkest night,
when the moon was covered
and I roamed through wreckage,
a nimbus-clouded voice
directed me:
"Live in the layers,
not on the litter."
Though I lack the art
to decipher it,
no doubt the next chapter
in my book of transformations
is already written.
I am not done with my changes.

The professionalization of poetry is not unlike the professionalization of politics, and the consequence is similar: the art part is not diminished, just subsumed, though by what? Social ambition that has little (though that bit is important) to do with artistic ambition. The change that I've most recently experienced is from a mild concern for career status to virtually no concern. I am, at the tender age of sixty-six, consumed both by the terror of extinction and the perverse joy of self-expression. But then I can afford, literally, such a shift in perspective, in goals, in fundamental values. I've been tenured for years.

The Magic Book
Why I Thought Publishing a Book
Would Change Everything

The following is the transcript of a lecture given at the Prague Summer Program in July 2009.

One brisk Saturday morning, in Norfolk, Virginia, mid-autumn 1965, I shuffled through the parking lot of the Giant Open-Air Supermarket, a few blocks from the projects. I wore a tattered black leather jacket I'd procured from the local Salvation Army, where my family acquired all of our clothes. It just so happened that the Salvation Army was conducting a used-book sale in that parking lot, and without thinking, I grabbed two books from one of many piles, lined up on folding card tables at the rear of the lot, and ran like hell. I was more than halfway back to the projects when I pulled up, gasping, and studied what I'd filched, stolen for no other reason than the thrill of doing so. Both, ironically, I would years later notice, were Taiwanese pirated editions: *Louis Untermeyer's Treasury of Great Poems* and *The Complete Poems of Robert Frost.*

What if I'd stolen books about high finance, architecture, or landscape gardening? Would my life have taken a different path? Would high finance, architecture, or landscape gardening have saved my life? I don't know, but I doubt it. I think I'd have found poetry one way or another. I think that one way or another, I'd have found my poet fathers to slay and poet mothers to long for. I'd have found my poet brothers and sisters, my tribe, my spiritual home. But that moment of puzzling over those books, as I stood beside the huge drainage ditch between Comstalk's Drug Store, where I bought and stole my DC and Marvel Comics, and the projects where I lived, I knew I held in my hands something truly marvelous. I'm not sure I'd ever even seen a "poem," words lined up like *that,* words sounding like *that.* At first, as I read randomly and ambled homeward, I was puzzled yet intrigued. I would soon fall in love with those books and seek others. Poetry was my secret for years. Within months of that same year, I somehow got my hands on Ferlinghetti's *A Coney Island of the Mind,* and so poetry closer to my urban experience, and something gloriously tainted by popular culture, became available. I "understood" so little of the poetry I read as a boy, but I wasn't bothered by incomprehension. I took it in stride, even relished it, the mystery of what I could not fathom in poetry.

In 1976 a guy who'd picked me up hitchhiking south of Dallas woke me up and told me to get out of his little truck. I'd heard of the French Quarter, recalled that the previous evening the guy had told me the French Quarter would be the end of the road. As I'd drifted off, I'd recalled that I had a buddy, Bernie Gallant, who lived and worked there in the Chart House restaurant. Public phones were a nickel. That evening I was scrubbing pots and banging racks of dirty platters into a dishwasher.

Soon after taking up employment at the Chart House, I met the woman I would live with in her apartment on Dumaine and would eventually, ludicrously, marry. After my adventures in three graduate programs, interspersed with gigs at several upscale French Quarter restaurants, Betty and I moved into what our landlord insisted, on one occasion swore, was the original House of the Rising Sun, on St. Louis between Bourbon and Dauphine, across the street from Al Hirt, or "Jumbo," as he insisted we call him.

It was there, at the age of twenty-nine, in the early autumn of 1983, that I received in the mail the package containing two hardback copies of my first book, *Green Dragons,* winner of the Wesleyan University Press New Poets Series. I can look back now over the almost thirty years and realize how silly I was as I ripped the envelope open and held my book, gazed into the image on the dust jacket with a soulful intensity I'd never felt before and would not feel again until eight years later, when I'd gaze into the crinkled face of my swaddled newborn first daughter.

I'm certain that every published writer can tell a similar story of that first moment of clutching that first book, turning it over again and again in one's quavering hands, opening it and flipping rapidly through the pages, lifting it to one's face and breathing it in, all but inhaling it, indeed all but eating it, of feeling that the thing is magic, will magically transform human existence. That feeling is a narcissistic idiocy that soon passes, or at least ratchets down in intensity. And at some point one feels, at least I do, a kind of shame for having been so self-consumed, for having invested so much ego into such a simple, even humble object.

As one reaches the point when Peggy Lee's "Is That All There Is?" becomes something like the National Anthem of the Inner Life, of course all the remembered manifestations of youthful narcissism become a source of great shame, and yet such shame does not empty into regret. I can never regret feeling so marvelous as I did holding in my hands for the first time my first book. I did not yet fully fathom how lucky I was not to be in prison or swabbing the deck of an aircraft carrier; nor did I yet fully fathom how blessed I was to have published a first book with such a prestigious press. A decade earlier, I'd moseyed, my nerves sparking, through the Coronado Public Library, coming down from half a hit of Windowpane, and spied three thin books at odd angles on a table in the stacks. I paused to touch them and read the titles: *Not This Pig* by Philip Levine, *St. Judas* by James Wright, and *Helmets* by James Dickey. Wesleyan University Press had published all three, though at the time I didn't notice such things. At nineteen, I fancied myself a poet, would get stoned and listen to LPs in the tiny booths of that library, of Dylan Thomas declaiming "Fern Hill" and T. S. Eliot "The Hollow Men." But with the exceptions of Ferlinghetti and Ginsberg, I hadn't read any contemporary poetry. Feeling as though I had battery cables clamped to my ears and someone was revving the engine, I sat at the table and read those books, and when I'd finished reading every single word of all three, I felt gobsmacked, transformed. A window was opened, and I crawled through, and the first thing I saw on the other side, ten years later, was a little book with my name on it. The fact that my moment of narcissistic glory was strapped to the wonder I first felt as a thieving boy and that that wonder coalesced into an all but selfless love for those qualities of affection and vision and truth telling that I first encountered as a nineteen-year-old kid in a library on acid, renders my self-congratulatory moment of utter self-consumption forgivable. That is, I forgive myself for having been so happy that moment I held my first book and for being so happy about it for so long. I was probably insufferable to my new colleagues, especially my fellow junior faculty who had not yet published books. I was probably insufferable not because I bragged or passed among them with a swagger but because I was so happy. I'd spent the last decade climbing through a window, and I was finally on the other side.

But where was that?

Who has roamed through a university or big-city library and not felt profoundly humbled? Who has not contemplated the sheer volume of information contained in books, the unfathomable range of information, and not felt infinitesimal? What information did my first little book contain, what information have any of my little books contained? Well, mostly info about me, how and what I've thought and felt over a range of circumstances. Hardly world-rocking stuff. Whitman yelped, "Who touches this book touches a man!"—and the floodgates were opened to a century and a half of ego spew, Romantic self-consciousness with an American zest, a radical egalitarianism that is uniquely American.

It took me ten years to climb through a window, and once I was on the other side, it took me a long time to realize that I'd not climbed out but rather in. I'd broken into the House of Art but not to burgle, not to snatch, bag, and escape. I was there, remain there, because outside is pain and despair. Outside, suicide is an option, and love is only chemistry.

Holding my little book almost thirty years ago, I held my own life, my life affirmed, my life transformed from lead into gold, or shiny copper at least. I became a published author; my name was surely destined to become a household word in dozens of homes across America! I was skinny and kind of pretty back then. I had one chin so did not require facial hair. I gave lots of readings to promote my little book and actually sold a bunch, relatively speaking. During readings, I'd stare into my book, glancing up to make fake eye contact every few seconds. My "reading" was really a recitation because I had the whole book memorized. Of course, I wanted the women in the audiences to really like me. I gave readings at colleges and universities that never would have admitted me had I applied to them. I was a young man telling his life story in ragged verses. Many of my poems were about the suffering of others: my family; hookers in Sasebo, Japan; doomed marines on their way to Vietnam; wretched winos passed out on gaslit French Quarter stoops; young gay men desperate for love on the balcony of Laffite in Exile. I referenced their sadness, their suffering, with a goofy joy. Though I'd composed the poems of *Green Dragons* in a state of empathy, I performed them, gazing into the book, a commodity no one really wanted to purchase, full of pride in that object, that fetish, that catalyst to my transformation, that prize I'd climbed through a magic window to acquire, that very source of magic that had opened the window, had placed the window, opened, in my path.

Well, we learn that all textuality is intertextuality, and we learn as well that there is no author, not really. There is only what Foucault termed the "author function." I hadn't begun my decade-long autodidact's foray into cultural and literary theory and criticism, so on the occasion of gazing into my first book, I assumed it was all *mine,* that every word *belonged to me.* A few years later, participating in a literary theory study group composed mostly of my junior colleagues, I puzzled all by standing, kicking the table leg, and declaring, "OUCH! Thus I refute Derrida!" Though that group, whose intellectual candlepower was formidable, had read a ton of theory between them, none, it seemed at that moment, had read Boswell's *Life of Johnson* or recalled that the great curmudgeon, two hundred years earlier, had famously kicked a rock and exclaimed, "OUCH! Thus I refute Berkeley!"

Well, somewhere a tree had fallen in a forest, and whether or not anyone had been present to see and hear it fall, it was eventually processed into paper, and those pages littered with ink arranged into shapes that were letters I'd pressed into patterns, grammatical units forming sentences, my texts, my ragged verses. Whether it existed because I perceived it or whether it and I were merely projections of the glorious mind of God, that moment I first held it, I knew that I would never climb back through the window, out of the House of Art, a condition of heart and mind that does not require an occupant to compose and publish a book; it had simply required that *I* compose and publish one.

But what if I'd been born in 1993 rather than 1953? That Richard Katrovas will not turn twenty-nine until 2022. I imagine him receiving an email congratulating him for being chosen, out of more than two thousand young poets, to have his book published online by a prestigious university press. It will be immediately available, of course, for downloading onto the ubiquitous reading pads and will even be available through print on demand.

Though even over so relatively short a period of time, the book as a fetish, as a magical object, as a thing that an ego may attach to, be anchored or buoyed by, will likely be past. When that Richard Katrovas is my age now, the year will be 2048. Will the atrocious nostalgia that this talk is wafting from pertain to that writer's life? His first book will never, none of his books will ever, "go out of print," will always be available. Of course, the internet will by then be littered with tens of millions of poetry books, if it isn't already, but most of the ones that actually get read by discerning audiences will have been vetted by respected publishers, thoroughly peer reviewed, and this will be true of all types of texts.

So much of lyric expression, especially pastoral lyric expression in its various manifestations, is about loneliness. Reading, at its best, is an exquisitely lonely endeavor. As a kid in the projects, my old man in the joint and my mother dying, I read to escape in the most profound sense. We lived on $169 a month from welfare, not a hell of a lot even in the midsixties. Our end of the projects, the white end, butted up against a lower-middle-class neighborhood of Black homeowners. I knocked on doors and asked if I could do odd jobs, even mow lawns with a crappy push mower I'd extracted from a junk heap. I'd earn a quarter to fifty cents mowing a lawn, and some Saturdays, I'd earn as much as three dollars, more than half of which purchased comic books. Of the hundreds I'd collected, kept in the third drawer of a battered chest of five drawers, was included *Daredevil* 1 through 8, in pristine condition. Oh, that I had sealed just those eight in plastic, then encased that bundle in something enduring, and buried it somewhere accessible though remote, I might return to the projects of Norfolk, Virginia, and exhume those comic books—which are neither "books" nor particularly funny—sell them on eBay, and pay off my 2006 C-class Mercedes! The exquisite loneliness of all pastoral expression and all passionate reading is simply that angst rooted in adolescence that, if we're lucky, never withers. With a stack of new comics and my two filched books, I'd sit half-lotus in the little field across a dirt road from the left bank of the Elizabeth River and give my life over to a summer day filled with that exquisite loneliness, that holy anonymity.

Well, I'm no longer anonymous in that same holy sense; indeed, I am ashamed to confess that I am an inveterate googler of my own name, a form of midlife onanism that may not cause blindness or hair to sprout from one's palms, though perhaps the jury's still out regarding its long-term dilatory effects. Suffice it to say that a fair chunk of the items associated with my name that get dredged up by that omniscient search engine have to do with people trying to sell used copies of my books. Terse descriptions of the books are always included, such that I know a hardback copy of *Green Dragons* exists somewhere on this planet with only a coffee cup ring marring the otherwise perfectly preserved original dust jacket.

There is no way to calculate the intrinsic value of any book. What value may we place upon a novel or collection of poems or history or philosophy or scholarly study, or comic book even, that changes or sustains an individual's life? What we are confronting now is that "book" is bifurcated along the conceptual fault line of content and form. We may now have purchase on the content of any book sans that very form that defines it. The extrinsic value of a book is purely a matter of market imperatives. I love that the first poetry books I ever read were Taiwanese pirated editions, that international copyright lawbreakers, Chinese ones at that, had calculated that Untermeyer's anthology and Frost's *Collected* might actually fetch some coin. I thought nothing of this as a kid, of course, but now I am mystified. Surely people who publish illegally are savvy about product. Those books were illegally printed in the late fifties or early sixties. What in God's name were those Chinese people thinking?

I would be delighted if one of my poetry books were thus disseminated across Anglophone Asia. I would love it if my name were a household word in more than a dozen homes across America, even if there were no monetary compensation. It's not as though I have actually made a living as a writer up to this point.

Intrinsic and extrinsic values merge in the enterprise of book collecting. When the content of a book has achieved an unquantifiable though very real transcendent value in the hearts of a coterie, or in the larger culture, that manifest content's "original" form may be assigned an extrinsic dollar value. In other words, such books enter the realm of visual art and baseball cards.

To lessen the book-buying burden on my students, I often cobble together reading lists that are wholly, or almost wholly, accessible online. It is easy enough to download everything from *Huckleberry Finn* and *Bartleby the Scrivener* to the poems and essays of T. S. Eliot onto one's laptop. Soon virtually all the world's books will be virtual, accessible, if the content is newly published, for a fee. Amazon will continue to trend toward the iTunes model, I suppose.

But my guess is that even as books become obsolete as the form in which verbal content is delivered, that form, the physical book, as an art object, will enter a protracted period of renaissance. Authors will seek to have fine, limited editions even of their best sellers produced by artisans. Indeed, to a much greater extent than is true today, many fine boutique printers, artists in their own right, will seek to print limited editions of the very best books in all fields but especially in the literary arts. The best books will have two lives, in mass distribution, or at least mass accessibility, in the virtual world but also in small fine editions for small discerning audiences of the writer's friends and loved ones as well as inveterate book collectors, a category of human endeavor that will grow exponentially but only up to a point.

On a flight home this spring from Prague, I met a couple of guys, roughly my age, who happened also to have Kalamazoo, Michigan, as a final destination. One of them was a colleague from another department at WMU whom I'd never met and whom I may very well never see again. I chatted up the Prague Summer Program, which he vaguely recalled having heard mentioned, and this year's theme. He talked about his Kindle, about subscribing to the likes of *Sports Illustrated* and how the "cover" now features not a static photograph but, rather, a video stream. "Just like Harry Potter!" he finished, chuckling.

My second daughter, thirteen, spends many hours on her computer, mostly on Facebook and on exclusively Czech-language social networking sites. When she is not exchanging cryptic, terse, misspelled messages with her posse of girls, her only other reading, usually, is of fashion and pop culture magazines. When we stand in line at the supermarket, in Prague or Kalamazoo, and she tosses a magazine on the pile of groceries, I will often pick up the magazine and page through it. My response is usually, "But, Annie, there's nothing here but pictures!" She'll protest that there's plenty of text, snatch the mag from my fingers, leaf through, and triumphantly point to a quarter-column of print, a caption to a photograph in which Brangolina is hauling clingy children through an airport.

A blending of image and text, in which the text is secondary to image, certainly did not begin with the internet. It is the very nature of print advertising, and I wonder if the graphic novel, haughty offspring of the comic book, will not in a generation supplant the traditional novel. The technology by which even a visual illiterate such as myself may produce vibrant, original, and complex images will surely be available. Indeed, the technology by which anyone may produce quite incredible cinemagraphic narratives will be available. Any schmuck will have the tools to out–James Cameron James Cameron. Isn't it the case that one of the reasons there are as many "writers" as there are today is because it's a cheap form of self-expression? When other more exotic forms of self-expression become not only available but also easy to access, won't there be a great migration toward such exotic forms of storytelling? The migration away from strictly verbal texts has, of course, already begun in the form of ever more complex and narratively rich video games, and some of the cheesiest sci-fi has already pointed toward a world in which alternative, virtual "realities" will be available, presenting quite staggering moral and ethical issues. As scholars have noted, the now classic and germinal *The Matrix* is a sinister cartoon of Bishop Berkeley's epistemology. The very nature of human intimacy is the ultimate issue. I am not one who believes that Facebook is a flash in the pan; rather, I believe that it is just a primitive beginning.

"We are the degenerate descendants of fathers who in their turn were degenerate from their forebears," proclaimed Horace more than two thousand years ago, and this degeneracy is particularly true regarding memory. The great storytellers of prehistory committed vast language constructs to memory, and so many of the conventions of "traditional verse" are but vestiges of oral traditions, the mnemonic devices that facilitated memorization of—literally—epic proportions. Textuality in preliterate cultural contexts is a matter of physical proximity, intimacy even. The presence of at least one other human being is necessary for the aural exchange to occur. And what we may call oral traditions did not, do not, exist within a simplistic, linear historical context. Clay tablets, Papyrus, wax tablets, and parchment scrolls held records of practical and cultural information in the midst of thriving oral traditions. The illuminated texts emanating from the scriptoria of medieval monasteries were the rarified products of isolated labor occurring in the midst of a bustling cultural life determined by folktales, superstition, and rumor, and likewise the more or less secular scriptoria that serviced the burgeoning university libraries of the twelfth, thirteenth, and fourteenth centuries. Even as Europe transitioned from manuscript culture to the printed book following Gutenberg's invention of the printing press mid-fifteenth century, the vast majority of people, through the Renaissance right onto the cusp of the nineteenth century, were not only unaffected by book culture but were illiterate. And even as we contemplate how truly rarified authorship was, as a social niche, up until only a couple hundred years ago, it is also interesting to note that authorship only relatively recently conveyed authorial rights. For many centuries, any text could be copied and sold or otherwise disseminated with impunity. Authorship that occurred outside systems of patronage offered little more than unremunerated glory. Even as today we observe the music business transforming as a business, becoming increasingly more diffuse, less profitable, more ad hoc, less secure in its mechanisms of exchange, so the e-book industry, as it evolves, will surely return us to that era of unremunerated, or under-remunerated, glory.

In his famous essay "The Work of Art in the Age of Mechanical Reproduction," Walter Benjamin mourns the loss of "the aura," what he characterizes as the moment of awe experienced by an individual witnessing a work of art for the first time. He argues that commercialization has subjected the aura to a grotesque warping of value, and the result is a cheapened "cult value." Of course, his emphasis in this formulation is on visual art, and throughout his groundbreaking essay, his focus, when looking back, is on the visual and plastic arts, and on photography, cinema, and performing arts generally when speculating about the future, though I think that his formulation regarding aura is more broadly applicable to include the literary arts, though the manifestation of aura has not to do, I think, with that rarified moment of discovery in the exchange between an "original" work of visual art and a discerning witness but, rather, with the very nature of the relationship between "author" and consumer of language texts. Quoting Benjamin:

For centuries a small number of writers were confronted by many thousands of readers. This changed toward the end of the last century. With the increasing extension of the press, which kept placing new political, religious, scientific, professional, and local organs before the readers, an increasing number of readers became writers—at first, occasional ones. It began with the daily press opening to its readers space for "letters to the editor." And today there is hardly a gainfully employed European who could not, in principle, find an opportunity to publish somewhere or other comments on his work, grievances, documentary reports, or that sort of thing. Thus, the distinction between author and public is about to lose its basic character. The difference becomes merely functional; it may vary from case to case. At any moment the reader is ready to turn into a writer.

Thus, the distinction between author and public is about to lose its basic character. Well, notwithstanding the fact that this passage seems prescient regarding our own time's burgeoning blogosphere, who cannot find the *about to* in the sentence just a little grotesquely charming, emanating as it does from the year 1936 and from Central Europe. We have all viewed the film clips from Nazi Germany of gargantuan piles of books ablaze against a night sky and Nazi citizens feeding those flames in a bacchanalian frenzy.

The aura of all books is a reflection of those flames and has everything to do with a history in which people have given their lives to the meticulous copying, husbanding, and preservation of sacred, secret, and forbidden texts and of texts that were the very touchstones of ethnic and cultural identity. "The People of the Book" survived thousands of years of persecution and Diaspora in no small part because of their reliance on the written word and their faith in the books, sacred and profane, upon which they have built their fundamentally alienated yet indestructible identity. The book as an object to preserve, to keep, to cherish even, goes to the heart of civilized life in a way that its disembodied information preserved and disseminated electronically never will. The soul-body dichotomy comes to mind. The book is the word made tangible, made flesh, if you will. Who touches a book, indeed, touches a human body. When I held my first little book, I held the body of my dead mother. I held the body of a child I would not know for eight years. I held the bodies of women I would love. I held the body of tragedy and the body of comedy. I held nothing less than my own corporeal humanity.

Or so I felt for those first blissful, self-loving moments as I pulled my leg through the window and set both feet squarely upon the floor. As I stood there, in the House of Art, my little book was every book, and I was every reader and every writer. My narcissism shaded to a profound humility, and I was happy.

Take My Wife, Please

Poetry Readings and Stand-Up

The poetry reading is a relatively recent form of entertainment and is rarely entertaining. A good reading can be edifying, interesting, but like a good lecture asks more of its audience than did, say, even the performances of those ancient singers of tales, the rhapsodes, or their lyre-strumming compatriots who were likewise unambiguously entertainers. Poets, unlike most lecturers across the spectrum of heady matter, occupy an odd niche; the chuckles that a lecturer on particle physics or seventeenth-century Swedish courting rituals may invoke are a kind of bonus, but poets are expected to embody a certain performative panache, though, alas, rarely do. Poetry readings, like stand-up routines, are a weird braiding of lecture and storytelling, lecture and musical performance even, but whereas a mediocre stand-up routine can be entertaining, there is no performance more stultifying, more painfully boring, than a mediocre poetry reading, and the great majority of such occasions are indeed mediocre.

I remember watching Henny Youngman on *Ed Sullivan*. I was eleven or twelve. A distant relative, ashamed of my family's poverty and moved to distracted pity by it, had given us a battered TV that usually worked only when we'd adjusted the rabbit ears, their tips wrapped in crinkled foil, at *just* the correct angle relative to one another, relative to the local broadcast tower, to the weather at that moment, relative to True North, to President Lyndon Baines Johnson's social agenda, relative to every child's fear of nuclear evaporation and the goofy gyrations of Fate itself. When we couldn't get the antenna magically configured, indistinct images faded in and out of an electric blizzard, and the sound modulated between gradations of

121

hissing. On most Sunday nights, however, in all seasons and regardless of most weather conditions, we didn't find the sweet spot so much as it found us, and—hallelujah—a talking horse, a Martian, and the great Ed Sullivan himself graced our heathen lives.

I laughed on cue. "Take my wife . . . please!" The implied "you" was plural and referred to the audience, the one to which the fuzzy old guy holding a violin was speaking directly, but also to all of "us" in TV Land, a commonwealth of which I was an albeit marginalized citizen. Where did he want us to take her? More importantly, what did he want us to do with her?

Some years later, I'd witness Buddy Hackett, chatting with Johnny Carson, distinguish comics from comedians: "Comics say funny things. Comedians say things funny." So, perhaps it was the quality of the pause between *Take my wife* and *please* that invoked mirth, though in my case it was primarily a matter of herd mentality. I laughed half a beat behind the studio audience, got swept up into that collective delight. It was actually not until I was in college that I "got" the joke. Henny Youngman's one-liner had seeped so deeply into the American psyche it would get repeated in the most delightfully odd contexts. A professor at San Diego State, one I didn't much like, would hang out with students in the main cafeteria, near the bookstore, and, cranked on caffeine, regale the more or less permanent audience of four or five that gained and lost members over the course of his routine, with his massive, if facile, erudition. One day, apropos of nothing worth recalling, he said, "Take my wife (*pause*). Please!" and I got it. One heard *take my* and knew it meant "consider," etc.

In the federal housing projects, where I'd first experienced the king of one-liners on *The Ed Sullivan Show* through the auspices of an evil Motorola, no one considered much of anything. *Take* for *consider* was not a locution native to the vernacular of that community or my family, and though eventually I'd enter the broader universe of discourse in which *take my* was comprehensible, it wasn't until that aha moment as an undergraduate that I truly got the joke.

And I groaned and smirked rather than laughed, which was precisely what my chain-smoking, coffee junkie prof required as feedback in the midst of cafeteria din. Whatever his point, it floated on his condescension to popular culture; he was that kind of second-tier, and (even by the mid-1970s) miserably outdated, intellectual.

If the world ends not with a bang but a whimper, surely that pathetic punchline will be followed by a rim shot ... *ba dum tis.* Eliot's deployment of a nursery rhyme in which innocents join hands and crab-walk in a circle was smirk inducing during that period when I was desperate to join the droll elite but now saddens me. Conflagration is no joking matter; neither are genocide and mass extinction, regardless of how pathetically submissive victims are conceived to be, and perhaps that was Eliot's point, or maybe it wasn't; speculating about authorial intention, we learn, is a fool's game. I know that apocalyptic humor affected me much differently after I'd become a parent than before and that Eliot never had kids.

Perhaps crazy-eyed Buddy Hackett's distinction is more relevant to the age of vaudeville than to the post-vaudevillian era, the latter marked at its beginning, I surmise, by Will Rogers stepping off the vaudeville stage and into movies and onto the page as a newspaper columnist. His oh-shucks aphorisms, whether he delivered them while doodling with a rope onstage or on the screen, carried unabashed sociopolitical content, and though he always managed to be antiseptically inoffensive, neither gangsters nor politicians, or any blending of the two, escaped his gentle critique. He famously never met a man he didn't like, and America adored him. But perhaps not until socially relevant humor (a phrase DOA by any comedic measure) was poured into the crucible of the 1960s did a tragic genius like Lenny Bruce (an accurate characterization that Bruce himself would have mocked ferociously) give up his body and soul onstage, stripped of persona, to say *funny things funny,* and create an art form; think Richard Pryor, George Carlin, and the cavalcade of social critics and satirists who have by now risen above all other forms of verbal expression that center on a single voice.

I have attended, that is, I have sat through, I mean, I have suffered through, hundreds and hundreds of poetry readings. I have suffered through hundreds of prose readings, too, but even the worst prose reading is not as painful to witness as an average poetry reading, especially when one considers that the very worst poetry readings are paradoxically a pleasure to attend, compared to any merely average one.

At San Diego State in the 1970s, I was that student who learned to work the university's arts events funding system, and so I was the go-to guy when a season's reading series was being organized or when a hotshot nosed around for another gig to supplement the one she or he had scheduled at another college or university within a two hundred–mile radius. Because I procured the cash, I was also expected to do the introductions, a duty I relished with the zeal of a True Believer, a gleeful apparatchik, a veritable dispenser of superlatives. Every goddamned poet with a book was one of the finest of her generation. Each one embodied the spirit of the age and could peer with X-ray eyes into the beating heart of the historical moment. I combusted so flamboyantly in my introductions that I left the poets I introduced choking on my rhetorical fumes.

Then, twenty years later, when I should have known better and was running a large study abroad program for aspiring writers, I continued to work very hard crafting introductions, for my hotshot faculty, that I assumed made angels weep and undergraduates glad to have gone deeper into debt to study creative writing in Central Europe for four weeks. That my intros were too long, too florid, much too much about my own investment in the proceedings, does not in retrospect embarrass so much as confound me. How could I, no longer a spring chicken or a newbie to the cottage industry of creative writing, have been so lacking in self-awareness? Whereas my twenty-year-old self simply relished the moment before an audience, my forty-year-old self was selling a product, or overselling it. I admired, truly respected, all of the writers I'd hired for my program, but my ego investment was in the program itself, and in pushing the prose writers and poets in my intros, I pushed my own grand design, my own good judgment, my own power to hire and organize. Mine was the pride of the impresario, and I displayed that pride by spilling fulsome praise on individuals whose accomplishments truly needed no introduction, certainly not that of a car dealer pushing Maseratis on tract home suburbanites.

And yet the most edifying, absorbing, deeply moving performances I have ever witnessed have been literary readings, especially poetry readings. That the ratio of transcendent literary performances to awful or average ones is something like three or four hundred to one is both beside the point and precisely the point. There are very fine poets who should never perform publicly, and there are some Florence Foster Jenkins–like poets who can be genuinely entertaining, in approximately the same way that extinction events in blockbusters can be delightfully distracting from the very real prospects of actual extinction events.

Charisma, not to be confused with a corporate boardroom "It" factor (a learned set of "interpersonal" strategies), is what Jay-Z, Meryl Streep, and Jesus Christ (we have to assume) as well as every petty dictator and drug lord have in common. Most performers, across the arts, don't need it, though for those in leadership positions seeking to persuade others to risk their lives, for glory or profit or both, it's probably a useful quality to radiate. It occurs in various degrees. One of my buddies from the early 1970s, who sang and played guitar quite well but became a dentist, had a dash of it. My Intro to Philosophy instructor at San Diego City College in fall semester 1972 had a pinch. That year, the first woman unrelated to me with whom I'd ever cohabit had a sprinkle. Over the years, I've known numerous folks blessed, more or less, with a measure of charisma, chief among them my third ex, who, under different circumstances, would have been a pulsing star in the firmament beyond me, her family, and her Facebook posse.

Relatively few poets have it, though, probably the same percentage as occurs in the general population, and yet there are very few poets who do not relish performance, standing behind a podium, usually, and reading aloud from pages on which are written words that they themselves composed. Even the most nasally chirper of original tunes in a coffeehouse bothers to memorize the chords, tune, and words to her heart's offering, and yet, with very few exceptions, even the most revered poets will look down at a page and literally *read* their poems to audiences.

The composition of poetry reading audiences is another matter altogether, but regardless, poetry readings are indeed the most bizarre performative configurations of which I'm aware. Some professors read lecture notes verbatim, though few who do are counted among the more successful disseminators of information and wisdom. Presidents, Oscar presenters, talk show hosts performing monologues, read from teleprompters; award winners, with shaking hands and voices, will read acceptances from crinkled sheets. But otherwise, and with few other exceptions, memorization is a necessary, wholly expected component of oral performance.

Poems and children's books (also, though to lesser extents and/or in different proportions, musical scores, sermons, speeches, and eulogies) have dual ontologies. They are texts to read silently and scripts for performance, but aren't most scripts memorized? When a poet stands at a podium and reads from a text, why is that performance not regarded negatively, as would be that of a lounge singer performing while reading from a music stand? When an award-winning famous poet is paid one, two, three, four, five thousand bucks to perform for fifty minutes his anthology pieces as well as nuggets hot from her noggin, shouldn't memorization be an expectation? It seems to me that even the most cerebral, abstract, nondramatic, language play–centric verse should be memorized by any poet who deigns to stand before an audience of seven or eight, much less two or three hundred, intrepid, sophisticated (by virtue of the fact that they are even in attendance), *elite* consumers of culture stuff.

Well, that sounds perfectly reasonable, but the tableau of the poet at the podium, flicking her eyes from text to audience and back to text, is now so deeply ingrained in our literary culture that those few occasions I've witnessed poets recite their own poems from memory have felt off-putting, self-indulgent. Of course, when a poet chooses to share another poet's work from memory, whether that other poet occupies the firmament or a duplex on the other side of town, the audience witnesses an act of humility and gracious celebration.

The poetry *reading* is a predominantly American cultural event. In other literary cultures, poetry performance often entails memorization and much grander, and more grandiose, presentation. The dubious Yevtushenko comes to mind, as does the entire Spanish-language lyric tradition. But in (North) America, poetry readings, as we now think of them, before mid-twentieth century were rarer than three-headed calves at county fairs. Dylan Thomas's sonorous Welsh baritone, steeped in whiskey, echoed across college campuses in the early 1950s and arguably was a major impetus for poetry readings becoming a thing, though surely it was the Beats, their infusion of radical egalitarianism into what became the counterculture, that transformed poetry readings from rarified into ubiquitous occasions.

Of course, no stand-up comic reads from a text or a teleprompter, and what aficionado of poetry readings has not walked away from a "great reading" more *entertained* by a particular poet's patter than by the poems she or he read from the book stacks of which a local seller was hawking at the rear of the auditorium? More to the point, when has a "great reading" (as in, "What'd you think?" Answer: "Great reading!") *not* been a dialectic between text and patter, poems and shtick? And during such performances—that is, great readings—when has the patter not seemed, weirdly, a *relief* from the poems, no matter how good, how edifying, the poems may have seemed?

I recall when "poetry slams" and "performance poets" and "spoken word" entered my regard in the late 1970s and 1980s, how easy it was to condescend to *all that* and how lavishly I did, with no compunction and, alas, absolutely no curiosity. If Laurie Anderson–esque performance art was engendered by the world of visual art and Marc Smith–esque spoken word by literary art, both had the Fuck You of surrealism as their Continental pater: Robert Desnos's trance compositions and Nerval (as popularized by Apollinaire) walking a lobster, among so many other texts/exhibitions, moved performance off the stage and into the street but then back onto the stage. It is my strong intuition that poetry *readings* (prehistoric shamanic rituals, ancient rhapsodic exhibitions, and all forms of public prayer in all times, notwithstanding) may have one historical foot in literary salons but the other in the street where workers gathered to air grievances, where citizens gathered around the booming voices of compatriots, standing literally on soapboxes, reading from treatises that excoriated bosses and bankers and the motherfucking police.

The same can be said for stand-up comedy. Horace reduced the role of poetry as either to please or educate, and, again, the same can be said for stand-up comedy, though of course, one may wish to change the *aut* to *et*. The best stand-up, as well as the best poetry reading, both educate *and* delight, though I would point out, and perhaps it is simply too obvious even to mention, stand-up comedy has had a much deeper effect on the culture than poetry readings ever could, though to say so is to slip around the historical fact that stand-up was engendered by modes of performance that lead back through the same prehistoric maelstrom of storytelling and lyric traditions. But in a modern historical context, who has deconstructed nasty talk more ingeniously than George Carlin? Who has laid bare more dramatically the absurd dynamics of racism than Richard Pryor? And what female stand-up, to my mind Sarah Silverman most acutely and recently, hasn't shattered gendered stereotypes, particularly regarding the female body?

"Performance" is a sticky wicket. One's workplace performance is rated. One's performance onstage evokes polite or thunderous applause.

Certain concoctions allegedly enhance sexual performance. A waiter's performance of the Heimlich maneuver can eject a chunk of sirloin from a blue-faced patron's trachea. An athlete's performance on a single play, breaking the plane of the end zone by a centimeter, can earn a championship for an entire metropolis. Performances of duties, hedge funds, roles, heinous acts, engines, motor oils, IRAs, magic tricks, pranks, and religious rituals all have in common at their ends the fact of success or failure, in the case of the last a mere fact of form: either you follow it successfully or you don't.

Performance bridges work and play, is a primary determinant of both, and as such blurs the distinction, *especially* regarding ritual, or, as Robert Frost famously characterized poetry, though as I would humbly apply to ritual itself, "play for mortal stakes."

Stand-up is clever patter without poetry (what comics perform) or patter *as* poetry (what comedians perform). Comics distract; comedians illuminate. Our best poets, the ones who are not ridiculously serious or seriously ridiculous, are comedians, comedy here conceived in its broadest sense, as union following disorder, as clarity following misdirection, as narrative that *does not* resolve in utter obliteration of an older order to be followed by a new one similarly fated.

Adorno's (in)famous pronouncement that lyric poetry is barbaric after Auschwitz has been chewed over by toothier minds than mine, but though Yeats, of course, didn't live to know of death factories, his playful yet ominous lines from "Lapis Lazuli" ("All things fall and are built again / And those that build them again are gay") are to me even more chilling and predictive of how the egocentric predicament—or however one wishes to tag the solipsistic bent of any mind roiled in the avalanche of market forces—quavers on the surface of postmodern (dare I say bourgeois) consciousness. Adorno walked back (as we now say of politicians moderating their more incendiary public pronouncements) his postapocalyptic judgment of lyric expression, how even so ancient and primal an impulse as ego song is enmeshed in the gummy fabric of history, though I would argue that, whatever Adorno may actually have meant, the barbarism is not contained within the human impulse to sing but, rather, in the ambition to sing, to perform ego songs, even when those songs are but fulsome introductions!

Henny Youngman was pushing forty when the revelations of the death camps were made vivid in the black-and-white newsreels of the mid-forties. His shtick was to assume the stage with a violin under his arm and a bow in his left hand. That is, he presented himself as a performer of music, and at some point in his act, he would indeed play the violin with obvious skill. But his musical performance was incidental to his patter, his rapid delivery of one-liners, the mostly anapestic rhythms of which he traced on the air with his bow. Is stand-up barbarous after Auschwitz?

There wasn't much social relevance in the routines of the old midcentury stand-up comedians, and yet given the fact that they were almost all Jewish, I wonder if, at least subliminally and upon assuming careers in the entertainment business, just before and through the Second World War and on television in the two decades following it, they weren't paying homage to the dead; I wonder if pouring secular silliness into the old *formulae* of the Jewish humor tradition they weren't giving breath to the dead, though to put it so is still to question whether comedy itself wasn't rendered grotesque, even to the Jewish heart, by all that "Auschwitz" embodies. Youngman's violin was that of every Jewish kid whose mother, over the centuries, had to account for the possibility of rapid flight. Its portability rendered it at once aspirational and practical. It was a more or less universal icon of cultural achievement, one recognized and respected by the established, fixed, Christian majorities, but also, unlike a piano or even a cello, small and durable enough to accommodate hurried relocation. Youngman said funny things funny—his one-liners were firecracker-terse as discrete compositions, his delivery motor-mouth mordant—but he did so as a peripatetic Jew, as a Jew on the run, alas, as a Jew who got away at least this one time, to stand on *that* stage at *that* moment.

The quintessential American Jewish poet of our time is Gerald Stern. There are even more Jewish poets than there are Jewish stand-ups, but that's only because poetry is easier in its performative dimension, which is simply to say that audience expectations are less, shall we say, demanding, which is odd given that most audiences for it are composed primarily of folks fancying themselves poets. I say "odd" because when I imagine an audience composed of working comics at a comedy club, I don't envision a particularly easy crowd.

I recently hosted an event in New York that was meant to promote my study abroad program for writers, the Prague Summer Program. Stern, a spry ninety-one, was one of the readers, a group of former teachers in my program that included the terrific poets Stanley Plumly, Richard Jackson, Anne Marie Macari, Alison Deming, Beth Ann Fennelly, and Patricia Hampl (who smuggles poetry into luminous prose). Stern performed with the nimble wit and erudite yet folksy wisdom that I'd seen him exhibit on at least twenty other performative occasions over the years, and as before, the transit between poems and patter was often barely distinguishable; speaking extemporaneously to any audience (of other poets mostly), he has always been flat-out funny, very much a stand-up declaiming poems that are *his* violin, his prop, his connection to arguably the richest discursive tradition on earth.

If poetry is, among other things, measured speech, Stern's unit of measure, even or especially when he is being dead serious, is the joke, sometimes the one-liner, sometimes the anecdote. Freud's hilariously grim, and by now discredited, formulations regarding jokes notwithstanding, the dialectic of Stern's poetry and patter has less to do with unconscious content than timing, in both the poetic (meter) and the stand-up comedic (that pause between "Take my wife," and "please") senses.

On the page, Stern's poems are as deceptively simple, as psychological records, as any Talmudic interpretation that illustrates, and so celebrates, pluralistic over monological authority, that is, a conception of deity as speaking out of innumerable sides of His mouth at once, so to speak, a regular comedian, as a Jewish mother might quip as she slaps you lovingly on the back of your head. The Jewish tradition is the only one that I'm aware of that questions whether God has a sense of humor and, rather than answering the question, simply characterizes Him as such.

In the early 1960s, when I was a kid in the federal housing projects in Norfolk, Virginia, a white kid in a predominantly Black neighborhood, I didn't know Jew from Al Capp's Shmoo, but I felt that the funny guys who made the *Ed Sullivan* and *Tonight Show* audiences laugh were cool and that they connected among themselves into a kind of community whose defining feature, besides being funny, was outsider status. Poets, too, upon my discovering their stuff in two books I swiped from a Salvation Army used-book sale, seemed to possess similar status, though they were surely even farther outside, given that nothing like that stuff appeared on our decrepit Motorola.

Among other Jewish poets, the only *intentionally* and pervasively funny one who was consistently so (well, besides Ginsberg at his least pretentious, non-Orphic best), as a performer, was Philip Levine, though there was always something of the oddly Puritanical about Levine's verse that contrasted oddly, sometimes to quite dramatic effect, with his caustic, often hilarious patter. Gerald Stern, I believe, stands alone as our only true stand-up poet and therefore connects to both powerful Jewish traditions, one ancient and the other modern, though both with roots in a prehistoric past, of poetry and stand-up. Stern says things funny, says funny things, and says funny things funny. His weaving of poetry and patter hangs not just on performance but in his poems as texts, best exemplified by his great lyric "The Dancing":

In all these rotten shops, in all this broken furniture
and wrinkled ties and baseball trophies and coffee pots
I have never seen a postwar Philco
with the automatic eye
nor heard Ravel's "Bolero" the way I did
in 1945 in that tiny living room
on Beechwood Boulevard, nor danced as I did
then, my knives all flashing, my hair all streaming,
my mother red with laughter, my father cupping
his left hand under his armpit, doing the dance
of old Ukraine, the sound of his skin half drum,
half fart, the world at last a meadow,
the three of us whirling and singing, the three of us
screaming and falling, as if we were dying,
as if we could never stop—in 1945—
in Pittsburgh, beautiful filthy Pittsburgh, home
of the evil Mellons, 5,000 miles away
from the other dancing—in Poland and Germany—
oh God of mercy, oh wild God.

Gerald Stern doesn't recite his poems; like almost all poets, he reads them to the audience, and sometimes his searching for a poem in a book, on a page he probably should have marked more clearly, offers an opportunity for some of his sillier-seeming, digressional shtick as he rifles through pages, pauses here and there, until finally he finds the poem for that moment.

And the segue from patter to poem is an integral aspect of the rhythm of the performance per se. That slight transformation in the tone of voice, the posture of the body, the cadence of the spoken words, the rhythm of the rhetorical repetitions, is a subtly powerful contrast.

This contrast, this repeated transformation over the course of a performance from patter to poem and back, is of course true of all manner of performances; indeed, we witness it at every poetry reading, though usually, even in the very best poets, it rings at least slightly false, contrived, melodramatic even. When Gerald Stern performs, the tonal modulations between poems and patter can be by turns so subtle and so pronounced that it seems he is testing, probing, the very limits of performance. Any expression of a range of emotions, from sorrow to exaltation, no matter the nature of the artifice in which we experience it, may achieve a rhythm, a prosodic depth, that becomes the signature of that moment, scrawled on the dark with a flashlight, its ephemerality both the essence and the limit of performance.

AWP and Me

A Meditation

Groucho Marx's famous one-liner about club membership speaks to the part of me that fancies itself a writer. For example, I am a member of the Academy of American Poets and the Associated Writing Programs and feel deep disdain for both organizations precisely because they stoop to have the likes of me as a member. Why do I pay dues? Why do I participate? Because not to would be to deny myself the healthiest, least painful opportunity for self-loathing, a condition I find necessary to maintaining my bona fides as a writer. If hell is other people, for me those folks are other writers, but only when we are bound together in any official capacity. There can be no such thing as an official poet, an official artist of any kind, and sanctioning organizations in the arts, be they academic or in any way government affiliated, even tangentially, are the bane of whatever temperate zone of the human spirit where Truth and Beauty cohabit in conjugal bliss. Shelley's unacknowledged legislators are, more to the point, unofficial, and that quality is an existential value whose denial is a flagstone on the path to bad faith. However, though the human heart may be tainted by tax-exempt status, there are no pure motives in Heaven or on Earth, and no blossom should be shunned just because its roots are in shit. Far superior writers, far more courageous people than I, have submitted their papers for official stamps of approval.

Arnošt Lustig survived the Holocaust because he was young, strong, lucky, and could acquit himself usefully at manual labor. The last train he was forced upon was from Buchenwald—following his stint in Auschwitz—to Dachau, where he was scheduled to perish in a gas chamber; however, his doom was forestalled when an Allied plane bombed the engine. The bomber had probably mistaken the train for a troop transport. Arnošt and a friend escaped into the woods even as the others, the story goes, were machine-gunned. Both boys made it back to Prague and joined the resistance.

This anecdote was the seed of Arnošt Lustig's novel, the English-language title for which was *Darkness Casts No Shadow.* In the novel, the boys are killed before they reach Prague. I once asked Arnošt, now dead for several years, why the boys in the novel die when in fact he and his friend lived. "Because they had to" was all he answered.

Most of the German words I recognize I learned watching *Hogan's Heroes* and movies about World War II, but I know that *lustig* means "joyous" and that no Czech misses the irony in the fact that one of its great twentieth-century writers (and that such a small nation indeed produced several world-class writers is remarkable) wrote exclusively, for more than sixty years, about the Holocaust and happened to be one of the most joyful people on earth.

I've many stories about Arnošt Lustig because I was his boss, for nearly twenty years, for four weeks each summer, but to define the relation thus is misleading because Arnošt Lustig laughed off all authority and did pretty much what he wanted, which always far exceeded my expectations as the director of a study abroad program for aspiring writers. On those rare occasions when I felt obliged to insist that he be here or there at a certain time or to suggest that he alter this or that aspect of how he taught his class, Arnošt would smile and change the subject or just ignore me. How does one "direct" a person who has occupied not a metaphorical but an earthly hell? How does one exert any kind of authority, no matter how well meaning and professionally administered, upon a Holocaust survivor?

There are many questions I wish I'd asked Arnošt. For example, I wish I'd asked him at what age he decided to become a writer. When he was in Auschwitz, did he know that he wanted to become a writer? Well, there was no "becoming" in Auschwitz, but did he dream of a life after, and in that life, was he a writer? Was such dreaming possible in Auschwitz?

From what I've read, and what I know about the heart, a boy could dream of a life after Auschwitz and Buchenwald, but at what point did the capacity to dream, to fantasize a life after all of that, cease to be possible?

Did teenaged Arnošt fantasize a life after the camps even as he boarded that last train? Was the Allied bomber a dream come true?

One of the stories that Arnošt told me was of arriving at Auschwitz, after an extended period in the Nazi "show camp" Terezín, and being told to strip with the other prisoners, all older men. It was winter, and when the guards left that group of prisoners, of Jews, standing naked in the freezing air, the older men gathered tightly around the boy to keep themselves warm but with the skinny boy at their center. Many of them no doubt had, or had had, children. That was what they could do, as fathers, in the moment. I've recounted this anecdote elsewhere and, frankly, feel a little dirty recounting at all such an event so distant from my own experience and so bloated with . . . oh, let's call it Hollywood potential, though judging it so is an indication of my own corruption by the Dream Machine of postmodernity. Suffice it to say I am at a phase of life when I do not identify with that boy but with the doomed men constituting the minyan pressing warmth into him. No one I've ever known has embodied Auguste Comte's paradoxical formulation that the goal of humankind should be the achievement of maximum individuality within maximum community as saliently as Arnošt Lustig. No one I've known has managed survivor's guilt with greater aplomb. He told stories, on the page and off, out of a moral imperative but also to deliver the good news that, yes, hell is other people, but even within the most corrupted precincts of life in extremis, there may be—albeit fleeting—moments of redemption.

Arnošt joined the Party, was a member of the Czechoslovak Writers' Union, as were Milan Kundera and Ludvík Vaculík, indeed, as were most of the country's writers. Publication depended upon one's being a member. In the midst of the Prague Spring, he became one of the strongest, most vocal critics of the Communist regime at the 1967 Fourth Writers Conference and gave up his membership in the Communist Party following the 1967 Middle East War. Soon after the Soviet invasion of his country, in 1968, he bounced from Yugoslavia to Israel and finally to the United States, where, after a year at the vaunted Iowa International Writers' Workshop, he took a teaching gig at American University in DC; he taught there until his retirement in 2003, after which he once again became a more or less permanent resident of Prague.

I didn't comprehend Arnošt's stature within Czech society until one day in the early 2000s I happened upon my second daughter, Annie, sitting before the TV but not paying much attention to the kids' show that was in progress. Two hand puppets were chatting with a handsome, smiling, white-haired old guy. "Annie, look, it's Arnošt!" I said. She looked up from fabric she was destroying with round-edged scissors. "Oh, yeah. They're talking about fairies," she informed her father, whom she knew could not fully follow even the baby Czech that Arnošt was exchanging with the puppets.

I often wonder what I would have done: (1) joined the government-sanctioned and therefore government-controlled Writers' Union; (2) become an unabashed dissident; or (3) fled. There was certainly no dishonor in numbers 2 or 3, particularly number 2, but the first option was more problematic than is immediately obvious; some Party members, writers and not, indeed tried to work within the system to change it; Dubček's "socialism with a human face" was the motto for such efforts that resulted, penultimately, in the Prague Spring, though ultimately in the Soviet invasion.

I can't recall with much clarity the first time I attended the annual Associated Writing Programs conference. I'm fairly certain it was in the mideighties and must have been a year when the convention was in New Orleans, where I lived and worked at the local state university; I doubt I would have bothered back then to travel to another city to attend it. All that I can recall with certainty, without doing a little digging, which I refuse to do, is that it was much, much smaller than it is now.

God Bless America for innumerable features of our pluralistic society, our dynamic culture, our vibrant if at times goofy democratic processes. God bless this country for the mechanisms by which it more often than not nurtures its better angels. God bless its idealism and especially its innovative spirit. I give this blessing with only a smidgen of irony, only a tad. I am thankful for my good life, my incredible Czech American daughters, and a job I love more the longer I do it, a job that would have been unimaginable, say, the year I was born, 1953, only eight years after the end of the Second World War and as armed conflict on the Korean peninsula ceased. Universities and colleges were still being fueled by the GI Bill, and television was experiencing its golden age, though I've never fully understood that characterization. It was the beginning of the age of mutually assured destruction, a characterization I do understand and which shaped the consciousness of a generation in ways that we're probably only now beginning to comprehend. Creative writing is but one of innumerable manifestations of nuclear dread, being a creature of counterculture, itself a pink mushroom cloud of hysterical affirmation of life's essential value.

Repression occurs on an individual psychic level but also in the body politic and generationally. I recall the Cuban missile crisis vividly, and I recall the terror that all sirens invoked. Most vividly, I recall sirens going off in Sasebo, Japan, just days after I'd arrived there, at the end of the summer of 1967, with my new family, two adults and three younger children I didn't really know; I recall how I lay in the dark on a cot, still jetlagged, and was certain that I would soon be vaporized. I can't recall if I understood how near I was to Nagasaki or even knew of the event that had seared the name of that city into modern consciousness. I understood that my stepfather, whom I'd met just three months earlier, was a naval officer whose new billet was as the skipper of a wooden-hulled minesweeper, the USS *Phoebe,* a tiny ship with which he would trace the treacherous coast of Vietnam. I lay on that cot, my muscles tensed, my eyes tightly squinted, awaiting the flash and heat as the sirens squealed upon the utterly foreign darkness. The next day, no one spoke of the sirens, what they may have signaled, and they never again popped on over our three years in Sasebo.

The 1989 fall of the Berlin Wall and all that it represented was perhaps a false dawn. The planet is no safer regarding the reality of mutually assured destruction and is a hell of a lot less safe in terms of the lockstep-march of climate change. And yet I intuit a diminution of terror even as we live now in what may reasonably be called the age of terror, a time of guerrilla actions, suicidal mass murders meant to obliterate the reigning order, however one may conceive it, by a thousand relatively tiny slashes. Life under a smoldering volcano is not conducive to long-term planning; the sense of an ending infuses each day, each moment, with giddy dread. As urgency shades to resignation, threats become as abstract as the sense of an ending propagated by popcorn movies flaunting apocalypse as ephemeral as spring fashion. The apocalyptic imagination, which is to say the capacity of any single mind to conjure an image of the volcano, the fount of doom, even as one averts eyes from it, is drained of alacrity by the bastions of divine distraction, the saccharine puffs of silly hope we know as entertainment, art, religion.

Each year, I attend the Associated Writing Programs (AWP) convention. An assistant and I purchase our little table, among many hundreds. We decorate it with Prague stuff and sit for hours chatting with the same folks who stop by each year to catch up and with some prospective students, though more often with folks schmoozing to teach in the program, folks who, because they have to schmooze, are not qualified to teach in the program, bless their hearts. If we are lucky, one or two, maybe three, good writers will attend our program after having talked to us about it at the AWP convention. Our participation is not particularly cost-effective, but it has become a downbeat in the rhythm of our lives.

I am happy to be irrelevant if relevancy entails the kinds of decisions that Arnošt and his friends had to weigh as they considered the authority of the Czechoslovak Writers' Union and, by extension, the Communist Party. I am a member of AWP, and if I quit it tomorrow, the Democratic Party, of which I am also a member, would not likely be notified. Irrelevancy, even more so than ignorance, is bliss. The fact that I can make a living being irrelevant, and training others to be likewise, is a feather in the Yankee Doodle cap of the republic, an indicator, albeit a lagging one, of the glory of American exceptionalism.

During the years that Václav Havel was president of Czechoslovakia and then the Czech Republic, Arnošt Lustig lived in an apartment in Prague Castle those weeks and months he was in Prague. Havel was his buddy, his old friend, and made sure that Arnošt had comfortable digs, free of charge, when in Prague. Havel had been in prison just months before the Velvet Revolution, and his subsequent ascension to the presidency required him to reside in the Castle, a space he often seemed to consider simply a more opulent confinement than the one to which the old regime had assigned him. Though Havel had never been a member of the Communist Party, as Arnošt had, he'd been a disgruntled member of the Writers' Union up until 1968, the year both he and Lustig, and many other writers, quit that sanctioning organization.

In America, the arts got gobbled up by colleges and universities at about the same time that behind the Iron Curtain the division of the arts between state sanctioned and outlawed was occurring. In a totalitarian state, such a bifurcation is always a reality, though the Prague Spring painted the distinguishing line darker and created conditions in which joining the dissenting team, the Washington Generals to the Harlem Globetrotters, did not ensure defeat, no matter the final score of any given encounter, considering that everyone knew the game was rigged. Being a high-profile dissident was often a cagey career move rewarded with translation into, and publication in, major languages and hero status in the West. Dissident status reverberated in the West and bounced back as an echo in the totalitarian state. Václav Havel and other diehard dissidents were not bulletproof exactly, but they were at least waterproof; their voices could not be entirely drowned out by the martial music and party line rants of the regime. They were profoundly relevant, and that some of them were actually quite good writers was a kind of bonus. None had to submit to the scrutiny of tenure review, though constant surveillance and occasional incarceration were ordeals no less vexing to the creative spirit and, unlike tenure review, had no foreseeable end point. Was "official" status for writers, membership in the Writers' Union, the moral equivalent of tenure? Were the signatories of Charter 77 staking out a moral high ground equivalent to writers, artists, and intellectuals assuming status outside the academy?

The answers are "yes, but . . ." and "of course not." The *but* simply acknowledges that, at bottom, it's an apples/oranges comparison, and the simple fact is that totalitarian conditions render relevant any expression that is even implicitly critical of the reigning order. Charter 77, whose 242 original signers represented the cream of Czech culture, was a merely liberal document touting basic principles, many of which even Stalin could have applauded in the abstract. The fact of its existence, not its content, was its oppositional authority.

A pluralistic society may ding-dong back and forth between Left and Right extremes that, in broad historical terms, are anything but, which is not to say that it will never dislodge from its pendulum mooring. But as long as the pendulum remains firmly attached to its fixed point of what is variously named, but which we in America know as First Amendment rights, personal expression—the value of which is calculated within a market determined, usually, by the lowest common denominator of puerile, primitive taste or by a cultural elite that is dubiously so—will be gloriously irrelevant.

The paradox, as I see it, is that the value of art, especially of literature, in a totalitarian system that touts the good of the many, centers on the individual artist, and in a pluralistic system that places a value on individual rights, its value is in the aggregate, even cumulative, dare I say collective, force of its presence in the midst of, and perhaps in spite of, market forces.

When we arrive at whatever mammoth convention space that the lords of AWP have requisitioned and set up our little table, we take turns walking the rows, scoping out where Wesleyan University Press or Carnegie Mellon University Press are displaying their wares this year. When it is my turn to roam, I pause here and there to say howdy to folks I see only for this one four-day stretch each year; we regulars have watched one another age, mellow. I learn that so-and-so has died or retired or simply said screw it. I marvel at how much time and effort some organizations, presses and writing programs, expend upon looking good at AWP, and generally, I note how incredibly sincere, earnest, dedicated, my fellow conventioneers seem. Everyone is a little bit on the make, as we say, and by Thursday and Friday, when the great halls are buzzing the loudest with literary ambition and a general love of books, of sitting alone and reading, and of stringing words together to compose verse or prose or some hybrid thereof in the hope that a few people will read those language constructs and think well of one for having taken the time to cobble them together, I am humbled.

When it is my turn to cease pushing my little program for a few minutes, my assistant plies her considerable charms solo in my absence as I meander through the rows, avoiding eye contact with folks whose books I do not wish to purchase or whose programs have absolutely nothing to do with me. And meanwhile, I wonder just how long this odd-duck, beautiful, humane, and life-affirming system can continue. Is it a kind of Ponzi scheme? I doubt it, but I don't know. On a fundamental level, in whatever Grand Scheme one is able to wrap one's head around, what enterprise isn't?

In the early 2000s, I was once invited to participate in a literary festival in Singapore. They paid for my ticket, put me up in a very nice hotel, and gave me a handsome stipend. They asked me who, among the Czech writers I knew, they should also invite, and I told them Arnošt Lustig.

I was bowled over by the Singapore Literary Festival infrastructure, if not by the organizational acumen of its proprietors. I was impressed by the press and media coverage and by how much money had gone into putting on such an event, especially given that, as far as I could tell, the festival seemed not to have a revenue stream.

They had invited me not because they were particularly interested in or much impressed by my numerous little books but because they were intrigued, I think, by the study abroad program I direct. They clearly wanted to pick my brain, which, given the severity of the jetlag between the American Midwest and Southeast Asia, was probably rather like plucking mosquitoes from the air with chopsticks.

Arnošt arrived with a fetching forty-something, a statuesque, strikingly pretty woman who, I seem to recall, was the vice president of the Czech Goethe Society or some such thing. She and Arnošt smooched unabashedly, usually sitting in the front rows at readings and presentations, packed on the PDA, as the gossip mags now characterize such behavior, for the entire three-day program. Arnošt had somehow talked the organizers into paying for his friend's ticket and then proceeded pretty much to ignore all of the festival's sincere attempts to celebrate and promote Anglophone Asian literature, opting rather to love up, publicly and gloriously, a beautiful and, I was to learn, extremely bright and cultured, Goethe-loving fellow Czech.

The organizers of the festival were furious at me for recommending that they invite Arnošt Lustig until it was his turn to talk about his work, talk about his life, or I should say his life up until he was nineteen, because for more than sixty years, he wrote almost exclusively about that boy whose skinny, naked body had been kept from freezing by the naked bodies of old men, who had known starvation, who had seen more death and misery than any human being should ever witness, and who escaped by the sheerest luck from a death train. One could not be in Arnošt Lustig's presence and not eventually understand that he had died and been reborn, or that he should have died and simply didn't, and that he felt every minute of his life since escaping into those woods to be an undeserved blessing and that to live simultaneously in the hell of his boyhood and the relative comfort of his life after was a radical yet easy decision. Life after was friendships, family, a sense of belonging to something beautiful and good, even if it turned to shit. It was unfettered erotic play and opportunities to act on principles. It was conflicts in which he engaged and conflicts he ignored or laughed off. It was living in the midst of absurdities and calling them such. It was the melancholy he expressed when recounting his enthusiastic embrace of communism so soon after emerging from the woods, reentering Prague, and joining the resistance.

Once, in the late 1990s in Prague, he and I were waiting for colleagues to arrive for dinner. We gossiped a little, joked around. There was a moment of quiet as I checked my watch and he stared out the restaurant window. He sighed and said, as wistfully as I'd ever heard him speak and apropos of nothing about which we'd been chatting, "They fucked up a beautiful idea for a hundred years."

I knew what he meant, and that evening, as he and I and our colleagues, mostly American poets and novelists and their significant others, dined on hearty Czech fare and the wine flowed and wit was unleashed and laughter rang out, Vera, Arnošt's wife, also a survivor, berated him loudly and mercilessly, joking even about his manhood. Arnošt laughed with her and at himself, and when she castigated him for his numerous affairs, he continued to laugh sheepishly as the rest of the group roared, for the roasting she gave him was full of love, and he deserved it and took it like a mensch, of course. He was with her when she passed, in Prague, more than a decade later, and he passed very soon after.

Mao Tse-tung, responsible for the deaths of many millions, fancied himself a poet. The Rogue's Row of other literary artists, from François Villon to Richard Savage, is quaint by comparison, but the fact that bad people can make beautiful, at least vaguely interesting, literary stuff is indisputable. However, though I know that poets and writers can be incredibly petty, vain, self-deluded, cowardly, and passive-aggressive (especially that), none has registered, thus far, upon my regard as possessing an ugly heart; I've met none that I thought enjoyed the physical or emotional pain of others. Even my worst enemies, as loathsome as I may judge them in my little world, have not seemed ugly hearted, have not seemed the sort who would murder or defile, have not seemed sadistically inhumane, at least not in the sense that drug cartel henchmen, neo-Nazis, and right-wing politicians usually are.

Creative writers—terrible and brilliant, idiotic and transcendent, famous and anonymous, principled and unscrupulous, visionary and myopic, profound and profoundly mediocre—despite the pending death of literature as we know it and the ascendance of virtual realities and other heretofore unimaginable extensions and augmentations of the imagination, are charmed, special, oddly indispensable, whether organized or not.

A Privateer in the Arts

Arnold Johnston's *Where We're Going,*
Where We've Been

A "career criminal" is a lucky citizen! She makes money doing something that, even if she doesn't love it, she's at least good enough at doing to secure a steady, if occasionally disrupted, income. If there were a space, such as a federal corrections facility, to which career artists were likewise sent, to be fed and sheltered during those fallow or unlucky times, the world would indeed be a fairer one. Of course, the most successful careers in crime and the arts converge in those bastions of blurred distinctions, Washington, DC, and Hollywood, California. But in most of America, especially Flyover, USA, the career criminal and the career artist are most often institutional creatures, the former, intermittently, of state and federal penal systems and the latter more or less permanently of academe. Of course, both career paths entail the management of risk, as do all endeavors, to some degree, though most indubitably in art and crime.

Careers in the arts, like the arts as such, are divided between "popular" and . . . what? Not popular? Serious (God, I hope not)? Sophisticated? What is art that is not popular? The kid pushing his rap CD (I understand that this is still done, despite the demise of compact discs) on Muscle Beach tourists is working in a popular form but is as marginalized as any poet working in a non-popular (not to be confused with unpopular) form of that stuff we call poetry.

Perhaps I am compelled often to consider the relation of art to crime because my father was a con artist who spent most of his adult life in prison; as a con artist, he was one kind of poet, and because he so often got caught and institutionalized, clearly he wasn't a very good one. I've been a poet in academe—that is, I, too, have been institutionalized—for thirty-seven years, which means absolutely nothing regarding any measure of success or failure. But I am not joking when I characterize myself, and any other academic artist, as institutionalized. Among institutionalized poets, notwithstanding kids in the joint busting out rhymes, are those in academe who are there through the auspices of the cottage industry of creative writing (and I don't at all mean to disparage, bite the Feeding Hand, by deploying the phrase *cottage industry*) and those who are trained scholars who happen also to be poets. Arnold Johnston is the latter, and I want to riff a bit on his career as well as his verse, though also on the idea of arts careers as such.

Full disclosure: Arnie, who chaired the English department for ten years, hired me at Western Michigan University. He was my neighbor in the Marlborough on South Street in downtown Kalamazoo for almost a decade. He and his Beloved Collaborator, Deborah, are my friends.

Arnie has published an important monograph on the novels of William Golding, who gave us that famous one about English schoolboys going ape on a desert island. He's also published a novel about Robert Burns in which Arnie duplicates the spoken English of eighteenth-century Scotland. Arnie has published also two poetry collections and has another novel forthcoming. His list of acting credits is formidable (his Lear, several years ago, to my untrained eyes and ears, was stellar), and his list of dramatic publications and productions (many in collaboration with Deb) even more so. I've known perhaps half a dozen true Renaissance persons in my institutionalized life; Arnie is one.

Here's a deliciously dirty little secret: every scholar dedicated to the study of any era or flavor of poetry has a sheaf of poems in a bedroom drawer tucked under her/his/their unmentionables. As sweeping generalizations go, this one's a sword on which I'd giddily fall. Of course, I can't prove the frequency of this secret, but I don't have to. I'm not a scholar; I'm an artist. Like the forty-fifth president of the United States and other truly audacious criminals, I wield hyperbole like a privateer's cutlass.

And when I think back over my years in academe, I can't help noticing a difference between the 1970s and 1980s—my years as a student and my first decade as a professor—and now: when I was a student and then a baby prof, creative writers, particularly poets, were Yahoos among the Houyhnhnms. Now that I'm an Old Dude in the English department, I am among colleagues most of whom have no memory of such a time; my more junior scholarly colleagues, most of whom are deep into their own careers, simply accept the presence of creative writers because the Yahoos were already ensconced in English departments by the time these junior colleagues became university students. They're used to communing with privateer rabble.

You'll have to take my word that most (well, many . . . some) scholars of poetry—or fiction or drama or memoir or the personal essay or any combination thereof—also write the stuff covertly. I can't tell you how many scholars, friends much smarter and God knows more erudite than I, slipped sheaves of poetry into my cubby at the University of New Orleans and at the several places where I've been a visiting poet. What the majority of those efforts have in common is glittering intelligence and undeniable technical acumen. What sets these efforts apart is that they are, well, apart, outside the concentric circles of period styles that define the state of the art as it has evolved, is evolving, within the cottage industry of creative writing. Such bodies of work usually exist on a periphery where the traditionally formalist poets such as Richard Wilbur, Howard Nemerov, and Amy Clampitt sought to achieve the Sublime or exist as homage to the iconoclastic gesture at the heart of the Modern.

Arnie Johnston is not one of those folks. He was in the creative writing maelstrom his entire career and indeed shepherded creative writing at Western Michigan University into something like a golden age that lasted for seven or eight years, during which WMU, arguably, housed one of the more prestigious creative writing graduate programs in the country.

Arnie, even as he managed a large and typically diverse department— alas, more in terms of the range of aesthetics and skill sets than in terms of how categories of people are represented—also caucused with the creative writing division within that department and served as a kind of bridge between the department's scholarly and creative missions. As such, Arnie Johnston was a victim, in a career sense, of his own considerable managerial gifts: it is too often the case that a talent for organization will draw one into the realm of institutional leadership, a Phantom Zone in which one may, over time, compose significant creative work but from which one may not, usually, with impunity, conduct much of a literary, or for that matter scholarly, career.

And we in the world of creative writing must understand that the life of writing is one thing and the life of the writer quite another, and the latter is the province of self-promotion (How many literary agents specialize in poetry?), especially concerning poets who, as a motley and far-flung social unit, are a pirate ship of private contractors, or *privateers,* that is, pirates with papers, outlaws sanctioned, usually only temporarily, by a government. Spain, England, and France held their snuff-numbed noses and hired privateers as a matter of expediency, and such has been the case concerning poets inside the academy, which is to say almost all of them, for roughly sixty years.

I have been privileged to know, a few deeply and many in passing, poets from all over the world, and what even the most famous—the likes of Yevtushenko, Ginsberg, Heaney, Walcott, Levertov, Angelou—have had in common with the more obscure of us is a penchant, no, a passion, for self-promotion, a task as interminable as a narcissist's ego requirements, and though many lyric poets, good, bad, and mediocre, are narcissistic, they are usually so in the most benign sense: the narcissist who wishes to rule the world is one thing, the self-absorbed poet who wishes, even more outrageously, to move the world in a non-Euclidean sense quite another. The emblem of that about which I speak is the famous photo of Whitman holding out his finger upon which a butterfly has alighted; on close examination, we see what the contemporary viewer may have missed in that more innocent phase of this protracted age of mechanical reproduction: the bug is attached to the bard's finger by a wire. Yes, the Great American Poet (well, the other Great American Poet, along with Dickinson) was a huckster.

And Ginsberg was a huckster. And Angelou. And Borges. And Rich, even, was a huckster. And Milosz and Herbert. And (Carlos Drummond de) Andrade and Akhmatova. All hucksters, like my father, the check-kiting con man. Unlike Dickinson, true, but like the forty-fifth president of the United States. Like . . .

Well, in a thoroughly corrupted capitalist system, we are all cons and hucksters but most indubitably in the arts and most egregiously, and charmingly, and even innocently, in the community of poets (akin to "gang

of priests" or "herd of bears"). Yes, poets are "unacknowledged legislators," and all legislators, with the rare exception of a few statespersons,
are hucksters, cons, though what poets hawk, the elixir they are selling, is
the Sublime, what an orgasm would be if it were entirely in the mind. Yes,
that substantial! The poet, like Dickinson, like Weldon Kees, like Elizabeth
Bishop, who does not or cannot, off the page, fly the flag of her/his/their
own disposition, is the ringing exception.

As are those who are not sanctioned, so to speak, within the cottage
industry of creative writing, as is the case with most poets whose identi-
ties are rooted in the world of scholars and/or whose unfortunate talent
for organization and leadership causes them to be cut from the herd and
prodded into administrative positions. The scholar-poet, the academic
poet with scholarly credentials, straddles two traditions within the literary
tradition, or two narratives within the institutional tradition of English
departments. She or he is at once of the world of literary writers and of
academic scholars, which is rather like having one foot in the world of
hunters and the other hoof in the world of deer or, from another angle,
one foot in the lab and the other in the petri dish . . . or something like
that; being a literary artist in the academy is one thing and being an artist
who is an academic administrator quite another; for some artists, to accept
a managerial position within an academic bureaucracy is to crawl into a
roach motel from which views of neither the moon nor any other natural
beauty are accessible. Though one may dream, as Arnie Johnson does here:

> She circles me, keeping her distance,
> Knowing I'm under her influence, a little crazy.
> My tides rise to her changeable aspects;
> Her distant calm fazes me constantly.
> Her face, the one she always shows,
> Wears its beauty well; I never tire
> Of that complex topography.
>   *—from "Moon Goddess"*

This is funny, though to say how a poem is funny is as stultifying as to
describe the mechanism of one of Dave Chapelle's or Sarah Silverman's
jokes. One need only peruse Freud's theory of humor to note indeed *how*

stultifying. Suffice it to say that Johnston goofs here on the archetypically feminine moon and the over-determined tradition of male poets swooning in her sway. Poets prodded into administrative positions check in, but they rarely check out of the roach motel for the duration of their academic careers; rather, they retire to a room with a view, at least the lucky and truly gifted ones do.

Johnston has mastered all three major forms of the English-language sonnet.

THE POET VISITS LAKE MICHIGAN

Hunkered, he's here beside her, picking stones
Along the wind-chopped margins of this lake
They've found their way to, where they've come to rake
Through memories like ash or blackened bones.
A lone fly bats his temples, backs off, drones
Away. He looks up, sees the lighthouse bake
Under the late summer sun. Will this make
A difference? Will it modulate their tones?
Or will they file away this weekend, chalk
Another try off the list as they edge
Their way to nothing? "Is it going to rain?"
She asks. Now they've come down to such small talk;
They shore up their civilities, a hedge
Against inflated hope, to keep them sane.

The Petrarchan sonnet has always for me been the more challenging of the three major sonnet forms, if only because its rhymes jangle more, are more insistent. In an age when most folks assume (erroneously) that originality trumps convention, managing such an insistent scheme (*rhyme scheme* has always put me in mind of some duplicitous behavior) is a task of the cat-herding variety. Every such poem, to the degree it is deemed successful in a technical sense by anyone qualified to judge, is a tour de force. And technical success centers on, of course, the management of prosody ("rhythmic cognition," by Harvey Gross's wonderful definition), including the jangling scheme, and one manages the extrinsic form of such a lyric by the judicious manipulation of extreme enjambment, a feature that, so prevalent here, would have been anathema as late as the early twentieth century. Extreme enjambment restrains the cascade of Petrarchan rhymes, is an aural dam the result of which is the energy of tension between the doggerel that such unabashed rhyming becomes to the jaded postmodern ear and the off-handed, conversational tone that is the dubious mark of sincerity.

Johnston's exquisite ear, when he presses it into the service of (rather) free verse, affirms an incontrovertible, if fuzzy, truth: with relatively rare exceptions (these are the sources of the fuzz; think A. R. Ammons, Frank O'Hara, Robert Creeley, and all other anti-lyrical lyric poets), a successful free verse composition will proceed from one or more, what I call, ghost meters; that is, whether most contemporary poets proceed consciously or not regarding the relation of stressed and unstressed syllables within their English-language free verse compositions, the line as a unit of measure will, like the tides relative to the authority of the moon, feel the pull of the Past, the gravitational force of the English-language prosodic tradition that is itself anchored to a prehistoric, preliterate tradition (though "prehistoric tradition" is nonsense) that linked the discrete minds of rhapsodists and shamans to their audiences by virtue of aural paradigms rooted in the necessity for mnemonic organization. Simply put, those guys Plato's sock puppet Socrates ushered so politely yet resolutely out of his ideal city-state were singers of stories and snippets of stories and songs of mourning and celebration that were rendered memorable, in both the practical and aesthetic sense, by virtue of aural structures that were the stage upon which the dance of the intellect, with the heart, was performed. Whether it was Pound wishing to compose "in the sequence of the musical phrase, not in sequence of the metronome," or his acolyte Charles Olson charting the circuit between the head (ear/syllable) and heart (breath/line), they were not presuming to obliterate tradition but to build a new stage upon it. It would always be *there,* the feet below one's feet, so to speak, the heaving iambs and trochees and trisyllabic substitutions quantified in patterned clusters, the foundation of all those dynamic structures that constitute the best of modernity.

Or if the tradition is not the foundation, it is buried in the foundation and from there rises through the floorboards to haunt even the most iconoclastic, and blissfully ignorant or merely intuitive, free verse compositions. Most short lines of free verse will approximate dimeter or trimeter, most medium lines tetrameter or pentameter, and those longer will have embedded in them dimeter, trimester, tetrameter, or pentameter resonances. In Johnston's "Old Debts,"

> The sky freshens, light blows through the clouds.
> I feel my face soften in the damp wind.
> The ocean shifts, poised between gray and green.
> And I say nothing.
>   Waiting is my game.
> Somewhere on this same water, years ago,
> I stood fixed in the great vibrating bell
> Of sound that fell, heavy, out of the first
> Queen's foghorn. I had asked to be there,
> Blown along her deck one night
> Like a drunken sailor, hanging
> In the rush of air like ill-pinned laundry.
> Did I learn then to lose myself,
> Waiting for the wind's turn,
> Or was it later?

This is blank verse composed by a craftsman who is confident enough to truncate or terrace lines as the rhetorical moment requires. He utilizes rather than pays homage to the most ubiquitous, and enduring, measure in English-language meditative verse. The poet is experiencing a Wild Swans–at–Coole moment, and though I question whether a clothes item may be "ill-pinned" and remain on its line or if being so it would appear any different than if it were well-pinned, I delight in the kinetic energy of these lines in which the speaking subject is "fixed" and the environment vibrant. When he transitions from blank verse (including the truncated second and third lines) to a nervous seven-syllable tetrameter in the heavily enjambed eighth line and into another heavily enjambed tetrameter ninth, the effect of the return to ten syllables though within a four-beat line is that the metaphorical laundry indeed blows across all four stresses of the ten syllables, especially given the updraft created by the initial anapestic "In the rush."

Elsewhere I've written about a Victorian literature prof with whom I studied sometime before the last Ice Age—well, in the mid-1970s—and who voiced unabashedly what his contemporaries simply assumed: the only good poet is a dead one; by this, of course, he meant that only the efforts of poets ensconced in a misty past are the appropriate objects of academic scrutiny. He and his ilk, as I experienced them as a student in the seventies, were barely two generations removed from a time when American literature as such was the ugly dog in the pound and three removed from when English departments as such were controversial and when writing pedagogy was the exclusive province of expository prose composition and held similar prestige within humanities education as bowling and darts have always enjoyed in the world of sports ("Is bowling a sport?" "Yes, and barbering is an art!"). Professors who taught composition, in the misty flats of the early twentieth century, did so as high school football coaches teach woodshops or high school math teachers, who themselves never made varsity, coach JV football; I imagine that most took such course assignments in stride as more a matter of professional service than of professing and even as the rabble was putting its aggregate shoulder into the barred gate of the university English department, the Victorian, Romantic, Neoclassical, Elizabethan, and Medieval literary scholars (as well as ... gulp ... the Americanists); the philologists and linguists et al., under threat of the counterculture tsunami and wary of the cracking whip of the institutional Bottom Line, acquiesced to the rabble but not happily. That the ascent of creative writing within English departments occurred even as the—by turns vaunted and vilified—canon was being tinkered and toyed with by some and damned to hell by others and even as literary theory was the solution in which all the subdisciplines roiled is testimony to the dynamism of postwar higher ed, the oddly entrepreneurial nature of humanities education in particular, as it competed for resources with the postwar science and technology juggernaut. Perhaps only dead poets are worthy of scholarly regard, but live ones put warm bodies in the seats.

In "Two Tramps in Mud Time," Robert Frost gave us the famous dictum about careers and their relation to what one loves and, by extension, their relation to identity:

But yield who will to their separation,
My object in living is to unite
My avocation and my vocation

As my two eyes make one in sight.
Only where love and need are one,
And the work is play for mortal stakes,
Is the deed ever really done
For heaven and the future's sakes.

I do not wish to burden Arnold Johnston's wise and lovely book of verse with such boughten wisdom paid for with the metaphorical sweat from a dead poet's noggin, though doing so allows me to note that Frost is indeed Johnston's precursor among the early-twentieth-century giants and that Frost, a fine self-promoter in his own right, was, arguably, our first professional American poet as well as our first academic poet. A dropout of both Dartmouth and Harvard, Frost made his living primarily as that hothouse flower of academe, the poet-in-residence; he thrived at Bread Loaf and at Amherst and Harvard, among other institutions, including the University of Michigan in Ann Arbor, where the professorate was divided between the literary scholars housed on the main quadrangle, and who resented a college dropout being on the English faculty and getting paid as much as they (and who got showered with national recognition), and the "nonacademic" yahoos who taught rhetoric, composition, and journalism and bivouacked on the campus's wrong-side-of-the-tracks side of State Street. As that of the first privateer to emerge from the motley ranks of yahoos and thrive, Frost's vocation was not blended seamlessly with his avocation so much as it represented an incursion into the Elysium of full employment. Artistic endeavors under the auspices of academe are akin to coastal raids by dreamy marauders; thus sanctioned, however, are such efforts diminished, or tainted, by the vagaries of market imperatives? Were the products of some Renaissance masters diminished for having been enabled, and consequently shaped, by the church's patronage?

The answer is above my paygrade and beyond my capacity to count angels on the heads of pins or discern poets' hearts solely by perusing their CVs. Suffice it to say that life is short and art long, and one's career isn't even the half of it. If Arnold Johnston had chosen to attend medical school, he still would have been a poet, like William Carlos Williams. If he had chosen to enter the world of personal liability insurance, he'd have thrived within that corporate environment because he's gifted at working within complex social systems, like Wallace Stevens, and still would have been a poet. If he had chosen to buy a piece of land in southwestern Michigan and work it, he probably would have been a hell of a lot more successful than Robert Frost at coaxing sellable plant matter from fecund dirt. If he had chosen to attend a fine arts graduate program in creative writing rather than a PhD program in modern literature . . .

Poets, alas, are born, as are criminals unlucky enough to hatch possessing double Y chromosomes or into funky neighborhoods and/or into heart-warping families. The world of creative writing, my world for most of my adult life, is one soaked in false or dubious pedagogy: one may not be taught how to make art; one may, however, be taught to appreciate it and the always sloppy process by which it comes into being, and the fact is that scholars and artists appreciate literature differently, and both ways of appreciating literary art are profoundly humane, life-affirming, necessary. Both ways of appreciating literature, unlike in the past when scholarly hegemony defined literary education, exist relative to the other, and the resulting dialectic is the dynamism of the twenty-first-century English department at its best. That dialectic renders English departments the goofy, slippery, uniquely beautiful loci of language, feeling, and thought.

Soul Retrieval

"What you have told us is rubbish. The world is really a flat plate supported on the back of a giant tortoise." The scientist gave a superior smile before replying, "What is the tortoise standing on?" "You're very clever, young man, very clever," said the old lady. "But it's turtles all the way down."
—STEPHEN HAWKING, *A Brief History of Time*

Three years ago, my then twelve-year-old daughter was in the giddy throes of existential dread, a condition that compelled her to scoff at the term *agnostic,* particularly her father's marshaling it to describe his relation to the idea of deity. She held that as an oppressed majority, nonbelievers should embrace *atheist* as their binding agent and dispense with all hedges against the sorry nature of the human condition. She had come to the conclusion that life has no transcendent meaning and scanned fervently her jaundiced horizon for less lofty sources of such. We were in that phase of the annual cycle of our relationship when she is in Prague with her mother and sisters and I am in the States, a time block when we Skyped (now FaceTime) almost every day; I'd sent her a PDF of Camus's "The Myth of Sisyphus," and later we would argue, amicably, about whether we should in fact imagine the sorry bastard happy.

As I write, I am in two space-times; in the 2020 Salt Lake City space-time, I am in a new beloved's home. Although the coronavirus pandemic is raging, I am cozy in the intellectually and erotically stimulating presence of a brilliant and beautiful new friend, and I am also in Room 107 of the Salt Creek Inn on the outskirts of Nashville, Indiana, whose cultural relation to Nashville, Tennessee, is only a bit less disparate than that of Cairo, Illinois, to Cairo, Egypt; country music seems the common touchstone for the former pair, if the crowded gallery of country stars' framed photos in the Salt Creek Inn lobby accurately reflects the musical soul of Nashville, Indiana.

In that second, earlier space-time, it is 2017, and I have accompanied my wife to her weekend seminar for shaman practitioners; this session's theme is soul retrieval, and not the metaphorical sort we may attribute to municipalities such as the brassy-jazzy soul of New Orleans, the Broadway show tuney soul of New York, and, yes, the country-fried soul of Nashville, Tennessee. The metaphorical soul of Black America, as it characterizes kinds of food, music, and cultural pride, is retrievable only by those—Black, white, and other—who acknowledge its beauty and for whom such a potent metaphor makes a tuning fork of the spine.

In 2017, my wife has come here to learn to guide loved ones, discombobulated essences of the recently kaput, from the Middle Realm to the Lower, where wise and loving animals cavort, or to the Upper, where all our deceased beloveds and "spirit teachers" endlessly mingle at the ultimate cocktail party, a symposium more edifying than even Plato could have imagined. The distinction between metaphorical and actual souls seems strained at best, yet it is a vital one for a person such as she, from whom I am divorced in the Salt Lake City space-time but who, in 2017, has signed the Empathetic Contract, I'll call it, with the "universe," the more diffuse, multifarious term she substitutes for a monological (if perennially mute) "God."

My Salt Lake City companion, with whom I am sheltering as the world rides out the 2020 phase of the contagion, is an intellectual, as my wife in 2017 is not. However, my new amour is no less a student of the paranormal than my ex; indeed, I would argue, she is a more disciplined, certainly more systematic explorer of the Other Realms precisely because she applies a true intellectual's skepticism to the enterprise of seeking, and then touching, the Question Mark at the Heart of Existence. When I first encountered my new lover, I had no idea that the Venn diagram of her way of being and that of my ex would illustrate an overlap regarding matters spiritual. These women share qualities of phenotype as females who are attractive to me, but that's about it, beyond the fact that both are poets as well as lifelong learners of astrology and New Age spirituality—what my new lover prefers to call "adventures in consciousness." This commonality was not apparent to me until my friend and I were quite deep into the initial stage of our courtship. I have been perplexed and delighted to have moved from one spooky intimate to another, though these two people remain quite different in many significant ways that are incidental to this meditation. I'm frankly puzzled by the coincidence implicit in the fact that I've always eschewed New Age stuff yet was married to a New Age explorer for a decade and recently, certainly unintentionally, have linked my heart to the heart of a mystic.

I am in dangerous discursive territory centering a public meditation simultaneously upon a failed marriage and a new relationship that will not be "new" by the time these musings are published, and I wish to express at the outset my respect for each woman's privacy and beliefs. I simply wish to understand how I, a flaming agnostic, a Doubter to the bone, have tethered these bones, consecutively, to two faith-full, deeply intuitive, and wonder-full people. My ex was (I shall hereafter refer to her in the past tense because she has passed from my life, not from the world) a naive poet, naive in spite of having garnered an MFA in poetry a decade or so before we were together; I express this judgment not intending snark and add that my favorite poets have indeed been those who cultivated their innocence, Blake and Whitman most luminously, but must add that I feel a similar reverence for every woman who has ever been burned at the stake, literally or figuratively, for witchcraft or any other form of self-empowering self-expression beyond the auspices of male authority.

I've always envied those for whom the Leap of Faith is an easy choice and am lucky that, though I have never possessed the courage to make the leap myself, I have managed twice to link my life to women for whom faith was never a difficult decision but an act as inevitable as opening a door onto a perfect spring day. Ella, my intrepid atheist, alas, liked her former stepmother just fine and does not remember a time when my ex was not in her life. When she was three and my future ex had just emptied the U-Haul of her earthly belongings into our sprawling Kalamazoo condo, Ella had no compunction about handing the charming interloper a wad of tissue, bending at the waist, drawers around her chubby ankles, and presenting her backside to her new housemate. Now she scoffs, affectionately and respectfully, at the idea of a soul, of a nonphysical essence that each living thing possesses and that projects beyond physical degradation into timeless realms. My precocious preteen atheist, blithe scoffer at thin-gruel agnosticism and pie-in-the-sky spirituality alike, benefited profoundly, as did I, from the presence in our lives of a Believer.

My ex was one of those New Age believers who cannot stress too strongly the difference between religiosity and spirituality, a distinction I'll not belabor here beyond opining that it makes sense for a female, allowing herself the choice between any lockstep God Squad and a decidedly more democratic condition of transcendent being, to choose the latter. All major religions are patriarchal because they coalesced in Patriarchy's temporal wheelhouse, that is, over the past seven thousand years or so, and my ex proudly declared to me that she daydreamed through history classes in high school because, as she put it, Betsy Ross was the only female given much play, "and all she did was sew." My ex's mother, heroic by virtue of grace she embodied despite physical frailty and chronic pain and discomfort in her final days, watched Sunday Mass on TV and lived in the midst of glass and porcelain knickknack angels; stationed at her kitchen table before a TV, her oxygen tank full throttle, my ex's working-class Catholic mother melted the pre-blessed host on her tongue and clicked a rosary from the Infant of Prague's home at Our Lady Victorious in Prague's Malá Strana, a rosary my ex gifted her a few years before our divorce and her mother's transition. My ex accepted that history is written by the victors and that, numbered as they were among the defeated, neither she nor her devout mother needed to count the angels on the tip of History's sword even as they assumed that hordes of the glorious little dickenses were dancing there. She postulated that spirituality trumps religion and that the latter is a subset of the former, patriarchal history be damned.

At *this* stage of life, I am agnostic not only regarding a Higher Power, a Prime Mover, a Big Daddy, a god, *the* God; I am agnostic as to whether poetry is a valid receptacle, or an adequate antenna, for receiving communications from the truth-beauty continuum and whether Art possesses transcendent value beyond crass therapy, beyond entertainment even.

But my agnosticism was a condition of mind I took for granted until my ex came into my life. I now find it a dynamic, rather than passive, aspect of who I think I am. It is rather like "quantum weirdness," at least in the sense that Desire to Believe and Inability to Believe are a rapidly spinning polarity that defies easy distinction. Its dynamism notwithstanding, my agnosticism, alas, is as spooky as the left panel of a secular triptych through which bleeds a palimpsest image of faith.

And I wonder if that ghost undertow isn't shadowed into my biology (and therefore, by virtue of an obvious syllogism, into everyone's)—I wonder if that wisp of faith isn't the organism compensating for self-awareness, that disease of higher consciousness that isn't higher at all but merely defective, a cosmic "oops." *If* is a disease of consciousness in the sense that consciousness is a disease of life that has metastasized out of creature programming into the fevered realm of choice.

Before patriarchy, before gods and God and all the history that followed, the same history my ex eschewed in a Catholic schoolgirl kind of way, there was song, and whether songs were pretty or scary or sad or funny or sexy or majestic, whether they were mournful or giddy, they weren't *just* songs; they were spells of sorts, assertions of magical power. They were practical attempts to affect creature needs and desires, attempts followed by randomly positive events often enough to keep prehistoric folks singing.

Mary Martin implored me to clap my hands and bring Tinker Bell back from death or its brink. I refused. It was 1960ish, and I sat half-lotus before a motel TV somewhere in a southwestern desert. A grown woman was pretending to be a flying boy, and Tinker Bell was a flashlight beam. I refused to clap, not because I didn't believe that clapping would bring a fairy back from Heaven but because in Heaven nothing stank, hunger was never an issue, and no one got smacked or whipped with a leather strap. Why, I thought, would anyone *want* to come back?

I knew that Tinker Bell was a flashlight beam. I even grokked the ambiguity as to whether Tinker Bell was deceased or simply on the brink of being so before every child in America, except for little Ricky—yours truly—began to clap her back to exuberance. I think my not clapping had to do with my knowing that other boys and girls in other rooms watching other TVs were clapping, and of course, when Tinker Bell did return from death (or near-death), my suspicion was confirmed: I was not needed. Enough kids had clapped that I didn't need to disturb my resting father and mother or my sleeping toddler siblings. Yes, *maybe* clapping brings fairies back from (the brink of) death, but in that instance, it was either all show, as the saying goes, or had nothing to do with me.

When one's audience is God, or the gods, or a menagerie of spirits inhabiting organic and inorganic stuff alike, and when one sings for a practical purpose, to procure meat or rain or to hasten the cessation of deluge or wildfire, the aesthetic dimension is tinged with the terror of extinction. The beauty or majesty or catchiness of the song is subsumed by its purpose. That its auxiliary audience, the non-shaman members of the tribe, say, find it beautiful, even entertaining, is incidental to the hunger or generalized anxiety it is deployed to alleviate or in some way remedy. Beauty and wisdom for their own sake were revelations of complex social systems, and maybe that is why, with the exception of "Amazing Grace," Protestant hymns are so damned ugly and why so much of the greatest devotional music, art, and even literature seem to transcend their ostensible occasions, though, ironically, that transcendence is not skyward but earthward and by dint of the loins.

Michelangelo's *Pietà* is about, as much as anything else, that young corpse's right hand, how his life and death converge in its slight bend at the wrist, how a fold in the robe worn by the anything-but-maternal-seeming Mary is so delicately wedged, cigarette like, between the pointing and middle fingers. It is about how stone may be rendered to seem, visually, as malleable as cloth. It is about Mary's fine features and how marble may appear limp. It's about Mary's right hand, the fingers wrapping beneath the corpse's underarm, how the fresh corpse's skin is still supple, uplifted from the dead weight. It's about how subtly powerful Mary appears by virtue of the wide spread of her legs forming the lap that bears the weight of a grown man's body. It's about the angle of the corpse's head and the inscrutable, anything-but-mournful expression on Mary's face. It's about a great artist showing off by both mobilizing and undercutting a narrative steeped in hocus-pocus; the Christ beautifully dead in Mama's sexy lap will, soon enough, reanimate and, after forty days of aweing Mary Magdalen and various combinations of his Gang of Twelve, ascend. The *Pietà* in no way, by no feature I can discern, foreshadows resurrection, the defeat of death. It rather posits death as beautiful precisely for its finality. *Ars longa, vita brevis,* no ifs, ands, or buts about it, though if Christ *were* the cosmic *but,* Michelangelo chose to veil that exception in the gauze of his own humanity. Did the great artist identify more keenly with the sexy mama or the sexy son? Alas, artists never identify with the dead even when they do, and the good ones rarely presume to speak to God. The *Pietà* is not a prayer; it praises nothing supernatural. It requests no intercession with nature. It is the pinnacle of camp: Michelangelo, I submit, fancied himself a pretty, androgynous woman holding, displaying even, the beautiful body of a young man. There is no motherly anguish on Mary's mug, only muted lust, at least by my wicked reckoning.

Mary Martin's Peter Pan resurrecting a fairy was camp of similar co(s)mic proportions, though implicating children in the process seems deliciously sinister, in a campy kind of way, and the big difference is that we actually got to *see* the magic trick of resurrection, participate in, indeed facilitate, the glorious event simply by applauding Flashlight Tink alive and witnessing her flit about the colorless stage set. Jesus's reanimation was, for no clear reason, much sneakier. A certain plausible deniability seems to have been cooked into that miracle.

My problem (well, one in the midst of a thick cluster) is that I cannot see how Art requires faith any less than God or Spirit do. I do not understand how art is possible in a godless universe, in one that is not more or less haunted not only by Dark Matter but by Something Else. Perhaps it is a meaning thing, but I can hang with a godless universe in which existence precedes essence and in which consequently meaning is exclusively a posteriori, wafting from the stinking muck and blooming lanes of the everyday. I cannot, except in a kind of double mindedness where my agnosticism nests, conceive of art that does not implicitly advocate for First Cause.

But I am neither smart nor patient enough to follow this bunny through millennia of philosophical brambles, and if I fell down the hole after him, I'd end up in the Library of Babel rather than Wonderland. First Cause is the indispensable block in a game of Jenga; pluck it out, and thousands of years of head-scratching and prayer come clattering down. And what then becomes of Art? Empty forms. Husks. Mere artifacts. Perhaps "God," "Spirit," and "meaning" are three sides of the same coin, in which case Yogi Berra is God, which may explain both abstract expressionism and L=A=N=G=U=A=G=E poetry. But I recall reading Viktor Frankl's *Man's Search for Meaning* when I was young, puzzling over whether Freud or he had been right, and coming to the conclusion that hormones trump all abstractions. Meaning is malleable, at least linguistically speaking, but biochemistry is inexorable. Now, on the cusp of senior citizenry, I realize, or think I do, that meaning's the rub.

I mean, meaning is the rub and First Cause the Saussurean masseur or masseuse, though she or he may indeed be a figment of the collective imagination, the fragrant fart of the collective unconscious, which brings us to Carl Jung, who mapped the path between incredulity and fervor, science and magic, as dauntlessly as Lewis and Clark, bellies full of equine flesh, traversing the Lolo Trail. But the imagination, *this* sputtering wish machine, requires a cause to First Cause, and horror of horrors, it's turtles all the way down.

A week later, my ex and I returned to Indiana, this time to a freeway pit stop burg named (alas) Georgetown, twenty minutes from Louisville, Kentucky, my ex's hometown. That shaman-practitioner workshop's theme was "extraction," centered on the removal of "intrusions"; extraction should not be confused with exorcism, though the two operations are not unrelated. To parse the difference as my ex explained it would be an appropriation, and I'd probably get a lot of it wrong; she, not I, learned hands-on, over two intense eight-hour sessions, the shamanic techniques for that kind of healing.

The last night of that tutorial, after the second and final training, my ex retrieved me and her beloved Chihuahua from the Red Roof Inn and drove us into Louisville to surprise her mother. On the way, we bought four fish sandwiches from Cunningham's on the Ohio River; one was for my ex's brother, who was scheduled to appear in court in nine days and would subsequently be incarcerated. He had had a stroke eight months earlier and changed from being a gentle, decent, hardworking, mumbling drunk into one who all too often became verbally abusive, felonious, and downright dangerous. He should not have gone to prison but into long-term mental health care, but he was poor and inarticulate and, in the present version of America, would receive undeserved punishment rather than compassion.

After picking at my gruesome sandwich—it was greasy and over-cooked, the beige fries limp—I took a brisk, two-mile-plus walk around a nearby park. I wanted to give my ex and her mother some private time, but truth be told, I primarily wanted to get the hell away from that kitchen table; I especially wanted to forgo my ex's crazy brother's Jesus talk. Because he'd not drunk alcohol for a number of days, his love of God's Only Begotten was cranked up to 8.

When I returned from my 2.6-mile jaunt, Crazy Brother was gone, and my ex was weeping. It seemed Mr. Hyde had tagged Dr. Jekyll and then leaped into the ring, at which point the Christ had hit the fan.

Well, when a family's demons fly about their heads, the rotten magic is such that years compress and old wounds fester, especially if one of the family is cuckoo for Cocoa Puffs. I wasn't sure if my not being present had been a good or bad thing; if I'd been there, maybe Crazy Brother would not have verbally abused his sister and threatened physical violence, though if I had been there and he had acted thusly, I might have stomped his crazy ass. A conservative estimate has it probably a good thing I was engrossed in peripatetic ruminations during that particular family conflict.

I am not agnostic regarding the Judeo-Christian narrative. I know it is horse manure, at least in its concrete particulars. I am not agnostic regarding Hinduism, as such. I am not agnostic regarding flying saucers and ancient aliens. They are horse manure in similar fashion to the Judeo-Christian narrative. I am not agnostic regarding Bigfoot. I am only a little agnostic regarding ghosts. Ghosts do not exist (at least not in an ectoplasmic sense), nor do giant, shy, abominable snow folk. I am not agnostic regarding vitamins; vitamins are largely horse manure.

I am agnostic regarding the Question Mark at the Heart of Existence; that is, I'm agnostic regarding First Cause and the infinite stack of turtles on which the universe, without question, rests.

Where did my ex go when she journeyed, and gently led others, to the Lower and Upper Realms? I mean, what *are* those realms? She journeyed to where science and myth weep in one another's arms, where she attended to souls, the nonphysical essences we "know" we are, because souls are either the lie that is programmed into our chemistry or because they are the truth that hovers above our chemistry.

On the six-hour drive from Louisville to Kalamazoo, mostly on godforsaken Interstate 69 ("What's a Hoosier?" "I don't know. Let's google it."), my ex was down, shaken. After two luminous days of drumming and journeying, of a dozen believers practicing extraction on one another, she was in a brown study. The youngest of seven, she had always been "Goof 2" to her older brother's "Goof 1"; they had bonded, if tenuously, by virtue of their similarly free spirits. Crazy Brother had hurt her, had hurt their mother, hurt everyone in his family, by hurting himself again and again. It's a Jesus thing, if Jesus had managed to nail himself to the cross.

I am agnostic regarding art, particularly lyric poetry: I don't *not* believe in poetry, nor do I believe in it. When I was a kid, it saved my life in similar fashion, I have to think, to the way Jesus is said to save the lives of store owners, eighth grade PE teachers, insurance salesmen, landscape engineers, tugboat pilots, bartenders, stonemasons, hairdressers, bank tellers, chiropractors, flight attendants, alcoholic stroke victims, and poets.

Yes, poets! Not all of whom, needless to say, are agnostic, though none of whom, despite glib assertions otherwise, is an atheist. There are no atheist artists, no atheist poets. Born of contagion magic, the primal song, steeped in irrational practicality, is a yearning for the divine that settles for the sublime.

It is my fatherly duty to guide, deftly, my precocious darling, my brilliant teenage cynic, from the Mars-scape wilderness of the Impossible toward the shimmering green vistas of the Improbable, from locked No Exit to condemned Fire Escape, from grim certitude to flickering hope. It was my duty as a romantic partner to be guided by a manner of being in the world that affirms imagination as a kind of breeding place of stars and worlds and sentient, soul-bearing occupants of those worlds, as a source not merely of chimeras but of wishes and dreams no less essential than water.

Imagination is where we are stalked by, and stalk, the predator Despair. It is as real as love, and by real, I do not mean actual but effectual; by love, I do not mean the transcendence of biochemistry but its organic consecration. Doubt is the bedrock of sanity, but I doubt that flinty aphorisms, weaponized abstract nouns, can do much more than wound the snarling, purring, or grunting gray denizens of our waking dreams.

When my ex spoke of her journeys, always careful to keep confidence regarding anything she learned in either the Lower or Upper Realms about others' inner lives, she embodied negative capability, what Keats famously, if cryptically, posited as the primarily enabling quality of literary art. My ex drummed, danced, and chanted in the midst of "uncertainties, mysteries, doubts, without any irritable reaching after fact and reason," and regarded healing as an activity rather than a condition. In the most ancient and profound sense, she was a poet.

And so is my new beloved, though she is not intellectually naive, and possesses a historical sense that is subtle, deep, and richly nuanced. She is a serious student of the art, and scientific underpinnings, of divination, past lives, and "spirit" as such, which is to say the "science" of how any of that can be efficacious beyond "mere" imagination. Of course, she is a student of history, and particularly women's place in it beyond flag sewing, with a lab laser focus on the mysteries of healing and that activity's grounding in the Ultimate Mystery.

But whether one is naive or intellectually grounded in any shaded notch on the ideological spectrum, one's search for meaning is as noble an enterprise as any hero's quest or protector's vigilance, though both the faithful and faithless are bound by finality that I doubt is the baseline of my youngest daughter's heart. I pray to the Nothing that is the pedestal upon which the Question Mark at the Heart of Existence flashes neon that my baby learns to cultivate exquisite doubt, that she only believes fervently in the necessity for compassion, and otherwise lives a long life stunned by the beauty of it all.

Straight and Normal

Poets and Drugs in the New Age

I have not, until now, been involved, romantically or in any other intimate sense, with anyone who is, as we used to say, "straight." The adjective through the 1970s was associated more with illicit drug consumption than sexual predilection, and my dear friend and lover, who is socially and politically progressive and who is a true intellectual who happens also to be deeply wise about the heart, is straight. I am not. I am normal.

Parents, especially the military brass of my late adolescence in Sasebo, Japan, were straight. Teachers (we assumed) were straight. Suited madmen and their secretaries were straight. People who ran everything, generally, were straight. Narcs—those trolls under our rainbow Bridge of Sighs—were lethally straight. *Reefer Madness* cracked us up; straight people cracked us up, especially when we were high but only when we weren't paranoid, only when they weren't scaring the hell out of us.

It is a wonder that my sweetheart got through high school, college, graduate school, and life in general to this point, among the Yahoos of the arts and humanities, totally straight. Every bit as much as I am, she is a creature of creative writing, the tribe of writers in the academy. For my generation, the arts were, among other things, the tip of the velvet spear we thrust at the faces of straight people, mostly to keep them back, mostly to keep them away. Art was weird. Straight people were repelled by weird.

Straight people drank alcohol, and so did most of the normal people I knew, though not as much as straight people. Some normals drank a lot of alcohol on top of drugs of choice, and some of them dropped dead, in increasing numbers when coke became a white tsunami washing over urban America, inundating lethally too many in the community of New Orleans service workers that I inhabited as the seventies bled into the eighties. Through the early seventies, I dropped a fair amount of acid, dabbled in everything else (never shot up; snorted heroin only once, with the late Darryl DeLoach, the first lead singer of Iron Butterfly), but stopped smoking pot in my early twenties for a time and didn't even drink much when I moved into the French Quarter of New Orleans.

Dicky was my favorite bartender at the New Orleans Chart House, the balcony-ringed second-story restaurant across from Jackson Square. I'd wait into the small hours at the mahogany bar, avoiding my reflection in the mirror running its length, for my cocktail waitress first wife to get off work; Dicky would chuckle and call me "the only sober man in the Quatas," as I sipped a single tepid beer for more than an hour, and I probably was, through the late seventies, the only sober biped, at 1:00 a.m., strolling rancid Bourbon Street. Sober but not straight. The distinction is important.

I am a father of three adult daughters who are multilingual and bicultural and who have thus far dodged addiction. Even my wild-child second is comparatively temperate. They accept the fact that I, an ex-drinker, smoke pot and ingest edible forms of THC not socially but medicinally. And let me add that I do not advocate for recreational drugs generally, though I am selectively libertarian in advocating for the decriminalization of all drugs and of course, especially, marijuana.

From my first to third divorces, I drank an average of half a gallon of whiskey every four days or so. I'm a largish fellow, physically strong from lifting weights religiously, and am generally in good shape notwithstanding type 2 diabetes, the result, no doubt, of all that alcohol, a condition I keep in check with metformin and exercise. When I quit drinking, it wasn't because of the diabetes. I just got tired of sometimes feeling mean and impatient, and besides, I simply knew it was time. I woke up one morning and announced to Charley, my third wife's Chihuahua, "I'm done."

It wasn't supposed to be that easy. Knocking back sixty-four fluid ounces of eighty-six-proof over four nights . . . well, the math *is* easy. The fact is that I have a preternatural capacity for alcohol, rarely in my life have I been stumbling drunk, or even slurry, and my good doctor, always impressed with my blood work numbers, never even asked me about alcohol consumption.

After more than four decades during which I'd toked only a few times, had not purchased weed since the mid-1970s, and after several months of sobriety, I bought some pot.

I liked it more than I ever did as a young guy. I'll not rhapsodize here about the beauty of marijuana, except to say that it is beautiful. As was true of my drinking, I never smoke or ingest socially or during daylight. I get high, in bed, during the one or two hours before sleep, usually as prelude to reading or watching Netflix.

My sweetheart is fluent in German and has never, I kid not, tasted *Bier*. She speaks Italian and hardly ever sips *vino*. She clearly has me by at least a dozen IQ points and possesses a flypaper memory and a fabulous sense of irony and humor. She is brilliant and resolutely straight only in part because of physiological challenges she has managed since childhood. Whatever her personal reasons, she's never ingested an unprescribed drug, with the exception of a few polite tokes in college, and is wary even of the most innocuous over-the-counter pain meds. Could the sharpness of her sophisticated and mystical mind be at least partially the result of a lifetime of teetotaling? (The etymology is murky, but I'd thought it was *tea,* not *tee.* She does consume vast quantities of the former.)

How could anyone destined for the arts, of our generation (we're in the same ballpark), not get sucked into the maelstrom, the kaleidoscopic vortex, of counterculture drug use?

Well, that's her story. The necessity for prudent management of hypoglycemia notwithstanding, she chooses to be straight, but I don't choose to be normal. I ceased being straight just after my eighteenth birthday, the very day I exited my stepparents' home on E Avenue in Coronado, California, November 4, 1971, never to return except to cadge meals. The transformation occurred over several weeks as I participated almost daily in a garage-apartment symposium moderated by Daryl and his adoring associate Wink.

Daryl presided in a massive royal-blue wingback chair; Wink attended in a princely smaller one, rolling joints on *Led Zeppelin 4* as Daryl held forth or strummed his Fender and whined derivative ditties about a peroxide blonde for whom he infamously yearned. The Pacific was audible from outside the door to that garage, and I would have to step out from time to time to escape Daryl's nasal keening, but he seemed not to take offense, probably assuming I had a weak bladder. Sometimes I did piss on his mother's China roses but usually just smoked a cig and listened to the waves a quarter-mile away, beyond the pricy bungalows, on the other side of the chain-link fence from the North Island Naval Air Station.

Within, we three or four acolytes, the representatives any given afternoon of a coterie of a dozen or so, lined up, legs sprawled or folded half-lotus, against a dark wall on fetid mattresses swathed in tie-dyed rayon, passing joint after joint after joint. Sometimes one or two or all of us were tripping, and the joints served the practical purpose of mellowing the trip; and on those occasions, when Daryl's older brother, Dirty Dave, an outrider with the Hell's Angels, ousted him from the throne chair, the group sometimes "whooped" toluene, drenched a rag with the poison, and shook it up in a baggie into which each in turn hyperventilated. I would not participate in that particular bonding behavior. I wasn't *that* normal.

In an asylum, madness is normal. In a warzone, killing is normal. To an infantilized generation defined by its opposition less to its parents and a war than to the Puritanism coating the core values of all previous American generations and whose embrace of hedonism in the midst of the gross abundance and absurdities of late-stage capitalism was all too convenient and disingenuous, indulging in altered states of consciousness seemed only natural. All forms of indulgence seemed natural, normal.

I read Andrew Weil's *The Natural Mind* in the midseventies, two or three years after it was published. I'm pretty sure I read it stoned, but that's beside the point, at least somewhat. I read it in the light from a recently cracked door of perception and was delighted that I grokked Huxley's reference to William Blake and that Blake seemed a thread stitching Leary to Huxley to Ginsberg to Haight-Ashbury to shamans to acid to Woodstock to peyote to Kent State to Buddha to the weirder aspects of the Old Testament and even to the Smothers Brothers. Blake rendered supreme antonyms singular—innocence and experience, Heaven and Hell—and Blake was easy to read stoned. I hefted in one metaphysical hand Weil's assertion that the desire to alter pedestrian consciousness is innate and the 1970 Comprehensive Drug Abuse Prevention and Control Act in the other (what I perceived as the latter's broad effects, anyway) and concluded nothing, really. There was no conclusion any more than there could be one regarding Heaven and Hell. Besides, I'd read Keats's letters and was pretty sure I had negative capability.

Counterculture and New Age blended in "the mind," a location not distinct from the biblical loins but in the Age of Aquarius was manifest in it. The "natural" mind existed in opposition to its unnatural incarnation, was more Jungy than Freudy, and propagated "alternative lifestyles" that would eventually be gobbled by the corporate behemoth, that most unnatural creature. Free Love was by turns unfettered libido and Lawrencian Sex in the Head, the latter a marker of generalized alienation and the cave in which the creature slept on its horde of trash bags, traffic cones, Barbies, and other petroleum products. The jumping jack flashy corporate "It" factor was a (natural) gas gas gas, and the mind-body unity idealized within those lifestyles that coalesced out of the revolutionary chaos of counterculture became the orthodoxy espoused by the mindful legions of a "spiritual" consumerism.

The natural mind, colonized by the angels dancing in Zippy the Pinhead's noggin, assumed a *Separate Reality* that the fraudulent explorer Carlos Castaneda exploited as a kind of academic conquistador. He was also a poet posing as an anthropologist, which is a hell of a lot more interesting than the reverse, and one can only hope that encoded in the charming lie upon which his edifice balanced is a Higher Truth (pun intended).

But I doubt it, maybe because I doubt just about everything. My sweetheart may be straight, but she is a New Age maven who talks the walk and walks the talk of spirituality. She is a sober mystic who has made pilgrimages to Delphi and Lily Dale alike; I am, a couple of hours many nights before sleep, a stoned skeptic. We occupy different mansions within the heavenly New Age–counterculture matrix. In mine, marijuana is in the medicine cabinet next to the metformin; it is resolutely outside the category "drug," if only because drug has been grotesquely adulterated by more than half a century of the sleaziest propaganda. In hers, the realm of spirit is something like an exercise room just off the kitchen. That she still regards marijuana as a "gateway drug" is forgivable if only because the straight combatants on the other side of the culture war, from both my straight sweetheart and normal self, deemed it so and, empowered historically to choose the battlefield, have met us in a discursive space where generic terms like *liberal, democrat* (in the place of *democratic*), *patriotism* (as a condition unavailable to those who oppose right-wing agendas), and *drugs* (any substance that empowered straights deem verboten) have been, to use a currently popular trope, weaponized. And besides, it is objectively true that an individual, for example, who ODs on heroin is likely to have smoked a joint before ever sticking a needle between her toes. It is also objectively true that the same tortured soul is likely to have smoked tobacco before toking or shooting up, but it's highly unlikely that a kid has ever stood in an orange jumper before a judge for smoking Kools or Marlboro box reds.

But I do my sweetheart a disservice characterizing her attitude toward pot in these terms. Being straight, for her, at least in part, is a matter of greater physiological prudence than for most other folks. The New Age consortium is as richly complex, as heterogeneous, as any political party within a binary system. At one far end of the spectrum are fatuous Lululemon New Agers who tote their rolled mats into vegan restaurants to commune with other European American suburbanites; on the other are intellectuals who seek to glimpse, even touch, the Question Mark at the Heart of Existence. A beneficiary, and victim, of a Catholic school education, my sweetheart discovered astrology in childhood, became an aficionado, and over the years has queried the range of topics that put the super in natural with the fastidious resolve of a scholar trained by two Ivy League institutions and at Oxford before she matriculated in the Iowa Writers' Workshop. She knows how to think about magical thinking and seems delighted to live at a time when the more cogent narratives wielding the cutting edge of cosmology and quantum physics, dummied down into a kind of poetry for those of us unable to grok higher mathematics (no pun intended) but hoping nonetheless to extract from them something like authentic understanding, are available to students of culture. But this is not to say that her interest in the paranormal is mere interest; I fancy that she is a gentle, postmodern version of Atalanta, the female Argonaut, a hunter and explorer but one aligned not exclusively with men but with a predominately female gang. New Age generally, like yoga specifically, emerged from patriarchy on a trajectory toward female empowerment. The original yogis, of course, were dudes, but enter any Western hot-or-not studio today or even leaf through any current issue of *Yoga Journal,* and you will feel the weather of a women's world, one welcoming to men but intolerant of masculine toxicity, the creepy "hot yoga" guru Bikram Choudhury both a case in point and notwithstanding. New Age, at its most innocuous as well as at its most profound, and despite its often-crass commercialization, distills spirit from religion, a sense of wonder from foundational patriarchal narratives. A young female, by some braiding of intuition, intellectual rigor, and wonder, may levitate into higher consciousness (pun more or less unintended) that is paradoxically both "new" and prehistoric, that jumps the patriarchal groove, veers from history as such, and presupposes human life before patriarchal artifices such as "church" and "state" and "history."

Sometime in the midseventies, I attended a poetry reading on the designer lawn of the La Jolla Public Library; folding chairs were lined up, and I recall a lectern, a piece of furniture that has always seemed to me zanily incongruous in pastoral settings. The ocean churned audibly in La Jolla Cove, and the weather was typically perfect. Jerome Rothenberg presided at the lectern, a warm breeze ruffling his several hairs in the long-shadowed golden light of the setting sun; perhaps two dozen of us in rows of folding chairs cocked our heads like Nipper listening at the gramophone to his master's voice as Jerome lugubriously chanted, for the first ten eternal minutes of his presentation,

All's I wants is a good five-cent cigar.

Each time he uttered the phrase, he placed an *umph* after a different syllable:

All's I wants (*umph*) is a good five-cent cigar
All's (*umph*) I wants is a good five-cent cigar
All's I wants is a good (*umph*) five-cent cigar
All's I wants is a good five-cent (*umph*) cigar
Etc. etc. etc. etc. etc. etc. . . . .

If Rothenberg, in any introductory patter, had offered context for his performance, particularly regarding why he chanted this sentiment in what vaguely seemed some form of African American dialect or why he seemed to be channeling some Black fellow from 1905, when one could indeed purchase a cigar for a nickel, I don't recall. I'd read his immensely important anthology *Technicians of the Sacred,* which had been published four or five years earlier, in 1969, and though I'd found much of its content engaging as cultural artifacts, I dismissed most of it as art. Of course, that judgment was a failure of imagination and an indication of deep-seated ignorance of the nature of translation and its transcendent importance not only to literary culture but to human survival as such. The judgment was also a marker of a colonial mindset nested inside my puerile, hippie-dippy noggin.

In the French Quarter, through the eighties, one of the "colorful characters" (homeless and psychotic) was the Button Lady (Leah Shpock-Luzovsky), whom some called the Bead Lady. Her shtick was to ply tourists and residents alike with the cheapest plastic baubles gleaned from the curbs and gutters after parades, the kind no one else ever bothered to stoop and scoop. "Lucky Beads! Lucky Beads!" she hawked with the aggressive charm of a bazaar proprietor, though her commercial dealings were not fixed but peripatetic; she roamed the Quarter, wearing always, or at least it seemed so, the same dirty-white blouse and ankle-length black wool skirt, no matter the weather, and I did not even try to imagine the olfactory abomination roasting beneath that skirt in the summer months. Her hair was silver, her face, obviously once pretty, was deeply tanned and grooved and shammy-soft with age and neglect. I saw her at dawn sleeping propped upright on Burgundy stoops beneath gaslight flicker and squatting in front of the A&P on Royal gnawing raw bacon like a squirrel an acorn. And I crossed paths with her at every hour on every other French Quarter *rue* from Canal to Esplanade, Rampart to Decatur.

"Lucky Beads! Lucky Beads!"

"No, Button Lady, I don't need any beads today," I answered multiple times over the years. But once she didn't just let me pass. I think I was on a meditative weekday stroll southward down Iberville on an early-spring early evening. Mardi Gras was a week or so past. Tourists were sparse. The entire city was still hungover, even the streets. Even the wrought-iron balconies and storm shutters and even the sky over it all. But not I. I was chipper from sobriety yet normal from the drugs, mostly pot, though also acid and peyote and psilocybin 'shrooms I'd ingested a decade earlier.

She pulled a knuckle of mauve chalk from an invisible pocket of her wool skirt, then squatted before me, barring my path, and began to scratch symbols on the sidewalk. I'd heard about her hexes. With the toe of my shoe, I rubbed out the figures as quickly as she could scrawl them, muttered, "Please don't hex me, Button Lady," and dropped a buck in her frog-legged lap before circumnavigating her.

I felt threatened. I felt her power, the power of her faith in herself to affect another life with magic I knew did not exist yet the efficacy of which I felt in that moment. In my heart, she was a descendant of the Voodoo queen Marie Laveau, who blended African, Native, and Catholic mumbo-jumbo into affective poetry. The Button Lady sometimes spoke in tongues, we locals would say, referring to those rhapsodies she sometimes entered while occupying a gaslit stoop with no interlocutor. She'd quaver between English, Cajun French, something vaguely Slavic, and something I'm told was Hebrew. She'd rasp and screech and sigh and exalt rapidly and seemingly at random from one to one to one, and I was too stupid, too self-involved, to engage her, at least to attempt to learn what must have been one hell of a story.

My normalcy is a lack of imagination but, more precisely, a lack of will. Into my thirties, I was as clueless as a baby fish asking a mama fish, "What's the ocean?" and once I figured out that I was in it and that it, unlike the actual ocean, was not an exclusive habitat, I was comfortably witnessing the world through counterculture ideology, particularly as that cultural lens was ground and calibrated by the Frankfurt Marxists, by Lefty cultural analysis generally. I chose, passively, not to imagine my life outside of ideological strictures of counterculture, the idea that one could, as an artist, ghost the corridors of power even as one critiques and thereby changes, renders more humane, those vaunted vestibules and antechambers. I was comfortable in the role of just another subversive brick in the wall of the Fifth Column. The New Age hippie and New Lefty in me fought to a draw. Though it wasn't much of a fight. The hippie, smug in his moral superiority, countervailed the Lefty's call to engagement by reveling in a schmaltzy Let-It-Be acquiescence to all forms of institutionalized brutality. Yeah, Mama, what's the ocean?

I stood on the shore of my own smug ignorance in the fall of 1989; I was not a baby fish but an academic artist, a poet making his living as a university teacher, a late-thirties white male gazing out upon a world I was able to see for the first time, one profoundly affected by the same forces, the same ideas, that had animated my formative years but reflected from a slightly, and delightfully, warped surface. Prague's Velvet Revolution matched the thumping paradox of my two-chambered, New Lefty–hippie heart, the oxymoronic base two / on-off matrix of social vision. I was an outsider, and I was normal. I was a normal outsider; my outsider status was my normalcy. In the fall of 1989, on a Fulbright not to Czechoslovakia but to Slovenia, having pursued a Czech woman to her shabbily majestic hometown of Prague, I witnessed, over the course of that season, her and her compatriots pry themselves from under a totalitarian boot.

The Velvet Revolution was a realization of the fact that the spirit of counterculture haunted both communism and late capitalism, that it spanned both a pristine libertarianism and no less pristine "socialism with a human face," and that it embodied gentle, even passive-aggressive resistance to institutional authority. It distinguished the good individual from the good citizen and indeed redefined citizenship in terms of resistance to all forms of authority that are for authority's own sake. The beauty of the Velvet Revolution was that it was self-consciously beautiful, that it manifested and fostered an aesthetic dimension, one that favored a comedic over a tragic sense of history.

The dissident is not noble self-sacrificing Sydney Carton at the end of *The Tale of Two Cities* but, rather, the Good Soldier Švejk throughout Hašek's novel about a canny, beer-swilling fatso who bumbles through the Hapsburg war effort subverting bureaucratic authority at every juncture. By that model, well over two-thirds of the Czech population were dissidents, but the fact is that there are dissidents and then there are women and men possessing the courage to absorb the petty wrath of a disintegrating state, people such as Václav Havel, who did hard time as a political prisoner, and Ludvík Vaculík, the English title of whose folksy and dyspeptic collection of feuilletons, *A Cup of Coffee with My Interrogators,* implies the whimper that issued from the dying state in the decade preceding the Velvet Revolution.

Allen Ginsberg famously mused as to when he, a poet, may indeed purchase sustenance with his good looks. Corollary to that rhetorical question: when will one's beauty, or simply one's humanity, be valued for its own sake?

Dominika, the mother of my three grown Czech American daughters—

when we were in the midst of an affair more giddy than lurid, before we could even have imagined the dirty diapers and sour-milk scent and cobbled-together meals and frenetic bedtime routines and weeping and laughter and soul-scraping worry, before we could have imagined the excruciating joy of parenting—led me one gray day in the fall of 1989 onto Wenceslas Square.

Nothing had been announced. There were no makeshift signs with arrows pointing where we should go. Dominika had heard someone chatting on the street after we'd espied the spontaneous memorial for Martin Šmid, the Charles University math student whom everyone thought, at that moment, had been killed by the riot police the night before. He hadn't, but it didn't matter. Everyone was pissed off at the police. And folks followed folks from that wad of flowers and mementos near the National Theater onto the lower end of the square, near Můstek, farthest from the National Museum and the mounted figure of Saint Wenceslas.

It was that first day, or perhaps it was the second or third, following the faux assassination of poor Šmid, who'd actually left the November 17 demonstration early, that Havel and Dubček came out onto a cramped balcony overlooking the square, and Václav Havel held Alexander Dubček's right hand in his left and raised both. The motley crowd went wild. There was not yet a sound system for the protests. The famous dissident and the famously disgraced *nomenklatura* needed only to make that single gesture of solidarity. The rest is history.

And from that historical moment, I proceeded Gump-like, ignorant but infused to the gills with goodwill for those people, who are now, through my daughters, my people, the Czech people, whose language is so familiar to my ears and yet so foreign to my cognitive facility (such as it is). I bore witness to a people changing their life through one collective and protracted act not of revolution so much as soul making.

The Czech soul of the autumn of 1989 was akin to Rabbi Löwe's Golem (Arnošt Lustig once told me that the Jew in him felt very close to the Czech in him, that the non-Jewish Czechs were in fact very Jewish, and I'm still trying to figure out what he meant by that). The reconstructed Czech soul was, is, a work of art, a thing to contemplate and spill forth awe upon. It is the protector of all that is Czech, and as such, it is more effective, more powerful, than any army or navy or palace guard. It is the self-effacing glory of a fat, beer-swilling noncom whose incompetence is hilarious and beautiful and wholly intentional, an iconic soul whose existence is steeped in, is pickled in, a nakedly human and oceanic resistance to evil, by Hannah Arendt's famous reckoning, the essence of banality.

In the postmodern American context, the nexus of spirituality (distinct from religion, that is, from institutional authority) and lifestyle is the crossroads of New Age and counterculture. It is the heart of existence where the Nothing That Is and the Nothing That Isn't animates another golem, Wallace Stevens's snowman, that spiritual essence who guards and strews flashing lights all over and around the towering Question Mark that is the source, and emblem, of all wonder.

"The Raggedy-Ass Masses"
Poets and Democracy

When the people shall have nothing more to eat, they will eat the rich.
—JEAN-JACQUES ROUSSEAU (maybe)

Ooo eee ooo ah ah ting tang walla walla bing bang . . .
—DAVID SEVILLE (creator of *Alvin and the Chipmunks*),
    "Witch Doctor"

Even when she or he espouses democratic principles most passionately, the poet and democracy are not a natural fit; the poet, since the Romantics established the role as that of a quintessential outsider, seems disingenuous espousing egalitarian values. The lyric impulse is narcissistic, and there is healthy and unhealthy narcissism, the former a condition of manageable pathology. Few well-adjusted, integrated personalities glom onto the role of poet in adolescence, that phase when a personality must glom onto something, when many feel compelled to connect to a higher purpose.

Poets in high school may relish brushing against the grain of the popular elite but less in the service of democratic principles than to play a more romantic role than Homecoming Queen or King: that of "the poet," the outlaw, the outsider. The Homecoming Queen may look down on her subjects, but that's her role; she is very much of the community that elected her. The poet is that kid lurking, probably smoking, under the bleachers, yearning for the queen and wholly inhabited by that yearning. The poet is such a gaudy freak that she or he is almost cool. Almost. It is important to note that the poet's yearning for the queen is not a matter of projection.

The poet doesn't want to *be* the queen, and that charming narcissist under the bleachers doesn't want to ravish her either. The pimple-faced poet, taking in the half-time ceremonies from a slit in the bleachers, wants to consume the queen.

Though not in the Rousseauian sense—the adolescent poet scarfs the queen by praising her, lavishing praise upon her beauty, grace, and utter inaccessibility in ragged verses scrawled with a Bic and stashed under the tighty-whities Mama folds and stacks in the second drawer on the left. The adolescent poet is a veritable yearning machine.

Not lust: too nasty. Not desire: too generic. Lust is pornographic and, as such, democratic. Because it is a function of biological imperative and not nasty intentions, desire is also democratic, in the sense of undifferentiated masses, though, on the order of bacteria and the profferrings of the internet. Yearning, by contrast, is the domain of self-sanctioned privilege on the order of criminal intent. It is obsession in a ballgown and tiara. In the throes of yearning, the poet maintains a rhetorical distance from the object of her or his yearning that is analogous to the physical distance between the dark, urine-reeking, paper cup–littered space under the bleachers and the Friday night–lit, cheer-drenched half-time spectacle of a homecoming ceremony. The poet, wherever the creature falls on the spectrum of gendered identity, is a discerning cannibal: she or he consumes by praising, and she or he praises only royalty.

An idealized husk is left after all that praising, that yearning. Praising and yearning . . .

"Whitman!" shouts the crowd of dead poets in my noggin, including the gray bard himself. But Whitman was a small-*d* democrat whose cosmic self-praise had nothing to do with you or me or even that fellow behind the tree Senator Russell B. Long joked is the one we should want to tax. Singing humanity, Whitman proceeded from a common "I" that resonated rather more like an imperial "we." Whitman's democratic lyricism was kissing cousin of the royal pronouncement, the hieratic tradition in which a single personality presumes to choose and speak for the collective. We who are praised by Whitman are consumed; we, as a collective, possess only an authority that is absorbed by the poet's praise because it is, finally, self-praise. The object of praise is consumed by the egotistical act of praising it. The poet's praise is self-congratulatory, self-centered, by its very nature. Walt Whitman is the King of Democracy, and unlike the Homecoming Queen, no one voted for him.

The raggedy-ass masses, as he referred to them, are those people from whom my criminal father sought to set himself, and his family, apart. The criminal and the artist, particularly the lyric poet, are of the people, and the self-loathing narcissism (yes, that's a thing) that both exude includes, is primarily directed at, those from whom they have risen, or sunk. Shelley's pithy formulation is rank with irony: as legislators, poets are unacknowledged for the same reason that the Soviet-era writers' unions were farcical. A poet's narcissism, even in the healthy range of the scale, dwarfs that of the most acquisitive politicians. Lyric art is fundamentally fascistic at its worst (on the grandiose end of the narcissism range), charmingly self-absorbed at its best. Its relation to audience is its relation to the raggedy-ass masses whom even the most democratic poet expects to be obtuse; the democratic poet, deep, really deep down, feels her or his own genuine identity, relative to audience, to be as opaque as that of a bounty hunter or tax auditor to their respective constituencies. The lyric poet perceives the raggedy-ass masses as the Ultimate Other, as a monolith she or he exists not to illuminate or edify, certainly not to entertain, but in spite of.

The roles of poet and shaman are intertwined. The shaman-poet possessed transcendent prestige within the tribe, prestige born of practical value: she or he was a healer. Access to the Other World—in which all believed—was for the practical purpose of physical healing. Poetry was one aspect of how the spirit world was accessed; poetry/prayer, the voice of multifaceted ritual, was therefore therapeutic, and the shaman was no democrat. She was *not* (I'm projecting to a misty Neolithic past) the tribal leader, though in significant respects was more powerful. He was a doctor. She was a priest. She or he was a poet. They had a pneumatic tube to the divine.

When I was a child living in the back seats of automobiles and in motels, the car radio was a constant companion. Certain tunes from the late fifties will echo from the desert static of my childhood when I lie dying; one is David Seville's 1958 "Witch Doctor": "Ooo eee ooo ah ah ting tang walla walla bing bang" is what the witch doctor (and I assume he's a cannibal) tells the forlorn lover he should do to win the heart of the woman to whom the song is addressed.

I recall my father and mother and three of us kids singing, "Ooo eee ooo ah ah ting tang. . . ." I was six, Chuck four, Terry barely able to stand by holding on to the back of our mother's seat. There was an infant brother in our mother's lap and a fifth sibling glittering in the corner of our criminal father's eye. We three in the back seat couldn't stop singing that refrain!

And it seemed like excellent advice. We kids chanted that sagacity like scratched vinyl. Our father, a handsome young man with a larcenous heart, screamed that he couldn't take it anymore, that we had to stop or he would stomp the brake and just walk into the desert and never come back. I recall being intrigued. I knew that our heroic father was nuts; I just didn't know if that was the standard condition of fathers. I didn't press.

I can't recall particular instances of his deploying the phrase *raggedy-ass masses* but recall it as a refrain from my early childhood and assume now that pretty much everyone not in our family was included in that group. The raggedy-ass masses were a huge, inclusive collective from which I assumed we were escaping. The bad police would take our father away and stick us among the raggedy-ass masses if we ever got caught, and we eventually got caught. Richard Page Harris, my father, spent the next thirty years shuttling in and out and between federal and state penitentiaries, and my mother, Joan Marie née King, four siblings, and I lived in federal housing projects on welfare through much of the sixties. We lived at the "white" end of the Norfolk, Virginia, Chesterfield Heights projects; that white ghetto of brick and cinder block bordered a predominantly Black neighborhood of lower-middle-class Colonial Revival and Queen Anne–style single-family homes, and I would troll that neighborhood of economically superior folks, knocking on doors and asking if I could do yardwork, any kind of manual labor, for a quarter or fifty cents. As an eleven-year-old independent contractor, I did okay; my Black employers surely relished their neighbors espying an adolescent Caucasoid huffing behind a rust-encrusted push mower (a boon I'd extracted from a junk heap).

There was a time when "Caucasian" was more a matter of bone structure than skin tone, but in 1964 that racist designation rolled off my tongue. I was a Caucasian. The word sounded special, and I wanted to be special. I knew it meant "white," or "not negro," but I had no idea what or where Caucasus was, and one whole weekend in 1964, I announced to my family and friends, Black and white, that I was a Caucasian.

I grew weary of the word by that Sunday night, probably as I adjusted the tinfoil-wrapped rabbit ears of our battered Motorola to witness the shenanigans of a talking horse and an incognito Martian. I became obsessed with another fancy word, probably *disenfranchise*. I loved that word for at least a week.

Caucasian is a soiled term, but *disenfranchise* is as relevant, as applicable, as ever. In this moment, Caucasians—neo-Nazi white people—are attempting to disenfranchise people of color and their allies. But I digress.

After an early childhood on the highways of America, during which my father accrued warrants from forty-seven states for bouncing checks and pulling used-car scams, I did not doubt that I was ensconced among the raggedy-ass masses and that we were a motley mob indeed.

It was at this time that I discovered poetry and the role of poet. I've told the story elsewhere of stealing two books from a Salvation Army used-book sale in the parking lot of a Giant Open-Air Supermarket, *Louis Untermeyer's Treasury of Great Poems* and *The Complete Poems of Robert Frost,* both, ironically, Taiwanese pirated editions. I can add now that becoming a poet was my ticket out of the raggedy-ass masses; I left without escaping from that blob of humanity, without leaving it.

I left without leaving. There is no frigate like a book, Emily Dickinson proclaimed, and those two pirate ships, laden with a contraband cargo of inexplicable verse, patrolled my soul thereafter as well as the Elizabeth River, on whose bank I would sit reading, puzzling. When I tried to write the stuff, what squeezed out of me was the doggerel that sloshes in every adolescent heart, but perspicacity and sophistication are irrelevant to the role of poet, and becoming one entails an initial purging, the spilling forth of that adolescent sludge, and the moment the kid realizes she's a poet is when she feels herself levitating out of the scrum of humanity.

She or he goes nowhere, of course, but angels screech hallelujahs on the occasion of any adolescent finding a life purpose and knowing, really knowing, that *that*—painting, singing, cooking, running, dancing, throwing, punching, orating, gazing at the stars—is her or his purpose, but no other identity—not singer, athlete, actor, sculptor, scientist, president, CEO, priest, or circus clown—is as exalted yet ridiculed, as culturally entrenched yet inconsequential, as that of poet, and as a bugaboo to the Puritan work ethic, as a leper in the cabana of Commerce, the poet, perhaps especially the American poet, is profoundly abstracted from the body politic and therefore from the democratic fracas. This is especially true given the transition in status of the academic poet from exotic potted flower, poet in residence, to one bedding greenhouse plant among many, tenured professor. Who is more abstracted, *perhaps* necessarily so, from the commonweal than a tenured professor in the humanities? This is not to say that the poet-professor may not be affectively engaged in the political moment, only that, from an institutional standpoint, regardless of intention, she or he stoops to conquer.

Whether Marie Antoinette actually said, "Let them eat cake" (*Qu'ils mangent de la brioche*), the statement is a great poem, an utterance soaked in irony and set echoing down the ages, in similar fashion to Swift's famously immodest and poignant proposal that the starving Irish consume the succulent flesh of babies, but of course, there is intentional and unintentional irony.

What kind of irony, then, do we feel in our democratic bones when Ginsberg asks, in "America," "When can I go into the supermarket and buy what I need with my good looks?"

Perhaps the question is an ideological litmus test, but I assume that the doomed French queen was clueless, that Swift was joking from the midst of moral outrage, and that Ginsberg, well, Allen Ginsberg, bless his beautiful heart and beautifully ugly mug, was no less a criminal than my father, who parlayed his own good looks and silver tongue into daily bread for his family.

I am alive because I was fed, kept alive through childhood, by a criminal. In the very cells of my body are remnants of my father's criminality, my mother's acquiescence to his crimes. John Adams famously said, "I am a warrior, so that my son may be a merchant, so that his son may be a poet," but implicit in that progression is the beautiful, sad fact of mortality and that we exist past death (some would say only) generationally. This also begs the question as to what the daughter or son of a poet—and I would add "or a criminal"—may do with her or his life. Ooo eee ooo ah ah . . .

Some facts: work, how it gets organized, who gets to do it, is changing profoundly. Remuneration for work is changing profoundly. Human worth, our sense of it relative to what we do to sustain our lives daily, is changing profoundly. The idea of national boundaries, and therefore of national identity, is changing profoundly. The idea of difference, from one human consciousness to another, is changing profoundly. The planet, alas, is changing profoundly, and unless we—and we together, not the imperial we, which is I—are successful in managing the other changes, that apocalyptic one . . . well, not with a bang . . .

How, in the name of a God who does not exist in any anthropomorphic sense, do we begin to comprehend change on such a scale?

Pronouns. Lyric poetry is a record, among other things, of the evolution of the cogito in *Cogito ego sum,* ye ol' Cartesian pith; the *I* in "I think, therefore I am," raises the question whether the "I" of the subject is the same as the "I" of the predicate. By the time one has located one's belly button, self-awareness has shifted; "I think" is a startling revelation because it untethers thought from thinking; the subject is *embedded* in the copula: "I am" thinking until I realize that "I am" thought. Who hasn't awakened free of identity for two and a half seconds and for that duration been terrified? Only I? I doubt it. Past a certain age, who hasn't thought that thinking, and so being, ain't what it's cracked up to be?

I AM!

I am—yet what I am none cares or knows;
My friends forsake me like a memory lost:
I am the self-consumer of my woes—
They rise and vanish in oblivious host,
Like shadows in love's frenzied stifled throes
And yet I am, and live—like vapours tossed

Into the nothingness of scorn and noise,
Into the living sea of waking dreams,
Where there is neither sense of life or joys,
But the vast shipwreck of my life's esteems;
Even the dearest that I loved the best
Are strange—nay, rather, stranger than the rest.

I long for scenes where man hath never trod
A place where woman never smiled or wept
There to abide with my Creator, God,

And sleep as I in childhood sweetly slept,
Untroubling and untroubled where I lie
The grass below—above the vaulted sky.

Well, the tortured sensitive John Clare, by all indications, was a tender, beautiful soul and, alas, was loony tunes, thought he was Byron some days, Shakespeare others, and seems to echo across a century to our beloved American Caligula (his peeps called him "Cal"), Robert Lowell.

SKUNK HOUR

(For Elizabeth Bishop)

Nautilus Island's hermit
heiress still lives through winter in her Spartan cottage;
her sheep still graze above the sea.
Her son's a bishop. Her farmer
is first selectman in our village;
she's in her dotage.

Thirsting for
the hierarchic privacy
of Queen Victoria's century,
she buys up all
the eyesores facing her shore,
and lets them fall.

The season's ill—
we've lost our summer millionaire,
who seemed to leap from an L. L. Bean
catalogue. His nine-knot yawl
was auctioned off to lobstermen.
A red fox stain covers Blue Hill.

And now our fairy
decorator brightens his shop for fall;
his fishnet's filled with orange cork,

orange, his cobbler's bench and awl;
there is no money in his work,
he'd rather marry.

One dark night,
my Tudor Ford climbed the hill's skull;
I watched for love-cars. Lights turned down,
they lay together, hull to hull,
where the graveyard shelves on the town. . . .
My mind's not right.

A car radio bleats,
"Love, O careless Love. . . ." I hear
my ill-spirit sob in each blood cell,
as if my hand were at its throat. . . .
I myself am hell;
nobody's here—

only skunks, that search
in the moonlight for a bite to eat.
They march on their soles up Main Street:
white stripes, moonstruck eyes' red fire
under the chalk-dry and spar spire
of the Trinitarian Church.

I stand on top
of our back steps and breathe the rich air—
a mother skunk with her column of kittens swills the garbage pail
She jabs her wedge-head in a cup
of sour cream, drops her ostrich tail,
and will not scare.

I suppose we can forgive Lowell's homophobia, given the time in which he lived. He does admit that "[his] mind's not right." He hears his "ill spirit sob in each blood cell" and realizes that he himself is suffering in a Miltonian hell; this is quite different from whining that no one gives a flying funk about you, but both poets, clearly, as is true of many of us, were the self-consumers of their woes. Both were isolated. Clare was the Northhamp-tonshire peasant poet, a diminutive fellow, who was probably a victim of childhood malnutrition; Lowell was a Boston Brahmin, a child bully who grew large and strong. What they had in common was poetry and mad-ness but also isolation, Lowell by virtue of his sense of entitlement, Clare by virtue of his suspension between the literary world of London and his beloved community of rural illiterates.

The evolution of the "I" from Clare to Lowell is from a sense of self forsaken to a sense of self forsaking. Clare feels forsaken by his people, Cal forsakes his community, and the difference resonates beyond passive and active voice. The gloomy charm of Clare's lyric is that it so strongly im-plies the deeply personal through expression of conventional sentiments; the dark charm of Lowell's lyric is the revelation that human feeling, that which is the residue of thought, is a disease. Who, really, is better inte-grated into that tony if declining human community of Nautilus Island, the poet or the skunks? Of course, what we're observing are poets from different eras expressing alienation, that bedrock of the human condition; Clare assumes its cause to be exterior; Lowell knows better.

Or Lowell assumes he does; having gone through rigorous therapy at the pinnacle of the golden age of psychoanalysis, and whether we account for the evolution of that institution within the American health care sys-tem, Lowell and white lyric poets from the beginning of the twentieth century to the present may be understood to have proceeded from a sci-entized model of consciousness, one in which divinity has been drained from madness in the process of seeking to understand it systematically. On some level, Lowell's poem expresses nostalgia for *divine* madness, a condi-tion that set the shaman-poet apart from those to whom he administered. Such loss of reason was integral to the ritual process for which poetry was the voice, a voice sometimes conceived as being channeled from nether regions, sometimes bubbling from a dormant source within and spewing forth only when invoked. To the tribe, madness spouted divinity.

To the raggedy-ass masses, for whom psychoanalysis is not covered, certainly not entirely, by Blue Cross Blue Shield or Medicare, the scien-tized cogito, that glorious iceberg whose submerged girth is a matter of speculation, drifts near a landmass whereupon roams a herd of unicorns stalked by spear-chucking Teletubbies. Even that segment of the raggedy-ass masses we call the intelligentsia assumes a pre-Freudian lyric "I," a cogito that is fully integrated if overwhelmed by yearning or other pure emotion, because lyric expression from prehistory through the nineteenth century proceeded from the assumption that self-consciousness is singular and that emotions, though they may become grotesquely mangled, are nonetheless pure essences. Spelunking the depths of one's soul was an activity for which one only required a lantern, maybe a rope tethered to a tree at the entrance, but despite the biblical and Miltonic references oppressing "Skunk Hour" like the heft of cathedral tunes, Lowell's giddily despairing persona is a comedian goofing on himself. More specifically, he goofs on himself as a member of a community. Clare despairs for being shunned; Lowell laughs at the impossibility of being integrated. Madness, divine or otherwise, is incidental to the wisdom it affords Lowell, a granular understanding of the chief revelation of modernity, at least for the lyric artist, that there are depths to which one best not plunge without the assistance of a guide, that the "I" of "I think," up to its chin in thinking, can see very little in the miasma of lantern light absorbed by dark rock above and dark water below.

Therapy—though more saliently the pop culture appropriation of the scientific, intellectual drudge work of inquiry into the nature of consciousness and human behavior generally—has migrated from a bourgeois elitism to an any-boy-or-girl-can egalitarianism. A winner of multiple Olympic gold medals for swimming hawks telephone therapy on cable TV, and every kid who gets his tongue stuck to a flagpole in winter will likely be scanned for personality disorder. The lingo of therapy was propagated in the TV era first by Dr. Brothers, then Dr. Phil, and now by a herd of New Agey internet mavens, for my money the intrepid relationship guru Esther Perel chief among them. But as a university creative writing coach of verse and prose—the kind that purports to be true but usually only kind of is as well as the sort that flaunts not being true though usually at least somewhat is—I can attest that few late-teens/early-twenties tadpole scribblers have *not* passed through the digestive system of the froggy American (yes, frogs also eat their young!) mental health care apparatus.

Walt's response to an astronomer was to mosey out of the lecture hall and bask in starlight, and that seems like a perfectly healthy thing to do if the gesture is not a dismissal of science. I think it is often wrongly perceived

187

as such. Everything I feel in my hoary heart about our beloved progenitor suggests that he'd entered the lecture hall in good faith and marveled at the information disseminated to that sampling of the raggedy-ass masses, his fellow audience members, before drifting outside to marvel at those cosmic corpses, the remnants of dead and dying suns, littering the battlefield of the night sky, so unadulterated back then, untainted by megacity lights.

The most insidious phase of the history of democracy, and the most deviously clever circumnavigation of its essential value, is embodied by the *Plessy v. Ferguson* Supreme Court decision of 1892. Upholding the principle of "separate but equal," it rendered racial segregation canonical for several generations, reinforced the sabotaging lie attached to American democracy, that it may legitimately exist divorced from socioeconomic realities. "Separate but equal" sounds fine until one registers that the group separated, a minority, is therefore cordoned off from the mechanisms of wealth and prosperity. Homer Plessy, a fellow who, literally, was more white than Black by the ridiculous racial math of the day—he was one-eighth Black—offended Louisiana's Separate Car Act of 1890 by choosing to sit in the white rather than the Black train car, refusing to enter that mobile ghetto that the latter represented. The Court determined that segregation is not discrimination. The rest is our mucked-up modern history.

So much of the lyric expression defining modernity proceeds from assumptions slow-cooked in the caldron of psychotherapy, a power relation in which a cogito submits to the authority of a benign guide through a space more like a lush canopy-covered jungle than a biblical desert, a space in which one cannot venture forth situated by the location of the sun or stars, a space so crowded with fecundity that the condition of being lost is a tragic normalcy: the human condition.

The ethos of therapy renders most analysands both patient and client, and the dual designations, as roles within an economic dynamic, are contradictory. As a client, especially in the context of a customer-is-always-right ethos, the analysand plants a flag in his/ her/their own psyche, that claustrophobic jungle, and sets out mapping it, guided by a hired hand who possesses something like local knowledge but is otherwise blind.

The therapist, the guide, no matter the sanctioning letters following her or his name, is the muse of modernity.

The point of this is simply that a notable feature of white privilege is the luxury of tethering private troubles to public issues in lyric art that proceeds from an assumption of the profound complexity, and therefore richness, of their racially (to some) and/or culturally (to others) superior minds. People of color, particularly those of African heritage, for the most part, have not had, certainly through the first half of the twentieth century *did not have,* access to any more or less official form of therapy or to the oddly comforting assumption that mind sickness is, if not curable, manageable. Within the American intelligentsia, only a small subset of which was interested—in Marianne Moore's sense, as expressed in "Poetry"—in poetry, an inward gaze was through a psychoanalytic lens whether one submitted to the "talking cure" or not. The talking cure trope, and even the most remote possibility of a scientific, or in some sense systematic, response to unhappiness, to mental or soul sickness, was a white privilege of which most white American intellectuals and artists may not have availed themselves, but the basic tenets of which (the fact of an unconscious, the complexity and centrality of sexuality, the relation of language to the repressed content of the unconscious) nonetheless undergirded their fancy flights inward. But what about people of color? Voilà: the blues.

And all it spawned, including jazz and rock and rap and most culture stuff quintessentially American, and outside the bailiwick of American Poetry, and the greatest gift that oppressors have ever received from those oppressed, if one overlooks the centuries of free, followed by grossly under-remunerated, labor. However they are ranked, neither gift—labor nor soul—was given. Little Richard did not give Elvis a soul. Muddy Waters didn't give Keith Richards one either. Scott Joplin, Jelly Roll Morton, Thelonious Monk, Louis Armstrong, Dizzy Gillespie, Billie Holiday, Ella Fitzgerald . . . Mingus, Coltrane, Hancock . . . the list is a cavalcade of American genius, and the likes of Brubeck, Baker, Goodman, Getz, Corea, who followed, or at least the best of them as human beings if not as artists, were humble contributors to the dynamism of that genius. "O O O O that Shakespeherian Rag— / It's so elegant / So intelligent" alluded to a popular song of the era, and Eliot's deployment of it was in the spirit of massive condescension but also grudging, if unconscious, acknowledgment of the genius, as in spirit, of its origin. Neither Eliot nor Pound nor modernism as such would exist except for that genius, that spirit, that soul, that force from a time before the ideological burdens of the scientized cogito existed, a time when all thinking was at least tinged with magic, even when most rational, a time when most thinking was magical thinking.

Could there have been a *Waste Land* or *Cantos* or *Ulysses,* for that matter, or "stream of consciousness" as such, had there not been a shift of emphasis from product to process; if improvisation, at least the ideal, and as such a performative imperative, had not occurred with the force (if not the glacial speed) of the Great Vowel Shift? During the time when the races in America were least separate and most unequal, a profound cultural diffusion occurred even as white fathers were raping Black mothers, even as all the original American sins were being committed interminably and all at once, and as has been the hallmark of all forms of enslavement (including colonialism, slavery-lite), the victims schooled the perpetrators as to how to be more alive.

That way was enmeshed in the art that wafted from historical oppression, art that was a celebration of the ecstatic moment or the somber or wretched one, art manifested in improvisational performance.

The iconic works of modernity took improvisation as a structural metaphor. The (in)famous footnotes to *The Waste Land* are as humorously absurd as would be a running voice-over commentary to a Coltrane solo that notes each musical reference, each musical joke with the great artist's fellow musicians and aficionados. English-language American poetry, the sheet-white modern canon anyway, would not exist except for American slavery, that most undemocratic feature of American history. Yes, Lowell's "Skunk Hour" is one of innumerable manifestations of the scientized cogito defining modern American lyricism, but it is more fundamentally an example of the influence of the blues-jazz cultural matrix on lyric discourse.

The two defining influences on the modern and postmodern lyric are the scientized cogito and the ubiquitous and countervailing force of African American performative art. In particular, regarding improvisation, the influence occurred less in terms of practice than as an ideal that shifts emphasis from product to process. Modernity is white Euro-American. The iconoclasm at the heart of it is African American; whether it radiates from Ireland or Germany or Poland or Italy or merry ol' England or from the US of A, the African American influence freed—and oh, the irony—

the white imagination from the strictures of its colonial past and present, worked more than a little magic on the scientized cogito.

Like Elvis, Eliot, especially of *The Waste Land,* perhaps didn't understand that he was appropriating the original genius of African American culture. The expatriation of American artists in the first decades of the twentieth century was flight from a "half-savage country," in Pound's estimation. Such a condition was to no small degree a defining feature of genocide and human bondage. This begs the question as to whether the best and brightest white writers and artists of the first wave of expatriation fled what they perceived to be cultural aridity, a defining feature of which was the savagery of institutional racism, or whether they fled what they perceived to be the savagery of the victims. It is ambiguous as to whether the likes of Pound, Eliot, Stein, and Hemingway were even capable of conceiving the difference. The second wave of American expatriates included both African American jazz greats as well as literary titans such as Miles Davis, Josephine Baker, James Baldwin, Langston Hughes, and Richard Wright, and there is no ambiguity as to what they were fleeing: the savagery of a mangled democracy. The lyric "I" of African American writers was imbued with an alienation wholly unlike the existential, politically benign condition saturating the more or less serious literature of High (and white) Modernism; it was beyond ironic self-pity and was profoundly ironic in its democratic spirit.

The mechanism of that profound irony resides in the African American Singer of Self's relation to a segregated audience: even seventeen-year-old Langston Hughes was aware of a white audience being, alas, his primary audience; yet Hughes also proceeded from a moral imperative to speak truth to Black readers and, indeed, to speak their truth to that white audience in "A Negro Speaks of Rivers." Has any white writer, specifically any late-twentieth-century (and twenty-first, for that matter) white poet, ever been guided, *significantly,* by a concern for her or his nonwhite audience, what nonwhite readers might think and feel about his or her or their lyrical effusions? The genius, that is, the spirit of African American lyric, lends the lie to Whitman's democratic spirit as well as to the scientized, and colonizing, white cogito, even as it embodies and vitalizes that spirit. That paradox is the thumping heart of all that is grotesquely beautiful about America and American poetry.

The Dick and the Donald

White Privilege and Flimflam

> Poets and storytellers are wrong about men in the most important matters. They declare that many men are happy though unjust, and wretched although just; that injustice is profitable, if not found out, and justice good for others but plain loss for oneself. Such things we will forbid them to say, and command them to sing and to fable the opposite.
>
> —PLATO, *The Republic,* Book III

When she was nine and I was thirteen, in the spring of 1967, my sister and I were separated, not to know one another again for fifty years. One day, offhandedly googling the website of our mother's cemetery, located in Elizabeth City, North Carolina, I came across a terse though passionate eulogy I'd not previously noticed, one my sister had composed and which I was able to trace back to her. We began a spirited and voluminous correspondence, but only after she'd verified my identity, a process she did not engage in casually given that her court testimony over the years has been instrumental in the incarceration of numerous murderers and drug dealers: a retired forensic investigator who characterizes her stellar career as having primarily entailed "dumpster diving for body parts," my sister is funny and whip-smart; she is strong and decent and curious and full of joyful wonder. She is a humane and principled libertarian who, shall we say, did not vote as I voted in the 2016 presidential election, and blended into the sweet sunshine of our initial exchanges were some swirls of vitriol. Of course, we eventually agreed on ground rules, one of which forbids all overt discussion of politics.

Another does not forfend discussion of our father but does forbid any *nuanced* discussion of him; that is, there is an unspoken rule that we cannot discuss him without proceeding from the judgment that he was a monster, a banal and grotesque creature void of compassion and incapable of truthful self-regard.

I am clueless as to why my sister, who fervently supported the regime as it existed after the 2016 debacle, cannot perceive how similar that recent occupant of the White House is to our father or the irony of this. The main difference, besides the silver spoon and gold-plated toilet seat, is that our father indeed possessed a capacity for compassion; he simply didn't know what to do with it when he felt it. Every bit as sick a pathological liar as my sister's political hero, our father, Richard Page Harris (henceforth "the Dick," as my sister refers to him with no irony, not perceiving, it seems, the connection that the definite article extends to said hero) told rapid-fire whoppers from as deep an ego swamp of insecurities and social terrors as her hero so publicly occupies and from which he expounds so vociferously as he floats through his ridiculously charmed life in the throes of a lucid coma dream.

I will not further insult the memory of my criminal father, my lying, cheating, dim-witted pater, by further comparisons with my sister's political hero. Suffice it to say that the "Big Lie" has not been wielded so ham-handedly yet effectively since Hitler and Goebbels, that dynamic duo, goose-stepped across the proscenium of Western Civ.

My sister says that there is much she can't recall of our childhood because of a head injury she incurred in her teens, several years after we were separated. I must wonder if her slate is blank primarily because of the injury or because what she witnessed after the Dick took Chuck and me to San Diego, California—only to return to Norfolk, Virginia, and the rest of our nuclear family—so damaged her that memory and pain are braided in her heart and stashed there beneath a wad of sorrow, the residue of mourning for our mother.

She recently described to me how the Dick, soon after returning to Norfolk, ripped Joan from her wheelchair and beat her with his fists until she was unconscious. She described trying to stop him mid-punch and how he threw my nine-year-old sister across the motel room, breaking her arm. She recalled that event in granular detail but cannot recall life on the road, cannot recall much at all of our lives in Elizabeth City or later in the Norfolk federal housing projects. Of course, her blurred memory is also due to her having been so young, apart from the effects of healthy repression. The head injury, I suspect, is a gauze, a soft bandage around it all; her memory of the Dick's attacks is simply what bled through.

My sister has not told her husband that she and I correspond; I'm not even certain she has told him that we have found one another. She admits that she has told him little about her childhood, and he, she says, has talked little about his own abusive childhood. He is a retired army guy, a "lifer," and they live in a nice pastoral spread somewhere I can't reveal because of my sister's vulnerability to evil men she has helped put away. She and her husband have made a very good life for themselves as forward-looking citizens who have both survived abuses and who now give the finger to the past. I salute them for giving the finger to the past. I wish I could.

I gather that my sister met her husband when she was a sixteen-year-old runaway from one of a series of "foster care situations." She was panhandling and performing, singing in coffeehouses and on the streets of college towns in Florida, and he, a few years older, was gentle and kind. But all of that is her story, and I'll not presume to disclose, beyond this point much of what she has shared with me. What is important is that connected to that soldier's life, she finished high school, attended college and graduate school, and made a terrific career doing humanly important work. Together, they give the finger to the past, cultivate a kind of healthy forgetting, and take genuine pride in their mutual accomplishments and the worldview that has guided them to where they find themselves at this moment in history. The pride I feel for my sister's life, her fundamental decency, is more potent than my loathing of her worldview. When, early in our correspondence, we would argue about politics, when I expressed my gobsmacked incredulity regarding her judgments, she accused me of condescension, and she was correct; I condescended to her and upon being called out on my liberal biases felt terrible but not so much so as to recant. I certainly don't think that she is any more a racist than most other white people. She is only perhaps 12 percent the racist that her political hero is, and I suppose I fancy myself to be only 3 or 4 percent the racist that, say, the governor of Mississippi is, any given year up to and including the 2016 cycle.

What does it mean to harbor in one's heart only 3 percent of the racism that occupies the social essence of a generic governor of Mississippi? It means that white entitlement is the brittle shell of gooey racism. It means that even though Waldo is hidden, in plain sight, within the mayhem of Martin Hanford's zany compositions, he is there for anyone who takes the time to scan the scene, to see.

No matter how hard I try to camouflage it in humor and ironic self-loathing, the sentimentality I bring to the enterprise of understanding, processing the emotional entropy of my childhood is tinged with racism if only because the criminal lifestyle my parents embraced was enabled by white entitlement, though I'm beginning to loathe the phrase and all such jargon: Fucking "racism"! Goddamned fucking "white privilege"! Mother-fucking "sexism"! Goddamned motherfucking "misogyny"! Cocksucking cunt whore "homophobia"! Goddamned motherfucking cocksucking cunt whore "patriarchy"!

My bridling at overdetermined nomenclature notwithstanding, white entitlement, alas, is "a thing," and no Black family at that time in history could have lived, more or less with impunity, on the highways of America. When my sister and I were kids, no Black father could have pulled the scams that the Dick pulled to feed us, to keep us going. No Black family could have lost itself in the America of the fifties and sixties. No Black man in America could have gotten away for so long with being such a blatant, egregious liar as the Dick, and as my sister's political hero, because no Black American can lose himself, and a family, on the freeways and turn-pikes and boulevards and country roads and dirt paths of America, not in the same sense as we were lost and certainly not for so long.

But in what sense lost? Perhaps I mean invisible or so innocuous as to seem not worth seeing, not worth the search through the zany American mayhem. If Waldo were Black . . .

Though she is certainly smart and sophisticated enough to know bet-ter, my sister has written to me that in fact some of her best friends are Black, or something very close to that racist formulation. She would take umbrage at this critique, and I must admit that it is possible for a white person to say that some of her or his best friends are Black and not be *entirely* racist, though the utterance would have to be waterlogged with irony if only because any white person who has, say, diminished her or his racism down to a single-digit portion of the racism inhabiting the soul of a generic Mississippi governor is wholly aware that racism can be like herpes, manifesting rarely but always otherwise dormant and therefore an unremitting potentiality. Ironized racist verbiage can be a form of self-parodic humor. But such self-parody is not an indication of one's being "woke," just pathetically insincere. I'm thinking of guys I knew in an all-white high school I attended before dropping out to make my fame and fortune as a songwriter in LA and failing miserably. I'm thinking of the guys I worked with in restaurants in the French Quarter of New Orleans, the banter between white and Black waiters in line in the kitchen. Here's a verbatim example:

> Brad: Rudy, is it true *N-words* drill holes in watermelons and fuck 'em before they eat 'em?
>
> Rudy: No, Brad, I'm a N-word that fucks your mama and then has to eat watermelon to get her stank out of my mouth.

And so it goes . . .

And I'm sure my sister knows that asserting that some of her best friends are Black is at the very least problematic. She is a survivor who does not seek credit for having survived and thrived, even though she is a white woman whose penultimate ethical value is self-reliance, whose ultimate value is survival. I do not doubt that some of her best friends and fellow professionals are indeed Black, nor do I doubt that somewhere, deep in the dim valleys of the unconscious terrain of her psyche, slouches the assumption that she's doing those friends a significant favor.

I recently had a troubling exchange with an applicant to the study abroad program for writers that I've directed for a quarter-century and have owned as a limited liability company for the past six years. I found his work quite interesting and offered him a scholarship that is, in effect, a thousand-dollar reduction in the cost of the program:

> Your verse, for the most part, is skillfully wrought and thoughtfully con-ceived. You write about a social context that white/Anglo-Americans, in particular, have a moral imperative to understand better. My colleagues and I would love for you to be a member of our community in Prague this July.

I should note here that the poet's work sample centered squarely, unabashedly on race and social justice. I should also note that the bit about moral imperative rings now to my ears, as I imagine it must have seemed to the applicant, condescending and that such formulaic, PC rhetoric is an example of the process, alchemical or digestive, by which fundamental truth transforms into a golden pile of self-aggrandizing horseshit.

I went on to offer him the scholarship and to describe what services, beyond the classroom, the program would offer. He responded:

> Thank you so much for your speedy acceptance! Is there anything I can do to qualify for an additional scholarship? I am graduating from university in the next few weeks and already know that there will be a cap on what financial aid I can ask for from my home institution. I'd also like to know what past students of color have attended your program, and what reviews they have given the program. Knowing that there is support for writers of color both institutionally (being in Prague, after all) and academically (in workshop) is essential to my acceptance.

I was royally pissed and conflicted. I responded:

> I can offer an additional $500 reduction. I will not list the names of other students of color. Approximately two thousand student writers have passed through the program, and many students from Anglophone Africa, Asia, and South America have attended the program, as have scores of African American, Asian American, Chicano, not to mention Native American, aspiring writers.

> It's frankly up to you to acquire "reviews" from past students of color. I've no idea, at this point, how many students this cycle will be nonwhite, and if this is truly an issue I strongly suggest that you attend another program. I think you're bright and talented and would like to work with you, and I'm certain that the other mentors will want to work with you, but I'm not trying to sell you a used car or anything else. The program is going into its twenty-sixth year. You either want to be a part of what we've represented since Czechoslovakia's Velvet Revolution or you don't. I leave for Prague on Sunday. If I don't hear from you by the afternoon of the fifth, I'll assume you've made other plans.

The poet's response was, well, perfect:

> Thank you for so plainly illustrating the treatment I can expect in your program. It seems I will no longer need any reviews from the "scores and scores [*sic*]" of students of color that your program has previously hosted. This email is enough. If it is not already clear, I decline your offer.
>
> P.S. To have a writing program that dates back to the Velvet Revolution certainly sounds impressive. However, I am more impressed by the racism you have fostered in those twenty-six years. It must have taken hard work for the former and dedication for the latter.

Of course, I should have left it at that but responded twice, first:

> You're too talented and too bright to resort to cheap shots. This program has always been welcoming to all promising writers. We wish you the very best.

But after fuming a bit, I blasted back:

> Okay, pal, you may come to the program for free! How about that! All you have to pay for is the housing and travel. You may participate otherwise entirely for free. This is a sincere offer.

I then rattled off the names of a dozen African American, Hispanic American, and Asian American writers who have served as faculty, and at that point I was so angry I wanted to scream, "I love you!" I so loathed the fellow I could have given him five thousand dollars to attend the program. I was so pissed I could have spent thirty hours writing a detailed, compassionate critique of just one of his briefer efforts. I was livid and could have fallen to my knees and begged him to attend the program. I was so angry I could have signed over the title to my RV.

Of course, he declined my final offer. He'd been fishing, I'm guessing. What angered me was *his* own sense of entitlement, that he required that I not only offer an additional break on the program cost but that I also persuade him to attend. He asserted that "support for writers of color both institutionally (being in Prague, after all) and academically (in workshop) is essential to my acceptance." What did he mean by that first parenthetical? Well, the Czechs have a reputation for racism against Roma, but I suppose the distinction between *institution* and *academic* is what puzzled me, though what yanked my hair was *essential to my acceptance.* Most students over the years, white and Black and other, have been delighted to receive any assistance at all. This cheeky fellow was haughtily placing a condition on his acceptance that had nothing to do with money. My racism, I eventually had to admit to myself, did not emanate from my initial peeved response but from the subsequent mega–passive aggression with which I'd hammered him. Of course I'd have honored my offer to have him attend for free, and I'd have treated him like a fine crystal goblet at a frat party; I'd have been that worried, that protective, that dishonest.

Which flavor of racism is most gag inducing, I wish I could ask him, the militant racism of a skinhead or the passive-aggressive racism of a card-carrying white liberal? Well, it's not that simple, and the kid was certainly playing the "race card," and there's no way he should have expected me to send him blurbs from past students of color:

"The Program was not only not racist; it was downright welcoming!"

or

"The Program is absolutely color-blind!"

or perhaps

"The Program is a bastion of acceptance!"

But then I proved his point by attacking him with my white liberal guilt, bludgeoning him with a special deal—that is, one just for him—insulting him with an offer that was meant more to demean than to honor his dream of being a significant American poet.

Racism is the Gordian knot hitching the oxcart of American exceptionalism to the post at the center of the ideal polis, the one in each of our hearts, though it's not a puzzle so easily solved as Alexander is said to have solved it, with a whack of his sword. It must be massaged and pulled and plucked at, endlessly, in every heart. Our American humanity is in the endless plucking, I guess.

This is how the Dick, my profoundly racist father, was memorialized:

He was born March 8, 1932, in Norfolk, VA, to the late Irene and Charles Harris. Richard served in the US Army as a young man. Later in life, he participated in Prison Ministry which help [*sic*] bring the Lord into prisons. He also provided spiritual guidance to nursing home residents.

He is survived by his wife Peggy Harris of 28 years. His children Rick Katrovas, Charles Harris, Arthur Harris Mendamis, Christopher Harris. His stepchildren Christopher Cruce and Melisa Lloyd. His sister Barbara Johnson and a niece Jody Danielson. Eight grandchildren . . .

He was preceded in death by his brother Charles Harris and sister Myrtle Jakeman.

Memorial contrubutions [*sic*] may be made to Faith Radio "Radio for Prisoners [*sic*]," First Baptist Church of Havana, or Big Bend Hospice.

The birthdate and place are correct, and the names (though, except by an ex-wife and a few friends, I've not been called "Rick" since I was a child). But the two most salient details of his life are lies: (1) He ran away to join the army, with forged documents, when he was fifteen but called his mama, Irene, weeping, only a couple of weeks into boot camp, to come and fetch him. She did. His "service" is a lie in the same sense that a streaker, circa 1974, frolicking into left field of Yankee Stadium during the seventh-inning stretch, may not claim to be a Bronx Bomber. (2) "Later in life" he no doubt participated in prison ministries but only after spending nearly three decades in federal and state prisons. I suppose that this is an example of a lie of omission, one that most would allow but to my heart and to my sister's—she is mercifully omitted from the list of offspring—is a travesty. Prison defined him in our psyches. We waited for him to get out of prison for half of childhood, the other half having been on the road in the Republic of Burma Shave, though we never really got off the road.

I do not begrudge him those lies, however. I know that omission of such facts was in part to alleviate discomfort for the living, his wife and her grown children, and the extended community of solid white people who rallied to his salvation in the last three decades of his life. That I am proud he endured prison and was able to transition out of criminal life into a settled one, in a community for which he became a kind of pet, speaks less to his status within that community and more to my overdeveloped sense of corrosive irony. That tightly bound community of evangelical Christians occupying environs just south of Tallahassee, Florida, took pride in his transformation and credit for that fundamental change, but what they failed to see, or simply didn't want to know, was that the Dick's conversion had less to do with authentic transformation than with the simple fact that advancements in banking technology, changes in information management generally that have connected us all whether we want to be connected or not, had rendered his scams of choice obsolete. His fervent faith was his retirement plan. He assumed the role of the White Man Whom Christ Has Plucked from Ruin, the flesh-and-blood exemplar embodying the transformative power of Grace, and his community kept him on a leash but fed and somewhat pampered him for thirty years. He became that community's living proof that no one strays beyond the reach of redemption, that rebirth is available even to the most inveterate scallywag.

The Dick was eighty-four when he died from a fever propagated by a legion of errant amoeboid protozoans that broke through his otherwise hearty immune system. Indeed, his widow commented, almost wistfully, a couple of years after his passing that the Dick had possessed preternatural recuperative powers, that colds never lingered, that scrapes and burns healed rapidly, that even his stomach cancer had gone into remission so quickly that his doctors had been astonished. That final fatal fever had swelled his brain; he'd hallucinated and raved for days. He'd fought the squiggly little bastards heroically. But they overwhelmed him, like skinheads with tattooed penises in a prison shower. The Dick dropped the soap, and it was all over.

As a child, on the road, in the back seats of cars, I did not hear the word *negro*. I heard *colored* or, less often and always in a jocular tone, the N-word. The latter never, I'm certain, passed Joan's lips, always the Dick's.

He referred to Vashti, the Black maid who actually raised him, as "colored." Rolling down his window, the engine chortling, we kids clustered behind and Joan passive beside him, he'd request directions from a fat, pink, shirtless fellow in bib overalls and be sent to the Black bootlegger off the dirt road behind the gas station outside a tiny burg equidistant between Birmingham and Montgomery, Alabama; before thanking him and rolling toward two or three pints of Four Roses, the Dick would inquire of the farmer, "'N-word' got a gun?"

I understood that *colored* was polite talk and that the other word was just talk, was just the normal way of referring to those mysterious other people. Why there was a need for a polite word designating them I, of course, didn't know and didn't even know to question but must have assumed that the polite word was reserved for the really good ones, that is, the exceptional ones, of which, alas, there were few.

Since I have become more or less savvy—I'm too savvy to say "enlightened"—regarding race, in the sense that one peers beyond kumbaya sentimentality into basic structures of social relations, I, of course, am embarrassed that I have spent so much of my adult life taking racism for granted and giving myself credit for merely recognizing it as a defining feature of American identity. I have failed to *feel* racism, which of course begs the question as to whether any white guy, even the most virulent Triple-K cracker, can be wired to feel it, not the hatred that is a salve to self-loathing and not the fear that belies any true sense of superiority but the deep structure in which one is subject or object and in which the distinction has gotten gloriously, and grossly, mangled over time.

Perhaps the only manner in which I may feel it is by imperfect analogy.

I have spent long spans of time blissfully unconscious of being white, although I have for quite a while been savvy enough to feel uncomfortable even writing, much less uttering, "the N-word." I mean, I've taken my status as a white American so deeply for granted for significant stretches of time—hours, even days—that my whiteness is as incidental to my being in the world as are my most elemental longings and creature requirements. My national identity, my Americanness, has likewise blended into that Zen ocean in which the baby fish inquires of the mama fish, "What's the ocean?"

When I am abroad, I am American first; when my fellow Americans are abroad, white or Black, they, too, are Americans first. By "first," I mean that, when an American is abroad, national identity subsumes all other aspects of identity, including gender and race and sexual preference and even social class. I never feel so American as when I'm abroad, and I never feel my whiteness a less important feature of who and what I am than when I'm abroad. Also, I never feel so strong a bond with Black Americans as when we meet and interact in a foreign country.

I'm quite glad that the kid who accused me of racism didn't take me up on my offer but only because experience informs me that he likely would have been a massive pain in my ass, a distraction. I might have been able to persuade him that I am only 3 percent as much a racist as any generic governor of Mississippi, but he likely would have latched onto that 3 percent and interrogated it, by his very presence, a presence armed from the get-go by his blatant accusation of racism, an accusation that no doubt correctly invoked my white, liberal entitlement, a sword I'd have plunged into my own heart every time I opened my mouth to respond to his poems with an authority I grow less sure of and less comfortable wielding each passing year.

Six people of color, in addition to four African Americans, have attended the program the past couple of cycles, though two were subcontinental Indian, one Indonesian, two Anglophone Asian, and two Anglophone African; with the possible exception of the Americans, none of those aspiring writers, that I'm aware of, was a descendant of enslaved people, none was due, in a deep and abiding sense, reparations for the crime of slavery, though all were, at least historically, victims of colonialism, what I have to think of as something like slavery-lite.

Once, back when I consumed alcohol, I stayed up all night swilling vodka over an entire sunny summer night in St. Petersburg, Russia, with four young, brilliant Kenyan poets whose names have been lost to me for more than a decade. All I recall is the sky that never darkened, the endless toasts, the laughter, the recitations—the fact of those slurred and charmingly histrionic presentations and not their substance—and the fact that I was inhabiting, in their joyful presence, another world, not in the sense that St. Petersburg and its endless summer days were foreign to me, which they were, and not in the sense that those poets were foreign to me, which they so delightfully were, but rather in the sense that in that vodka-bright night, I was foreign to myself; I was another country unto myself, or a citizen of one, a citizen of the back seat of an American car that carried me and my fellow citizens, two criminal adults and their four other children, from motel to motel, bank to bank to bank, sunset to sunset to sunset.

A Dead Dog and a Boy

In the spring of 1990, my youngest brother, Christopher, whom I'd not seen in twenty-five years, since he was seven and I thirteen, made an unannounced visit to New Orleans and talked me into cosigning for a loan. Post-divorce, he needed a new vehicle for a new business he would mount upon his return to Roanoke, Virginia.

He missed the first two payments, and we were visited by two FBI agents, who inquired as to his physical location. I squirted them with the lies he'd poured into my gullible ear, then flew to Virginia in a rage that I barely contained and took possession of the vehicle. I'd had two brief encounters with our criminal father over the quarter-century since the dissolution of our family. Desperately, stupidly, I contacted "the Dick," as I have since come to refer to him, in a nod to his sickness, his compulsion to lie in similar fashion as the forty-fifth president of the United States; I told him of my predicament. He invited me to drive the pickup to his home near Tallahassee, Florida.

Having squirmed in his presence on just two other brief occasions in three decades, I was only a little more familiar with the Dick than I was with "the Donald." My estranged *pater* circled the truck, sneering like an expert. He popped the hood, kicked the tires, and paused thrice to stare meditatively, arms crossed, a thumb on his lips. It was a new white pickup with fewer than eight thousand miles on it; I couldn't figure what flaws he thought he was seeking. As a child, I'd seen him play the wary consumer with used-car dealers when actually his primary concern was getting off the lot in anything other than what he'd driven onto it. The most recent ABP would refer, of course, to the vehicle he was swapping, so he had simply to bamboozle the dealer out of some trade-in credit and write a check and we were anonymous again in the Republic of Burma Shave, at least until the check bounced the following day.

The Dick's workday began at roughly 4:00 p.m., close enough to the end of banking hours that, by the climax of any deal, a smarmy salesman couldn't phone a fractious assistant bank manager for verification. That a dealer couldn't immediately verify the veracity of the Dick's personal check usually killed a deal, though often enough it didn't.

We kids learned not to develop sentimental attachments to automobiles. We knew we could count on living in one for no more than a few weeks and as briefly as a few days, indeed once only a couple hours, though I can't recall the dynamics of that particularly weird and frenetic switcheroo; I only recall the Dick loading us into a different car after completing the deal, then racing from that lot to another across town, where, after some haggling, he hustled us into yet a different automobile and all but scratched sand over the late hour's scat of deceptions and drove all night through prairie into desert.

I wanted him to assume the loan, but of course, he wouldn't. He insisted upon keeping the truck in my name and making the monthly payments. That way he had me. If I angered him, he'd stiff the bank. I wanted nothing to do with him, but now I kind of needed him. On a Fulbright, I'd impregnated a Czech while in Prague, Czechoslovakia, during the Velvet Revolution, and for several weeks, since the 3:00 a.m. phone call from my Czech paramour announcing her predicament and soliciting suggestions as to what she should "do," I'd been living an immense lie with my wife. Awash in self-loathing and excited at having a child in my life (for even in my fuzzy-headed, shocked state I'd not doubted my illicit lover should keep the child), I was in no condition to negotiate. I accepted his proposal and thereby became connected to him, a situation I loathed and he relished.

I even tried to reconfigure my regard for him. He had mellowed and seemed to try not to lie—and for brief spells lied with less frequency than he had before. A lie would slip out every twenty minutes or so and usually had to do with how much money he was now worth. At one point, he casually dropped that he was worth four and a half million; I just nodded and said, "Wow," suppressing an impulse to query whether he was referring to

Serbian dinars circa 1989 or German marks circa 1923, but I couldn't even look him in the eye when he lied like that. I couldn't challenge him or ask for proof. He and the sweet and melancholy woman he lived with were obviously comfortable; they'd eventually sell her business and probably had other retirement funds. They patted into a neat little pile enough to live on in modest white trash comfort for the rest of their lives. I was happy for him, in a sardonic kind of way.

I'd driven from Virginia to Florida, relinquished a pickup, on which I owed more than ten grand in 1990 dollars, to a convicted felon in the ridiculous hope that he would keep his end of a ridiculous deal, and that evening, in his and his wife's single-wide that was cluttered with knick-knacks so ridiculous they seemed to have fallen through a black hole of banality and come out the other end bizarrely elegant, I sat across from him, avoiding eye contact by staring into the paunch of a pink porcelain pig frolicking on its porky hind legs just above his head and absorbed his Jesus pitch.

I tried to be polite, listening without comment. But his monologue each minute became incrementally more self-righteous and stupid. My anger swelled.

For a moment, I shifted my gaze from the pig paunch to him. He was still a handsome man and radiated a modicum of charm when he wasn't holding forth. But the longer he lectured, the more I lamented having splashed from any gene pool to which he had contributed. I wanted to leap up, rush him before he could grab the pistol he always kept within reach, and pound him unconscious. He was explaining how Jesus loves even N-words and kikes but only if they aren't Catholics.

He said *N-word* a lot, and I hate that word, though I hate almost as much the fact that I feel so strongly compelled to write *N-word,* though I have no compunction regarding *kike,* in this context, anyway; alas, I also love that I feel so compelled. I am therefore profoundly conflicted. I feel silly that the two syllables composing the epithet, combined, are in PC jail, but I feel silly not because the N-word is the Lord Voldemort of English-language epithets for wholly righteous and justifiable reasons (and it is) but, rather, because the word wears the mind-forged manacles of Liberal Guilt, and there is no impediment more brittle, less intellectually honest, than the False Flag of Feeling planted in the name of Liberal Guilt. But I digress.

As I sat absorbing the Dick's rant in which racism, homophobia, and sexism were filtered through a simplistic and profoundly stupid reading of Scriptures, I became more and more sentimental. I thought of my Black students, my gay neighbors and colleagues, my poor deceived wife and my pregnant lover, and my sentimentality filled the trailer. I shifted from fuming silence to my own rant in a blink.

I pointed out the inconsistencies in his argument. Of course, he changed the subject from scriptural interpretation to my particular soul being consigned to Hell. He was smug in his knowledge of my doom, forced back a grin that flashed, then receded again and again. The only way I could avoid the most wretched of fates was to fall on my knees and pray with him.

I informed him that I'd rather gobble a steaming pile of Satan's bloody excrement than fall on my knees in his, my father's, presence. I screamed that he and his fundamentalist cohorts are all fascists. He grinned and said that Satan was speaking through me. Satan, he informed me, is a liberal.

My anger melted into mirth. The ecstatic porker, frozen mid-frolic above his cowlick where a halo would have hovered, became the essence of delight, and I burst out laughing; I requested clarification.

His argument was simple: Satan encourages people to live according to a moral relativism; he didn't use the term, but that's what he meant. I suggested that what was moral relativism to some was simply tolerance to others, and besides, does Satan encourage a redistribution of wealth through tax codes and social programs? Of course he does, the Dick answered. So Satan had been responsible for Joan and us kids living on welfare while the Dick was in prison? Satan fed and sheltered us? Satan had us immunized and paid our medical costs? The Great Society was pure evil?

Yes, it was pure evil. Satan tricked him, the Dick, into doing evil things and consequently going to prison, and then Satan shepherded his, the Dick's, family into his, Satan's, evil sanctuary.

I laughed in gleeful sadness. His sweet, pathetic wife entered the main room of the single-wide where the Dick and I sat facing one another. She smiled to see her sweet, righteous husband—who had survived such degradation to find, finally, solace in the bosom of the Lord—getting on so well with his wayward oldest son. As a collector of swine effigies, she displayed catholic taste at least within that niche, such that flying and dancing pigs cohabited on display shelves with ultra-realist tableaux in which exhausted sows nursed rooting piles of hunger.

My eyes burned with suppressed laughter. His life tethered to such as she, in the midst of profound kitsch, he occupied his blond Naugahyde throne, forearms posed upon the chair arms, hands hanging regally off the edges, grinning like a smug despot, and I recalled how much I'd missed him as a boy in Elizabeth City, North Carolina, where we'd lived after the first time he was caught, and in the projects of Norfolk, Virginia, after the second time he was caught and put away. Always, when he was away, life would be better when he returned. Always, when he returned, life darkened.

I had adored him. He had conned me into believing he was superior to all other living creatures. I was a lucky boy to have a father such as the Dick, a man so fearless, so audacious, so, alas, misunderstood.

I was seven the first time he got caught. The sirens. The flashing lights. It was midday, I think, mid-spring somewhere in central Florida. He screamed and punched the steering wheel. The three youngest wailed. We'd been stopped before, and he'd always gotten out of it. This time, however, there were three police cars.

As he pulled to the shoulder, he arched in the seat, plucked something from his pocket, and dropped it in Joan's lap. He pulled his holstered gun from under the seat and placed it between them as we jerked to a stop and zipped the hand brake. He snarled instructions to her; holding the newest member of our troupe on one arm, she hid the thing he'd given her in her clothes and stuffed the pistol in a bag by her feet. The Dick got out of the car.

He was out there a long time, fifteen minutes maybe; then he climbed back in and fired up the engine. I don't recall the kind of car we occupied that day, except that it was large, probably a Chrysler.

One police car stayed behind us and two in front. Their lights flashed, but their sirens were silent. They drove slower than the freeway speed limit. Cars blew by in the left lane. The Dick sputtered instructions to Joan. He ordered her to say this or that if asked this or that. We kids were terrified and silent and, for the duration of that slow and permanent detour, did not exist in the regard of our parents.

Whatever it was the cops accompanied us to—perhaps a highway patrol station—was quite lovely. I recall a steep, grassy hill that a cop assigned to watch us kids eventually allowed us to roll down and play on. The white stone, three-story box was guarded by two flagpoles and was singular, the only structure amid freeway landscape. Cops flanked Joan and the Dick to the rear of the building, and our cop watched us quite a while before we were allowed to roll down that hill.

I shat my pants. I was seven and mortified. I don't recall how it happened, probably as I tucked in my arms and rolled, then jumped to my feet and climbed back, repeatedly, too scared even to ask to enter that building. I'll always associate the Dick's first capture with the discomfort of shitty drawers.

Stinking, humiliated, confused, scared, I was led eventually into the building, down steps, to a cell. As contrived and sentimental as it may sound, my father squatted and touched my face through the bars. He promised I would see him again soon. He promised that everything would be okay. He told me to take care of everyone. He wept. I loved him unconditionally.

That evening, after phoning her mother from the highway patrol station to beg her to wire money for tickets and food, Joan and the five of us boarded a Greyhound to Elizabeth City, North Carolina, where her mother and several aunts lived. All the patrolmen had been kind. Clearly, they'd felt sorry for us. While we'd waited for the money from our tight-assed, slightly Germanic grandmother, a chubby patrolman or policeman or whatever he was, they all were, had brought us vending machine vittles and RCs from a concession stand on the grounds of that bucolic bastion of law enforcement. He'd also suggested that Joan clean me up.

He'd been very polite about it, seemed sensitive to my humiliation. Joan had then taken me to the bathroom, and I'd waited there naked while she'd gone out to the car to fetch clean clothes. On the way out the door, she'd dumped my drawers in a trash can. I recall the lid rocking, squeaking, in and out for several seconds after the door had whooshed shut behind her.

The bus was packed, and Joan slept deeply, her head propped against the window. The three younger kids, even Chris, who was not yet a year old, slept as they always did in cars, lumped together like puppies. I don't recall where Chuck was, though he was probably right next to me, as always.

Ours is an unshockable age that has culminated in my father's patron saint being elected president of the United States. No single life's agonies have much resonance beyond the twenty-four-hour news cycle. An overwhelming majority of our population, particularly that huge chunk outside the intelligentsia and even a significant portion of those who occupy its glittering fringe, will sit before television cameras and webcams and offer audiences, huge and tiny, a Whitman's Sampler of grotesque abuses. Confessional poetry, an often maligned yet ubiquitous lyric concoction blended from nineteenth-century Romanticism and psychoanalysis (with a dash of the Catholic confessional), flourished through the fifties, sixties, and seventies and exerts wide if diffuse influence even today. The flood current of what Christopher Lasch dubbed the "culture of narcissism" carried poems and novels and other forms of elite discourse, including that from academe, along the same path where Oprah and Springer were giddily swept along and has now converged with the raging Facebook river. Confession has become boring, predictable, like a friend's or family member's tic that we no longer notice. Even so, the culture of narcissism has blended, disastrously, with the culture of public lies.

The point of a confessional poem is to present the speaker, the poet masked (Plath) or unmasked (Lowell, Snodgrass, Sexton) as a representative sufferer, someone whose diseased consciousness is the consequence of a sick society. Lowell sang class, Plath and Sexton gender pathologies caused by a deluded, aggressively exploitative culture. I am not inclined to claim that such poets have become for our time Shelley's unacknowledged legislators, if only because the culture no longer needs such representation. Almost everyone is eager to hold up bloody wounds to everyone else. We have transformed from a representative to an absolute democracy of the hurt heart.

Lyric art dances on the border between a culture's conception of appropriately public and appropriately private discourse. When the margin blurs beyond recognition, the authentic work of lyric is rendered grotesque. Angel fucking, of course, continues gloriously. All poets are angel fuckers, even the ones who are most solitary in their grief and joy. Perhaps this little vat of self-involved ejaculations, this little book you are reading, is merely an instance of such a national spasm, though I hope it is also about it, especially inasmuch as what I am remembering and misremembering herein has less to do with personal suffering than with my astonishment that I have been so blessed in a universe for which I may assume no transcendent agents of blessings.

I am on the downslope. If I have twenty more years of breath, and actuary tables project that I likely don't, half of them will be a slog through the muck of corporeal degeneration, culminating in a slow and humiliating descent into shitty diapers and absolute dependence. I am a minor poet of the twentieth century's twilight, one of thousands rather than dozens due to the ascendance, post-counterculture, of the cottage industry of creative writing within humanities higher ed. I have had an odd life. It has not been spectacular, and certainly not exemplary, just odd. Of the historical events that determined me, the Vietnam War was probably chief. That is, missing Vietnam has made me what I am as much as anything else beyond the familial peculiarities. I missed Vietnam by two hours. If I'd been born two hours later or earlier, I can't recall which, my lottery number would have been a single digit rather than 339. And I think I'd have been stupid enough to go, though by the time I'd have gotten there, it would have been 1973. How many nineteen- and twenty-year-old men-children were being shipped over in '73? How many got killed? The bombing stopped, and the Paris Peace Accords, yada yada. Vietnam is a moot point but only chronologically speaking; the only way I'd have gotten into the shit would have been if I'd volunteered the previous year, maybe, and that certainly wasn't going to happen. My—let's call it—prudence, and not a principled stand on the morality of the conflict, determined my easy-peasy decision not to volunteer in '70 (with parental consent I'd certainly have been granted), '71, or '72; as a consequence, my life cleaves from the lives of men-children only a few years older than I who indeed volunteered or got drafted and didn't sneak north.

But there is an important sense in which Vietnam was not a moot point. It is important to know if one is a coward or not. I suspect that sometimes I am a coward and sometimes not. I suspect that under some extreme conditions I would stand and face death, and under others I would run away, wretched and pathetic. I have faced relatively serious danger on several occasions and not embarrassed myself. But war is the Great Truth. We men and women who have not gone to war, or not had it come to us, must remain humble before those who have, even those we find repugnant.

The Dick declaimed—in the most banal and mangled, usually drunken, oral narratives—his war days like a rhapsodist glorying in a scrap of the *Iliad*. Pathological liars (I'm of course not credentialed to make this diagnosis but nonetheless know it to be true), even bright ones, usually can't keep up with their lies. Few keep impeccable records. My father, early in my life, told me he'd gone to war in a place called Korea but never repeated any version of that lie. I'm sure even he could not live with such a lie, so he pretty much stuck to the adventures of barracks life and the travails of basic training and how he made sergeant in six months.

A strapping lad of fifteen in 1947 or '48, he'd run away from his upper-middle-class home in Norfolk, Virginia, lied about his age with false documents he'd acquired God knows how, and enlisted in the army. Of course, after a few days, he'd called his mother to fetch him, a pattern that would continue for many years. The Dick was a mama's boy and could always count on his scrappy little Greek mater for emergency funds. She often wired us fifty bucks when we were on the road, sometimes as much as two hundred, until the Dick had gotten so hot she could not wire him cash without facing legal jeopardy herself. I rather liked her. She was raunchy and a little mean but had a great sense of humor. Her father had been a sponge diver from near Athens (it seems everything in Greece is "near Athens") and had founded and/or been the first mayor of Tarpon Springs, Florida, or so the story goes, and no stories that issued from the Dick were true except in the most oblique sense. That I have relatives in Tarpon Springs is no doubt true because I recall hearing that tidbit from Irene, my grandmother. However, the Dick once insisted that his Greek grandfather had been a sea captain who'd kidnapped a princess and another time bragged that the patriarch had founded a town and been its first mayor. As a young man, I had no problem effusing, stoned or not, that my great-grandfather had been a sea captain who'd kidnapped and married a princess, then founded Tarpon Springs, Florida, and been elected its first mayor. Family lore is the least reliable and most consequential history. How many Americans believe they are part Native American because family lore has enshrined that belief? All family lore is true as all dreams are true. Exactly like that.

Irene did not fit the profile of a doting mom. She seemed more the type who would have kicked a bad boy's ass early on and with sufficient vigor to keep him straightened out. But she'd spoiled her only surviving son, warped a character predisposed to narcissism such that he could never wrench away from the most lurid self-regard in the fun house mirror of her codependence. She was a tangy old broad who'd lost a twelve-year-old son to pneumonia when the Dick was only nine or ten; who'd married a forty-something-year-old man when she was twenty-three and produced four kids with him; who rolled up, rarely though usually to happy effect, on my childhood in a two-tone green Chevy those years the Dick was in the joint; who loved to play poker and adored *Perry Mason* and who cursed, indeed, like a sailor in Greek and in English. Irene was, I think, the kind of woman I'd like now as a friend.

But she was a terrible mother, with no intuition as to when it is appropriate to embrace and when to push or turn away. She raised a classic coward, a man who could never face himself, even as he remained in a constant reverie of splendid self-regard.

Perhaps even in prison, he remained thus afflicted, though I wonder how, with Lipless Louie's schlong pile driving so many nights in his bung, he could have. I wonder if a pretty man-boy, an inmate marked to be punked early and often, doesn't become his own mother in the joint and therefore come to regard his body as only his mother can. Poor man. Poor, poor man.

When I was ten and saw him for the first time since that late afternoon when he said goodbye to me from behind bars in central Florida, I knew immediately that something was terribly wrong. He was fifty pounds heavier, all muscle. And he was clearly insane, though I had no coordinates from which to locate the manner in which he'd changed. I couldn't affix *crazy* or *sick* or *bonkers* or *cuckoo* to what he'd become, but I knew he was the embodiment of chaos.

Yet he was the man, the very concept my being had existed relative to, for three years. "When Daddy gets home" was uttered numerous times each day in our ugly little domiciles in Elizabeth City. Even Chris, just a big toddler who couldn't possibly remember anything about the Dick, awaited intensely his father's return.

And what returned was a monster, a muscled-up, crazy-eyed thirty-one-year-old supercharged with a humiliation that whirred and crackled at the core of his soul. Whatever madness had propelled him onto the highways of America, to make a family there and drag it all over Nowhere, had not been replaced so much as augmented by a more sinister madness, a fury he did not so much control as dispense randomly. That is the father I hate and the one I must learn to pity. I must reach back into my life and touch, console, comfort.

In Elizabeth City, we stayed at first with Aunt Bertha, with whom Joan's mother, Bula (or Beulah—I've seen it spelled both ways), was already co-habiting, and I recall sensing that Grandma was embarrassed that she was having to live there, though I don't know why she would have been em-barrassed except perhaps for the obvious reason: she'd married badly and now possessed little of value, though her sons had bought her a quite nice house in Seattle, Washington, which I recalled having visited a couple of years previously, the last time I'd seen her. Perhaps she'd sold the house and was in transition. Bertha was one of several ancient great-aunts in that small town who'd buried husbands and lived quite comfortably, if mod-estly, alone in quaint houses on their dead men's retirement funds and life insurance. She had a prolific fig tree and an old-timey washing machine in whose rollers I immediately got my fingers smashed. She was patient and funny, and I liked her much better than I did my grandmother, who was whiny and high-strung and who tried much too hard to persuade me I should like her. What damned her in my regard were the ugly things she ranted about my father. She said flat-out that he was a liar and a thief and should be shot dead. She was right, of course, but I didn't want to hear such things from her or anyone else in those first days and weeks since the Dick had been snagged.

She was wrong, at least strategically, to have said those things, to have tried to turn me against him. If she'd not staked her relationship with me upon an agenda of vilifying the Dick in my seven-year-old heart, she and I would likely have gotten along just fine. We never did.

Joan and the five of us arrived in April or May, and I attended the last four to six weeks of first grade. Oddly, I recall that teacher's face and body. She wasn't pretty, but she wore dark-red lipstick that rendered her fat lips a stop sign, and I indulged in elaborate fantasies in which she stood before the classroom of kids naked, addressing us in that same fake-happy voice she used when she was fully clothed. Mrs. Maple, that woman's name was; I shouldn't recall but do. I was seven and wanted to do something to Mrs. Maple, an image of whose dumpy naked body is lodged in my noggin even though I recall neither face nor name of any other teacher I would have until sixth grade in Norfolk, Virginia. I think I was a little ahead of the curve regarding such matters.

I certainly wasn't ahead of my peers intellectually. I'd somehow learned to read a little with Joan's help in cars and motels, though I don't recall her ever tutoring me. I spent hundreds of hours reading to my daughters when they were small and then into their adolescence continued reading with them every night. My oldest, Ema, graduated magna cum laude from Western Michigan University with a double major in English and music. Annie recently graduated from Anglo-American University with a degree in humanities, and Ellie attends an elite French-language gymnasium in Prague. They have surpassed me in so many ways and will continue to do so, much to my delight, and I take a small measure of credit for their intellectual curiosity and confidence; the early years of intense engagement, of talking to them voluminously and reading to and with them nightly, was an important aspect of my investment in their lives. How I've engaged my daughters as thinking beings may be the only thing I've gotten absolutely right in my life.

Joan read to us a bit, but she did not become a voracious reader, did not read to us in earnest, at least that I can recall, until the Dick went to prison. Somehow, though, from the time I was learning to talk, I liked the idea of books and wanted desperately to know how to read. When I was four or five, I sprawled on motel linoleum and peered into an issue of *Humpty Dumpty* magazine Joan had pinched from the lobby; I sat for hours staring at page after page, taking small respite in the graphics, as though I could will myself to understand printed words; after much effort, I wept that my will had failed me.

A couple of years later, in one of three scattered schools I'd attend for no more than two or three agonizing weeks each, I was mortified that the other children could read and I couldn't. That first day, I took my reading book home and showed Joan the page I was to read the next day. We went through that page numerous times until I'd memorized it: "Up! Up! Up! Oh, Anne, look! Can you see it, Anne? It is red. It is for us." Those were the first sentences I'd ever read, and I was thrilled. The whole phonetics thing popped out of Joan's sounding the words with me, and I just got it. Of course the next day I didn't read the words on the page because I didn't have to. I recited those sentences with gusto. The teacher complimented me and asked me to read the next page.

I was terrified but stared at the words and tried. I didn't get through the page, something about Anne's dog eating the red toy plane, but I sounded out a few words and felt an odd triumph in the midst of failure. I didn't mind the humiliation as much as a kid would who knew he'd be hanging around. I knew that nameless school in that nameless city would soon be far behind me, and in a few days, it was. After that, I bugged Joan constantly. I tried to sound out every word on almost every billboard we passed. I'm not even sure how I learned the alphabet because I'd certainly not learned it at the three schools I'd attended for no more than five or six weeks total, but however I'd learned it, no doubt from Joan, I was okay with the protean nature of vowels, and when I couldn't sound out a word in a tattered magazine or on a billboard, I'd hassle Joan for help. Somehow I learned to read well enough that after only four weeks in Mrs. Maple's charge, she passed me to second grade. I was pretty much an unsocialized animal and couldn't write a lick. I'm not even sure I could count, much less do the simplest arithmetic, when I arrived in Elizabeth City. But in the last month of first grade, I somehow acquired enough of the skills necessary to move up a notch.

My first day of school had been in Montreal, where we spent three or four weeks in a nicely furnished apartment whose bourgeois propriety we diminished by our presence. The Dick had probably made a big score and was lying low. I'm sure he couldn't pull his scams in Quebec, and how he accomplished much of anything such as to rent an apartment in the heart of the provincial capital, given that neither he nor Joan spoke French, is a mystery.

I was excited. I wanted desperately to be normal. I didn't realize that that was what I wanted, but I knew other people didn't live the way we did. I lay in a dark room in that strange city where I'd already discovered that I couldn't understand people when they talked, the clogged breathing of my siblings all around me, and tried to imagine what school would be like. In the dark, I feared a particular shadow because I speculated that a witch puppet lurked in that blotch; she had cackled on a show hosted by a friendly bearded giant wearing a green jumpsuit and a Robin Hood hat that had a feather sticking out of it. Everything on the set was small to render the guy enormous by contrast, even the witch. I can't recall if the giant and witch spoke English or French.

The Dick had arranged for an older boy who spoke broken English to accompany me to school. I liked that boy but was shocked, upon entering the school from frigid air for which I was inadequately clothed, to learn that I couldn't understand anyone. I knew there were other languages because a few months earlier we'd spent some weeks in Mexico City. I'd watched Mexican television and marveled at the grainy, black-and-white bullfights and what seemed the most ancient cartoons.

But I'd never been on my own amid strangers, much less strangers with whom I couldn't speak. I spent, I think, a week sitting in a room with boys who spoke a language I couldn't understand, listening to a stern male teacher who held me in utter contempt and yelled at me in French. He stuck me in a corner with nothing to do for the entire schoolday, allowing me to leave my seat of dishonor only for lunch, recess, and toilet breaks. The other kids flicked glances at me as they may have glanced at a class hamster running on its wheel.

I wept to my parents that school was horrible. That freezing evening, Joan bundled me the best she could, donned a new black faux-fur full-length coat that must have been bullshit against the subzero wind chill, and took me for a stroll. She just held my hand and led me through the elegant snow-crusted city center. She wore bright-white boots, and I recall pausing below a movie marquee and staring at those boots as she read of future attractions.

I felt wonderful to be alone with her apart from the others. The next morning, I ate her terrible oatmeal and, when the nice boy came for me, accompanied him with dreadful resignation.

After a couple of weeks, we left Aunt Bertha's and moved into the top floor of a two-story house and got on welfare. Relatives we'd never known who lived on farms gave us fresh produce in season. Joan cooked beans, every kind—lima, black-eyed, navy, split pea, white—and collards with cornmeal dumplings, cabbage, and she loved to fry corn fritters. Everything got cooked with salt pork and/or smoked hocks. The house was across from and parallel to the elementary school, behind which was the high school football field flanked by creosote-stinking wooden bleachers. The white team, the Yellow Jackets, played there on some Friday nights, and the Black team, whose name I can't recall because I couldn't go to their games, though I could see fans streaming in and out of the gate from my bedroom window, on others. I don't have to comment as to which team had the better band. The school and the field extended parallel to what the whites called N-word Town, which was indeed *inward* in relation to white regard, inward from whites' most superficial assumptions of superiority, inward to a forbidden place where people of color lived and loved and conjured joy from circumscribed despair. Our house was literally the first occupied by white people. We were the border between Elizabeth City and its interior, its Inward Town.

The white people downstairs kept a white goat in our shared backyard. There was a large boy in that family who tormented me. His mother had seen the letters Joan received almost every day from prison. Joan had managed to persuade me that the Dick had gotten out of that bucolic holding cell in Florida, that it had all been a mistake, and that now the Dick was "learning a trade" so that we could all live well when he returned. The big, ugly, snaggletoothed boy downstairs chanted every time I saw him: "Your daddy's a jailbird! Your daddy's a jailbird," the meaning of which another kid had to explain to me. The same kid who explained that trope to me, I think it was Joe Brickhouse, also informed me that there was no Santa Claus.

I confronted Joan with these assertions, that the Dick was in prison and that there was no Santa Claus. She confessed.

What other lies was I believing? I recall at the age of seven asking myself precisely that question. If those times we paused from the road to rent apartments and put up trees and open badly wrapped presents on Christmas Day were a lie, if Santa was not a magic being who could track our movements as apparitional though very real uniformed authorities could not, if he did not exist, could everything be a lie? Could I be dreaming? Could nothing be real? Why had my life been so different from everyone else's?

That summer, I got cracked at my crewcut hairline by the backswing of a baseball bat. The Black kid who did it was not to blame. I'd stupidly sauntered through a pickup baseball game on the high school football field, got smacked for a dozen stiches in a quarter-inch-deep gash.

That same summer, I got my tonsils yanked. A rotund woman in white kissed me all over my groggy face as she wheeled me out of the operating room and as I emerged from ether and recalled the few seconds of horror when the doctor had placed a sieve over my nose and mouth and dripped that terrifying metallic odor on it. As she kissed me on my cheeks and forehead, I smelled her spit and recalled a weird, echoey feeling before I blacked out. I hemorrhaged several times over the next couple of weeks, scaring Joan as well as myself. One morning, the bed Chuck and I shared looked like a crime scene, and later that week, I almost choked to death on blood on the side of the house as I played sword fighting with Jigger from across Merrimac Street. The doctor told me to take it easy for a while.

But there is only one iterative event that defines that time in my life. Beginning that early autumn and continuing into the following spring, at least twice a week, a boy younger than I by a year perhaps, staggered at dawn through fog or rain and dimness naked, weeping, wailing, "Richard, Richard Lee . . . Richard, Richard Lee . . . ," right up to Merrimac, the brink of the white section of town, and always he turned there, still wailing that name, and returned, wailing, weeping.

Richard Lee, we learned that summer, by which time the ghost had ceased his transits, was the pathetic kid's brother, who, at least according to Jigger's older brother Cecil, got stoned to death down by the tracks. The kid was a sleepwalker and mornings rose, still asleep, to search for his brother. He returned to bed, awoke, and carried on through his days more or less normally, or at least that was already the legend.

He has haunted my life, and I know I'll never hear a more honest cry of love and loss. I have composed wretched, sentimental verse about him, and yet, even though he is the essence of lyric poetry, I know that I'll never write the poem he deserves. That first time I awoke to his cry was the most wondrous moment of my life. I heard my own first name shouted in the raspy high-pitched voice of a child not a child. I thought he was imploring me to leave, "Richard, Richard leave!" And I was desperate to discover where he wanted me to go. I was so frightened of him, though, I couldn't possibly run out the back door, down the steps, past the nervous, tethered white goat, to ask. It took considerable courage simply to look out the window, and when I saw that he was naked and how contorted with grief his face was, a mask of such torturous remorse no real child should be wearing it, I knew I was witnessing the miraculous and that the miraculous is tethered like a dog, or a nervous white goat, to the wheel of actual days and actual nights and all the blunt details of which they are composed.

Most of which are decidedly *un*miraculous. For example, I recall re-reading Henry Miller's *Tropic of Cancer* in my forties and thinking what a reeking plug of pretentious woman-loathing horseshit that book is. When I was seventeen, of course, I loved it and was wiser in my assessment than I would be a quarter-century later. Miller didn't hate women; he simply didn't know how to love them, as was true of the boy I was when I first read that book and, alas, as was also true of that middle-aged man I became. And I suppose the irony that how I just characterized the book was influenced not only by political correctness sentiments I've absorbed into my bloodstream, but also by Miller's boyish sensibility, will be lost on few who read this.

Boyish, yes. So much of American literature is boyish. But I'll not rant about that. Others brighter, more erudite, than I have already made and closed that case. There is a golden thread or a yellow arc, a stream of piss, between Twain and Miller.

Joe Brickhouse was Tom Sawyer. When I read Twain in my midteens, I recognized Tom because he was Joe, whom I'd left in Elizabeth City a few years previously, except that Joe had bragged about fucking his older sister and had a glass eye. When I was ten, just before the Dick was to exit prison the first time, Joe was my hero. He was tall, lanky, and honest because he was too stupid not to be. I often took his stupidity for profundity. I suppose Joe was not as glib as Tom, but psychically, he struck a similar posture.

Though I've not been a particularly conscientious student of American literature as serious students go, I have through the years been fairly persistent, if scattered, in my regard for it. I realized in my late teens that my weird life resonated in ways that seemed to echo, at least faintly, the transcendent themes of American literature: the Missing Father. The Open Road. The Charming Rogue. Frenetic Movement. Boring, unkillable optimism. Tears filled my eyes when I came to that last paragraph of *The Great Gatsby*. I was eighteen, in my first semester of college in San Diego, and I believed that the Dick, though much stupider than Gatsby and not nearly as soulful, as humane, as capable of genuine emotion, had himself seen a green light, though years later, I'd get a grip and simply accept that if indeed the Dick had even seen a light, it was probably just a red reflector on the back of a semi.

But back then, when I read the White Dudes of American Literature—

Twain, Irving, Hawthorne, even Poe, even, or especially, Whitman, and of course Melville and then Hemingway, Faulkner, Frost, Williams, Salinger—I felt how American I was, and for the first time, I could love what I was.

Joe's glass eye didn't fit very well, and this was surely because he was still growing and his family couldn't afford to keep buying him new ones. He was always taking it out and fiddling with it, even using it in games of marbles, "funsies" or "keepsies." He was quite a sport about letting us keep it for a day or two, but there was an unspoken rule that we'd give him ample opportunities to win it back. From a distance, when he didn't have it in, the left side of his face was darker, as though that darkness of his socket rendered the surrounding area by optical illusion to seem shaded or as though Joe contained some of the night and it sloshed out of him.

The morning I heard him screaming on Merrimac, he wasn't wearing it. From my window, I espied him clutching the dead head of the only thing he loved, a black mutt, to his black jacket and heard him wail. The animal was limp and bloody, and when Joe screamed—his ass on the asphalt, legs spread apart, face contorted against the fact of his loss—his sockets scrunched up and disappeared, but then he stared at the sky, and the darkness spilled from the hole in his face, and he was transformed into something miraculous. Like that kid who wailed for his lost brother, Joe's capacity for grief, and therefore for love, hulked enormous on the gray morning.

INDEX

Academy of American Poets, 133

Adamo, Ralph, 87

Adams, Abigail, 6

Adams, John, 6, 182

Adorno, Theodor, 33

Ahab, 79

Akhmatova, Anna, 146

Ammons, A. R., 149

Amphibious Base (Coronado), 42

Anderson, Laurie, 127

Andrade, Carlos Drummond de, 146

Angelou, Maya, 146

Antoinette, Marie, 182

Apollinaire, Guillaume, 99

Arendt, Hannah, 176

Argonaut, 170

Aristotle, 185

Armstrong, Louis, 189

Ashbery, John, 17, 18, 36, 37

Atalanta, 170

Atlanta (Georgia), 54

Auden, W. H., 19

Audubon Zoo, 85

Auschwitz, 20, 33, 34, 128, 129, 133, 134, 135

AWP (Associated Writing Programs), x, 17, 133, 138, 140

Baker, Chesney Henry "Chet," 189

Baker, Josephine, 191

Bakersfield (California), 88

Balboa Park, 72

Baldwin, James, 191

Bannon, Steve, 79

Baraka, Amiri, 88

Barnake, Ted, 70

Barnstone, Aliki, 45

Barnstone, Tony, 45

Barnstone, Willis, 22, 45

Barton, Frederick, 87

Baxter, Charles, 22

Beatles, The, 19

Beattie, Ann, 22

Becker, Ernest, 103

Bell, Marvin, 15, 21

Benjamin, Walter, 118

Berkeley, George, 117, 113

Berra, Yogi, 160

Berryman, John, 16

"Big Nasty, the," 38, 82

Biguenet, John, 87

Bilek, Petr, 21

Black Mountain, 17

Blake, William, 99, 156, 168

Blumenthal, Michael, 22

Bly, Robert, 32, 36, 107

Borges, Jorge Luis, 146

Bosch, Hieronymus, 7

Boston, Bruce H., 35, 39, 89, 90, 97

Boston, Marsha, 39, 40, 90

Boswell, James, 130

Bourjaily, Vance, 19, 22
Breadloaf, 15
Brigadoon, 59
Brokaw, Tom, 46
Brothers, Dr. Joyce, 187
Brubeck, David, 189
Bruce, Lenny, 123
Buchenwald, 33, 133
Buddha, 168
Bukowski, Charles, 64
Burdon, Eric, 53
Burns, Robert, 144
Bush, George W., 21
Butler, Robert Owen, 22
"Button Lady, the" (Leah Shpock-
    Luzovsky), 172
Byron, (Lord) George Gordon, 47, 184

Cabildo, 82
Café du Monde, 85
Cairo, Egypt, 155
Cairo, Illinois, 154
Caligula, 184
Cameron, James, 117
Camus, Albert, 154
Capp, Al, 130
Carlin, George, 123, 127
Carnegie Mellon University Press, ix, 140
Carton, Sydney, 174
Carson, Johnny, 122
Cassius Carter Theater, 72
Cassin, Maxine, 82, 87
Castaneda, Carlos, 169
Castro, Fidel, 19
Caucasian, 180
Chapelle, David, 147
Charles University, 21
Chart House, 54, 82, 83, 93, 110, 166
Charter 77, 139
Chesterfield Heights, 24, 50, 54, 180
Choudhury, Bikram, 171
Christ, 125, 159, 162, 201

Clampitt, Amy, 145
Clare, John, 184–186
Clay, Andrew Dice, 79
Clinton, Bill, 98
Codrescu, Andrei, ix, 22, 87
Cohen, Leonard, 94
Collier, Michael, 22
Coltrane, John, 189, 190
Communism, 20, 141
Comprehensive Drug Abuse Prevention
    and Control Act (1970), 168
Conoley, Gillian, 87
Conrad, Joseph, 79
Cooley, Nicole, 45
Cooley, Peter, 22, 45, 82, 87
Corea, Amando Anthony "Chick," 189
Coronado (California), 42, 54, 71, 167
Coronado Amphibious Base, 42
Costanzo, Gerald, ix, 22
Coward, Noel, 4
Crane, Stephen, 88
Creeley, Robert, 18, 149
Crescent, the (Amtrak), 54
Crone, Moira, ix, 22, 87
Crowe, Cameron, 71, 77
Cuban Missile Crisis, 68, 137
Cully, Barbara, ix, 22, 39
Czech Goethe Society, 141
Czechoslovak Writers Union, 135, 138

Dachau, 33
Davis, Glover, ix, 18, 26, 35, 48, 89, 90
Davis, Miles, 191
D.C. Comics, 24
Dean, John, 72
Debeljak, Aleš, 19
DeLoach, Darryl, 166
Delphi, 169
Deming, Alison, 21, 130
Democratic Party, 45
Derrida, Jacques, 113
Descartes, René, 183

Desnos, Robert, 127
Dickens, Charles, 79
Dickey, James, xi, 111
Dickinson, Emily, 146, 145, 181
Digges, Debora, 20
Dlouhá, 20
"Donald, the," x, 192, 205
Doty, Mark, 21
Doyle, Sir Arthur Conan, 79
Dr. Phil (McGraw), 187
Drakulić, Slavenka, 22
Dunn, Stephen, 88
Dubček, Alexander, 136, 175
Dybek, Stuart, ix, 20

Eisenberg, Deborah, 22
Egyptian Book of the Dead, 26
Eliot, T. S., 76, 102, 111, 116, 123, 189, 191
Elizabeth City (NC), 9, 100, 181, 192, 194,
    209, 210, 214, 215, 217, 219, 221
Elkin, Stanley, 15
Empson, William, 17
Engle, Paul, 90
Epstein, Helen, 21
Eversz, Robert, xi, 21, 34
Everwine, Peter, 35

Facebook, 58, 60, 116
Fagan, 99
Faubourg Marigny, 79
Faulkner, William, 62, 222
Fennelly, Beth Ann, 130
Ferlinghetti, Lawrence, 110, 111
Fertel, Randy, 22
Fitzgerald, Ella, 189
"Fonz, the" (Arthur Herbert Fonzarelli), 47
Forché, Carolyn, xi, 16, 22, 39, 53, 55, 58, 90
Ford, Gerald, 74, 77
Ford, Richard, 15
Foucault, Michel, 113
Four Roses, 32, 168
FOX, 62

Frankfurt Marxists, 173
Frankl, Victor, 160
Franco, 95
Freedom Caucus, 57
Fremont, Helen, 22
French Quarter, 37, 38, 62, 80, 82, 83, 84,
    110, 112, 166, 172, 196
Fresno (California), ix, 18, 26, 27, 35,
    38, 39, 40, 47, 59, 88, 89, 90, 91, 92, 95,
    96, 97
Fresno School, 26, 35
Fresno State University, 35
Freud, Sigmund, 57, 78, 130, 147, 160,
    169, 187
Frost, Robert, 3, 4, 5, 24, 46, 61, 77, 92,
    106, 109, 115, 128, 151, 152, 153, 181, 222
Fulbright, 174

Gallagher, Tess, 22
Gass, William, 21
Georgetown (IN), 161
Gery, John, 87
Getz, Stanley "Stan," 189
GI Bill, 41
Gilchrist, Ellen, 87
Gillespie, John Birks "Dizzy," 189
Ginsberg, Allen, 65, 88, 107, 111, 131, 146,
    174, 182
Glück, Louise, 22
Godfather movies, 6
Goethe, Johann Wolfgang von, 141
Golden Gloves, 30
Golding, William, 30
Goodman, Benjamin David "Benny," 189
Gordon, Jaimy, xi, 21
Gorgons, 50, 56, 57
Great Depression, 43
Greene, Graham, 19
Gregerson, Linda, 22
Grendel, 79
Gross, Harvey, 148
Gutenberg, Johannes, 118

Hackett, Buddy, 122, 123
Haight-Ashbury, 168
Hale, Ester, 52, 53, 54, 56, 57, 58
Hall, Donald, 22
Hampl, Patricia, 21, 130
Hancock, Herbie, 189
Hanford, Martin, 240
Hanzlicek, Charles, 35, 89
Harrisburg Federal Penitentiary, 23
Havel, Václav, 19, 21, 22, 138, 139, 174
Hawking, Steven, 154
Heaney, Seamus, 146
Heimlich maneuver, 128
Hell's Angels, 168
Hemingway, Ernest, 191, 222
Hemley, Robin, 22
Herbert, Zbigniew, 146
Hilsky, Martin, 76
Hiroshima, 56
Hirsch, Edward, 22
Hirt, Al, 19
Hogan's Heroes, 134
Hogue, Cynthia, 22
Holiday, Billy, 189
Holocaust, 33, 133, 134
Holub, Miroslav, 22
Hoosier, 162
Hongo, Garrett, 22
Hope (Arkansas), 98, 99, 100
Horace, 21, 69, 117, 127
Hotel Del Coronado, 54
House of the Rising Sun, 53, 84, 85, 110
Hughes, Langston, 191
Humbert Humbert, 79
Huxley, Aldoux, 168

Iago, 79
Infant of Prague, 157
Internment camps, 56
Iowa International Writers Workshop, 135
Iowa Writers Workshop, 15, 35, 37

Iron Butterfly, 166
Iron Curtain, 138
"Iron John," 32
Irving, John, 15
Ivy League, 170

Jackson, Richard, 21, 130
Jackson Square, 82, 84, 166
Jagger, Mick, 53
Jarman, Mark, 21
Jarrell, Randall, 65
Jim Crow, 56
Jekyll/Hyde, 162
Jenkins, Florence Foster, 124
Joey's Pizza, 54
Johnson, Diane, 22
Johnson, Geronimo, 22
Johnson, Lyndon Baines, 121
Johnson, Raymond, 37, 43, 44, 45
Johnson, Samuel, 91, 113
Johnston, Arnold, x, 143, 144, 145, 148, 149,
    150, 152
Johnston, Deborah, xi, 144
Jones, Robert L., 18, 35, 39, 89, 90, 92, 94, 97
Joplin, Scott, 189
Joyce, James, 76
Jung, Carl, 32, 91, 161, 169
Justice, Donald, 78, 90, 92
Jay-Z, 125

Kabuki, 71
Kafka, Franz, 66, 106
Kalamazoo (Michigan), 48, 58, 96, 97,
    116, 144, 156, 162
Kal-El, 24
Kamenetz, Rodger, ix, 22, 87
Karolinum, 21
Karr, Mary, 22
Kata, 31, 61
Keats, John, 92, 163, 169
Kekaula, Robert, 88

Kenya, 203
Kennedy, John F., 74
Kennedy, X. J., 88
Kent State, 168
Kidder, Tracy, 22
Kinnell, Galway, 16, 21, 36, 37
Kizer, Carolyn, 21, 36, 37
Klima, Ivan, 22
Kommunyakaa, Yusef, 80, 87
Korea, 44, 136
Kriseová, Eda, 22
Kumite, 31
Kundera, Milan, 168
Kunitz, Stanley, 135
Kurtz, 79

La Jolla Cove, 72, 171
La Jolla Public Library, 171
Lake Pontchartrain, 16
Lake Pontchartrain Causeway, 37
Lasch, Christopher, 211
Laveau, Marie, 84
Lawrence, D. H., 18, 76
Lea, Sydney, ix, 22
Leary, Timothy, 168
Led Zeppelin, 167
Lee, Peggy, 111
"Left Bank of the 90s, the," 19, 21
Leithauser, Brad, 22
Levertov, Denise, 16, 17, 18, 37, 146
Levine, Philip, ix, 5, 6, 16, 18, 22, 25, 26,
    27, 33, 35, 37, 38, 39, 41, 48, 59, 82, 83,
    89, 91, 92, 93, 94, 95, 96, 111, 131
Levine, Eddie, 41
Levine, Francis, 16, 18
Levis, Larry, 18, 35, 36, 37, 38, 39, 40, 43,
    44, 45, 47, 48, 89, 90, 129
Levy, Alan, 18, 19
LGBTQ, 29
Library of Babel, 160
Lily Dale (New York), 169

Livesey, Margo, 22
Long, Russell B., 178
Lopate, Philip, 22
Loren, Sophia, 19
Lott, Bret, 22
Louis and Clark, 161
Louisiana State University (LSU), 37
Louisiana's Separate Car Act of 1890, 188
Louisville (KY), 94, 161, 162
Löwe, Rabbi (Judah Loew ben Bezalel), 175
Lowell, Robert, 184, 185, 186, 187, 190, 211
Lucifer, 69, 79
Lustig, Arnošt, 19, 20, 21, 33, 34, 133, 134,
    135, 138, 140, 141, 175
Lustig, Vera, 142

Macari, Anne Marie, 22, 130
MAD (Mutually Assured Destruction), 137
Maddox, Everette, 62, 63, 64, 65, 66, 87
Madonna, 59, 60
Maisel, Carolyn, 87
Mann, Thomas, 102
Mao Tse-tung, 142
Maple Leaf Bar, 62, 63, 64
Mardi Gras, 19, 81, 172
Marvel Comics, 24, 102
Martin, Mary, 158, 160
Martin, Valerie, 22, 87
Marvel Comics, 24, 110
Marx, Groucho, 133
Marx, Karl (Frankfurt Marxists), 173
Matrix, The, 117
Matthews, William, 19, 20, 22
Mattison, Harry, 39
Maurier, George du, 79
McCracken, Elizabeth, 22
McElroy, Colleen, 22
McGovern, George, 45
Medusa, 56
Melville, Herman, 79
Meredith, William, 22

Merrill, Christopher, 22
Merwin, W. S., 37
Mezey, Robert, xi, 16, 26, 35, 89
Michelangelo, 159, 160
Miller, Elise, 95
Miller, Henry, 221
Miller, Rayburn, 81
Milosz, Czeslaw, 146
Milton, John, 69, 79, 185, 187
Mingus, Charles, 189
MLA (Modern Language Association), 105
Moctezuma, Edwardo, 95
Monk, Thelonious, 189
Moore, Marianne, 88
Morris, Mary, 21
Morton, Jelly Roll (Ferdinand Joseph LaMothe), 189
Moscaliuc, Mihaela, 22
Mr. Natural, 39, 72
Mrs. Maple, 215
MSNBC, 62, 71
Mukherjee, Bharati, 22
Multiple sclerosis, 50
Murphy, Kay, 87
Musky-Dukes, Carol, 16, 21

Nabokov, Vladimir, 19, 79
Nagasaki, 137
Naked Café, 94
Nashville (IN), 154, 155
Nashville (TN), 154, 155
Negative capability, 163, 169
Nemerov, Howard, 92, 145
Nerval, Gerard de, 127
New Age, 71, 157, 165, 169, 170, 171, 173, 176
New Jersey, 88, 89
New Orleans, 15, 16, 19, 20, 37, 38, 39, 54, 62, 63, 64, 66, 79, 80, 82, 83, 84, 87, 93, 95, 136, 145, 155, 166, 196, 205
New Orleans Poetry Journal, 82
New Orleans Poetry Journal Press, 82
New Yorker, 64

Nicks, Stevie, 73
Nixon, Richard, 19, 74, 77
Norfolk (Virginia), 9, 10, 25, 28, 30, 42, 50, 68, 109, 114, 130, 180, 193, 194, 200, 209, 213, 216
North Island Naval Air Station, 42, 43, 168
NPR (National Public Radio), 60
NRA (National Rifle Association), 57

O'Brien, 79
O'Hara, Frank, 59, 149
Old Globe, 72, 73, 76
Olson, Charles, 17, 18, 149
O'Neil, Tip, 60
Orange Avenue, 54
Order of the British Empire, 76
Orr, Gregory, ix, 22
Orwell, George, 79
Ostriker, Alicia, 22
Oxford University, 170

Page, Jimmy, 71
Paley, Grace, 19, 20, 22
Panza, Sancho, 91, 92
Pape, Greg, 35, 89
Parisi, Joseph, 22
Pegasus, 56, 67
Pehe, Jirí, 22
Pekárková, Iva, 22
Perel, Esther, 187
Phillips, Jane Anne, 22
Pied Piper of Hamelin, 104
Pietá, 159
Plant, Robert, 71
Plato, 69, 149, 155, 192
Platoon, 36
Plessy v. Ferguson Supreme Court decision of 1892, 188
Plumly, Stanley, xi, 20, 130
Poseidon, 57
Poulos, Michelle, 37
Pound, Ezra, 7, 19, 69, 149, 189, 191, 193

Prague, 5, 34, 58, 68, 79, 94, 96, 116, 134, 135, 136, 138, 141, 142, 154, 157, 174, 196, 197, 198, 206, 216

Prague Post, 18, 19, 20

Prague Spring, 135, 136, 138

Prague Summer Program, 16, 20, 21, 109, 116, 130

Presley, Elvis, 189, 191

Pritchard, Melissa, 22

Prose, Francine, 21

Provincetown Fine Arts Work Center, 20, 55

Pryor, Richard, 123, 127

Reagan, Ronald, 80

Redding, Otis, 53

Reefer Madness, 165

Rexroth, Kenneth, 65

Rich, Adrianne, 16, 37, 146

Richards, Keith, 189

Rimbaud, 39

Rosie the Riveter, 56

Roethke, Theodore, 31, 92

Rogers, Will, 123

Roosevelt, Franklin Delano, 30

Root, William Pitt, 22

Rosebud, 32

Rosenthal, Chuck, 22

Rothenberg, Jerome, 171

Roundup, the, 85

Rousseau, Jean Jacques, 177, 178

Šalamum, Tomaž, 19

Salinas, Luis Omar, 35, 89

Salt Lake City, 154, 155

Salter, Mary Jo, 22

Salvation Army, 24, 109

"Samoan Lawyer, the" 38

San Diego, 3, 5, 9, 10, 17, 26, 32, 39, 42, 52, 53, 55, 72, 75, 76, 82, 89, 90, 94, 95, 97, 193, 221

San Diego City College, 70, 125

San Diego State University, 15, 16, 53, 73, 89, 90, 122, 123

San Francisco Renaissance, 65

Sasebo, Japan, 29, 30, 42, 61, 71, 112, 137, 165

Saussur, Ferdinand de, 161

Savage, Richard, 142

Schmidt, Michael, 91

Schwartz, Lynn Sharon, 22

Schwartz, Steven, 87

Scott, Herbert, 16, 22, 35, 89

Selma (California), 38

Sermon on the Mount, 61

Seville, David, 177, 179

Shakespeare, William, 58, 68, 69, 70, 72, 73, 74, 75, 76, 77, 184

Sheen, Charley, 36

Shelley, Percy Bysshe, 133, 179, 211

Shmoo, 130

Shobukan Okinawa-te, 30, 43, 61

Shrive, Susan Richards, 22

Silverman, Sarah, 127, 147

Simić, Charles, 77

Simon, Maura, 22

Singapore Literary Festival, 140

Škvorecky, Josef, 21

Slouka, Mark, 22

Šmíd, Martin, 175

Smith, Carol, 22

Smith, Marc, 127

Smothers Brothers, 168

Snodgrass, W. D., 211

Socrates, 149

Solana Beach, 94

Somali warlord, 57

Soto, Gary, 35, 89

Spanish Civil War, 95

Spear, Roberta, 35, 89

St. John, David, 22, 35, 89

St. Louis Cemetery, 37, 84

St. Petersburg, Russia, 203

Stalin, Josef, 139

Stansberry, Domenic, 87
Stein, Gertrude, 18
Stern, Gerald, xi, 21, 33, 37, 38, 81, 129, 130, 131, 132, 144, 145
Stern, Steven, 22
Stevens, Wallace, 153, 176
Stewart, Rod, 53
Strand, Mark, xi, 15, 54, 77
Stránskí, Jirí, 22
Streep, Meryl, 125
Sullivan, Ed, 121, 122, 130
Svengali, 71
Swartz, Larry (and Harry), 72
Swift, Johnathan, 182

Tan, Amy, 22
Terezín (Theresienstadt), 20, 33
Tinker Bell, 158
Thomas, Dylan, 48, 98, 111, 126
Thompson, Hunter S., 38
Tulane University, 82
Tunstall, Mrs., 50, 51, 52, 56, 57, 58, 68

University of Arkansas, 16, 37
University of California, Irvine, 90
University of California, San Diego, 17
University of Iowa, 15, 16, 17, 26, 35, 37, 39, 61, 90, 135, 170
University of New Orleans, 64, 79, 80
University of Virginia, 16, 22
Untermeyer, Louis, 109, 115
Uschuk, Pamela, 22
USS Phoebe, 44, 137

Vaculík, Ludvík, 22, 135
Valentine, Jean, 22
Vaudeville, 123
Velvet Revolution, 138, 174, 197, 198, 206
Vietnam, 43, 44, 86, 112, 137, 212
Villon, François, 25, 26, 142

Walcott, Derik, 146
Waldo, 7, 195
Ward, Jay, 79
Waters, Michael, 21
Waters, Muddy (McKinley Morganfield), 189
Weil, Andrew, 168
Wenceslas Square, 175
Wesleyan University Press, 110, 111, 140
Whiplash, Sydney, 79
White, Betty, 29
Whitman, Walt, 27, 61, 63, 64, 65, 88, 112, 146, 156, 178, 179, 191, 211, 222
Wiesenthal, Simon, 19
Wilbur, Richard, 92, 145
Williams, C. K., 21
Williams, Robin, 86
Williams, Sherley Anne, 35, 89
Williams, William Carlos, xi, 61, 69, 88, 152, 222
Winterová, Dominika, xi, 21, 174, 175
Winters, Yvor, 92
Wojahn, David, xi, 80, 87
Wonderland, 160
Woodstock, 86
Woolf, Virginia, 76
World War II, 26, 43, 44, 52, 106
Wright, Carolyn, 87
Wright, Charles, 49
Wright, Franz, 45
Wright, James, 22, 37, 111
Wright, Richard, 191
Wronsky, Gail, xi, 21, 22

Yeats, William Butler, 128
Yevtushenko, Yevgeny, 80, 146
Young, Al, 21
Youngman, Henny, 121, 122, 129

Zagajewski, Adam, 22
Zippy the Pinhead, 169

imprimatur

CPSIA information can be obtained
at www.ICGtesting.com
Printed in the USA
LVHW032157091221
705808LV00001B/53

9 780807 176634